Motor Vehicle Calculations and Science

PART 1

R. C. CHAMPION F.I.M.I., M.I.R.T.E.
Head of Engineering Trades Department,
Paddington Technical College

E. C. ARNOLD M.I.M.I., M.I.R.T.E.
Former Course Tutor, Automobile Engineering,
Southgate Technical College

EDWARD ARNOLD (PUBLISHERS) LTD. LONDON

First published 1954
by Edward Arnold (Publishers) Ltd
25 Hill Street, London W1X 8LL
Second edition 1967
Reprinted 1968
Third edition 1970
Reprinted 1971, 1972

ISBN 0 7131 3230 2

Printed in Great Britain by
Cox & Wyman Ltd, London, Reading and Fakenham

Preface to First Edition

These books deal with calculations and science as applied to automobile engineering. They should give assistance to the motor mechanic or apprentice who is working in a repair garage or service station and also studying for a technical qualification. In many service stations special equipment is used to give rapid and first-class service to our cars and commercial vehicles, and the successful use of this equipment demands mechanics with a wide range of both practical and theoretical knowledge. As the technology of automobile engineering is already available in textbooks, journals and the comprehensive manuals issued by motor manufacturers, this present work is intended to help the mechanic on the theoretical side only by providing information on the aspects of mathematics and science which are necessary to supplement his technical studies.

Automobile engineering courses are now held at most technical colleges either as part-time day or as evening classes, and it is hoped that these books will prove useful to students taking these courses as a supplement to the instruction given in class. Many of the exercises and worked examples are taken from past examination papers so as to give the student practice in solving problems similar to those which he will meet in his examination.

Part 1 of this work covers the elementary calculations and contains sections on elementary mechanics, heat and electricity. The solutions of some of the problems in these sections require a knowledge of engineering drawing and the measurement of angles with a protractor—work which should be covered in the engineering drawing class. Part 2 deals with trigonometry, algebra and further calculations and science up to the standard of the Motor Vehicle Mechanics and Technicians Examinations of the City and Guilds of London Institute and similar examinations set by other boards.

In conclusion, we are grateful to the following examining bodies for

their co-operation and for giving us permission to print questions from
their past examination papers.

City and Guilds of London Institute, London.
The Institute of the Motor Industry, London.
Union of Lancashire and Cheshire Institutes, Manchester.
Northern Counties Technical Examinations Council,
  Newcastle upon Tyne.
East Midland Educational Union, Nottingham.
Union of Educational Institutes, Birmingham.

R. C. C.
E. C. A.

Preface to Third Edition

Although the subject matter of these books remains unchanged, it
becomes necessary to publish a third edition using the new SI metric
system throughout (see page vii). In consequence both books have been
thoroughly revised in order to meet the requirements of the motor
industry and the examining bodies who will be using SI units in the
future.

The name **Système International d'Unités** (International System of
Units) and the international abbreviation SI are used for the systematic-
ally organized system of units introduced by the *Conference Générale
des Poids et Mesures* in 1960. It includes the SI base-units, supple-
mentary SI units, derived SI units, and the decimal multiples and
sub-multiples of these units, formed by use of prefixes. The name 'SI
units' is reserved for the coherent units only.

R. C. C.
E. C. A.

Contents

SI Units

The SI is a logically consistent system of units in which the product or quotient of any two unit quantities is the unit of the resultant quantity. Thus unit **area** results from multiplying unit length by unit length, unit **velocity** results when unit length is divided by unit time and unit **force** results when unit mass is multiplied by unit acceleration, i.e. when 1 newton is applied to a mass of 1 kilogramme the result will be an acceleration of 1 metre per second squared.

The SI derives all the quantities needed in automobile and general engineering from only six units shown in the following table:

The Basic Units

Quantity	Name of Unit	Unit Symbol
length	metre	**m**
mass	kilogramme	**kg**
time	second	s
electric current	ampere	**A**
thermodynamic temperature	degree kelvin	**K**
luminous intensity	candela	**cd**

Many students will be familiar with the first four basic units; the degree kelvin is equivalent to the degree Centigrade absolute (now degree Celsius).

Other units with special names have been derived from the basic SI units and they are explained throughout Parts 1 and 2 as and when necessary. A list of these units, with abbreviations, follows.

Abbreviations for SI Units

A or amps	amperes
Ah	ampere hour
bP	brake power
°C	degree Celsius
cm	centimetre
cm^3	cubic centimetre
g	gramme (mass)
h	hour
iP	indicated power
J and kJ	joule and kilojoule
K	degree kelvin
kg	kilogramme
kg/1	kilogramme per litre
km	kilometre
km/h	kilometre per hour
kW	kilowatt
1	litre
m	metre
ml	millilitre
mm	millimetre
mmHg	millimetres of mercury
N and kN	newton and kilonewton
P	power
rad	radians
rev/min	revolutions per minute
rev/s	revolutions per second
tonne	tonne (mass)
W	watt

Abbreviations for Words

b.d.c.	bottom dead centre
B.M.	bending moment
b.m.e.p.	brake mean effective pressure
c.g.	centre of gravity
c.i.	compression ignition
i.c.	internal combustion
m.e.p.	mean effective pressure
S.F.	sheer force
t.d.c.	top dead centre

Fractions

A **fraction*** is one or more of the parts into which a quantity can be divided. Each of these parts is a fraction of the quantity, and if the quantity is divided into, say, eight equal parts (see Fig. 1.1), then each part will be one-eighth of the whole. This idea can be expressed also by writing $\frac{1}{8}$. If two or more of these parts are considered, these can be written:

$$\frac{2}{8}; \quad \frac{3}{8}; \quad \frac{5}{8}, \text{ and so on.}$$

These parts are called vulgar fractions, but it is usual, however, to omit the term 'vulgar' and say simply 'fractions'.

Two numbers are required to express a fraction, and these numbers are called the **numerator** and the **denominator.** The denominator is placed below the numerator with a line between them.   For example,

5 is the numerator

$\overline{8}$ is the denominator

The figure 5 shows how many of the eight equal parts are to be considered.

A **proper** fraction is a fraction whose numerator is smaller than its denominator; $\frac{3}{4}$, $\frac{5}{8}$, $\frac{7}{16}$ are examples of proper fractions.

An **improper** fraction is a fraction whose numerator is larger than its denominator; $\frac{15}{8}$, $\frac{19}{16}$, $\frac{37}{32}$ are examples of improper fractions.

A **mixed number** is a whole number followed by a fraction, e.g. $3\frac{1}{2}$ is a mixed number and is the same as $3 + \frac{1}{2}$. In order to express an improper fraction as a mixed number we divide the numerator by the denominator:

$$\frac{35}{16} = 35 \div 16 = 2 \text{ and } \tfrac{3}{16} \text{ over}$$

$$\therefore \frac{35}{16} = 2\tfrac{3}{16}$$

*With the extension of the metric system and use of SI units, the use of vulgar fractions will tend to diminish.

In order to express a mixed number as an improper fraction, we multiply the whole number by the denominator of the fraction and add the numerator to this product; the figure obtained is placed over the original denominator.

Let us take $4\frac{5}{8}$ as an example. Now 4 multiplied by 8 equals 32 and 32 plus 5 equals 37. Thus, the improper fraction is $\frac{37}{8}$, i.e. $4\frac{5}{8}$ equals $\frac{37}{8}$.

If both the numerator and the denominator of a fraction are multiplied or divided by the same number, then the value of the fraction is unaltered. The diagram Fig. 1.1 shows that $\frac{2}{8}$ has the same value as $\frac{1}{4}$, i.e. $\frac{2}{8}$ equals $\frac{1}{4}$; we have divided both the numerator and the denominator by 2, and in this example 2 is known as the **common factor.**

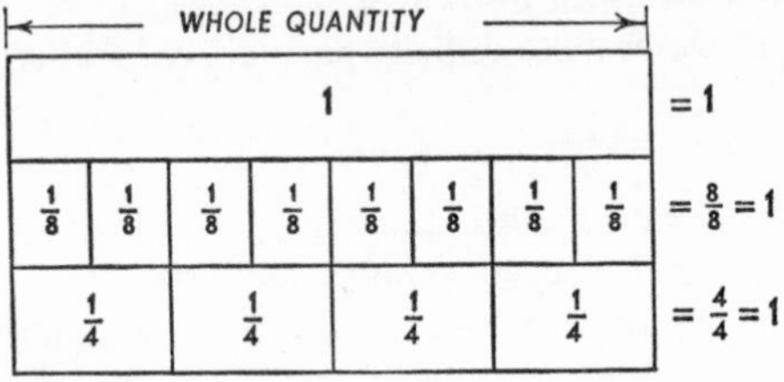

FIG. 1.1

A fraction is said to be reduced to its **lowest terms** (simplest form) when its numerator and its denominator cannot be divided by the same number without a remainder, e.g. $\frac{3}{4}$; $\frac{5}{8}$; $\frac{17}{32}$; $\frac{31}{64}$.

The following fractions can however be reduced to their lowest terms by dividing both the numerator and the denominator by a common factor:

$$\frac{4 \div 4}{8 \div 4} = \frac{1}{2} \qquad \frac{18 \div 2}{32 \div 2} = \frac{9}{16} \qquad \frac{6 \div 2}{16 \div 2} = \frac{3}{8}$$

$$\frac{4 \div 4}{20 \div 4} = \frac{1}{5} \qquad \frac{6 \div 3}{15 \div 3} = \frac{2}{5}$$

A **complex** or **compound fraction** has a fraction for both or either of its terms:

$$\frac{\frac{3}{8}}{\frac{5}{16}} \qquad \frac{\frac{1}{2}}{\frac{1}{4}} \qquad \frac{6}{\frac{1}{8}}$$

The line separating the terms shows that the top term is to be divided by the bottom term:

$$\frac{\frac{3}{8}}{\frac{5}{16}} = \frac{3}{8} \div \frac{5}{16} \qquad \frac{\frac{1}{2}}{\frac{1}{4}} = \frac{1}{2} \div \frac{1}{4} \qquad \frac{6}{\frac{1}{8}} = 6 \div \frac{1}{8}$$

The method of reducing complex fractions to their lowest terms is shown later in this chapter.

Multiplication and Division of Fractions

The **multiplication of fractions** is carried out as follows:

Multiply the numerators of the fractions together in order to form a new numerator, and multiply the denominators of the fractions together in order to form a new denominator:

Thus, $\dfrac{3}{4} \times \dfrac{5}{8} = \dfrac{15 \text{ (new numerator)}}{32 \text{ (new denominator)}}$

Whenever possible, reduce the products to their lowest terms.

In some examples the multiplication is made easier by **cancelling**, i.e. dividing the numerators and the denominators by common factors:

$$\tfrac{3}{4} \times \tfrac{16}{27} = \tfrac{4}{9}$$

i.e. both the numerators and the denominators were divided by 3 and 4.

Mixed numbers are first reduced to improper fractions before multiplying:

$$\tfrac{3}{8} \times 2\tfrac{1}{4} = \tfrac{3}{8} \times \tfrac{9}{4} = \tfrac{27}{32}$$

The term 'of' is sometimes encountered; it simply means multiply by:

$$\tfrac{3}{4} \text{ of } \tfrac{1}{8} = \tfrac{3}{4} \times \tfrac{1}{8} = \tfrac{3}{32}$$

The **division of fractions** is carried out as follows:

Invert (turn upside down) the divisor and proceed as in multiplication:

Thus, $\tfrac{3}{8} \div \tfrac{7}{8} = \tfrac{3}{8} \times \tfrac{8}{7} = \tfrac{3}{7}$ (the eights cancel out).

Mixed numbers are first reduced to improper fractions:

$$4\tfrac{1}{4} \div \tfrac{3}{4} = \tfrac{17}{4} \div \tfrac{3}{4} = \tfrac{17}{4} \times \tfrac{4}{3} = \tfrac{17}{3} = 5\tfrac{2}{3} \text{ (the fours cancel).}$$

Complex fractions are reduced to their lowest terms:

$\dfrac{\frac{3}{8}}{\frac{5}{16}} = \tfrac{3}{8} \div \tfrac{5}{16} = \tfrac{3}{8} \times \tfrac{16}{5} = \tfrac{6}{5} = 1\tfrac{1}{5}$. (8 will divide into 16, twice to

give 2, and 3 multiplied by 2 equals 6.)

$$\dfrac{\frac{1}{2}}{\frac{1}{4}} = \tfrac{1}{2} \div \tfrac{1}{4} = \tfrac{1}{2} \times \tfrac{4}{1} = 2. \text{ (2 will divide into 4.)}$$

Addition and Subtraction of Fractions

When two or more fractions have the same denominator their sum or difference is obtained by adding or subtracting their numerators.

$$\frac{3}{8} + \frac{5}{8} = \frac{8}{8} \text{ or } 1 \qquad \frac{5}{8} - \frac{3}{8} = \frac{2}{8} \text{ or } \frac{1}{4}$$

Fractions cannot be added or subtracted unless they have a common (same) denominator, e.g. we cannot add $\frac{3}{4}$ to $\frac{5}{16}$ or subtract $\frac{3}{8}$ from $\frac{9}{16}$ as they now stand, because the denominators represent different parts of a quantity. Eighths can be added to or subtracted from eights, but not to or from sixteenths directly. A **common denominator** of two or more fractions is a number which may be divided by the denominators of these fractions without a remainder, e.g. $\frac{1}{4} + \frac{3}{8} + \frac{5}{16}$; here the common denominator is found by inspection to be 16.

The operation of addition and subtraction can be made easier by using the **Lowest Common Denominator** or **Lowest Common Multiple** (L.C.M.). The L.C.M. is the smallest number that will contain each denominator of the given fractions without a remainder.

To Find the L.C.M.

The L.C.M. is sometimes found by inspection, e.g. $\frac{1}{2} + \frac{1}{4} + \frac{1}{8}$; the L.C.M. is seen to be 8. Where this way is not practicable the following method is used:

Divide by 2 as often as possible; then by 3 as often as possible; then by 5, 7, 11, 13, etc. The divisors and the remainder multiplied together form the L.C.M., e.g. the L.C.M. of $\frac{1}{4}$, $\frac{1}{3}$, $\frac{1}{9}$ and $\frac{1}{16}$ is:

$$
\begin{array}{r}
2)\underline{4 : 3 : 9 : 16} \\
2)\underline{2 : 3 : 9 : \ 8} \\
2)\underline{\cdot \ : 3 : 9 : \ 4} \\
2)\underline{\cdot \ : 3 : 9 : \ 2} \\
3)\underline{\cdot \ : 3 : 9 : \ \cdot} \\
\cdot \ : \cdot \ : 3 : \ \cdot
\end{array}
$$

$2 \times 2 \times 2 \times 2 \times 3 \times 3 = \underline{144}$, the L.C.M.

Example. Find the L.C.M. of $\frac{1}{6}$, $\frac{1}{8}$, $\frac{1}{7}$, $\frac{1}{10}$.

$$
\begin{array}{r}
2)\underline{6 : 8 : 7 : 10} \\
2)\underline{3 : 4 : 7 : \ 5} \\
3)\underline{3 : 2 : 7 : \ 5} \\
\cdot \ : 2 : 7 : \ 5
\end{array}
$$

$2 \times 2 \times 3 \times 2 \times 7 \times 5 = \underline{840}$, the L.C.M.

Before adding or subtracting fractions the following should be noted.

(*a*) Fractions should be reduced to their lowest terms.

(*b*) Improper fractions should be changed to mixed numbers.

(*c*) Add or subtract the whole numbers and the fractions separately.

(*d*) Divide the L.C.M. by the denominator of the given fraction and multiply this figure (the quotient) by the numerator of the same fraction:

Example. Add together $\frac{3}{4} + \frac{1}{2} + \frac{5}{8}$.

By inspection the L.C.M. is 8.

Now convert each fraction to eighths.

$$\frac{3 \times 2}{8} + \frac{1 \times 4}{8} + \frac{5 \times 1}{8}$$

$$= \frac{3 \times 2 + 4 \times 1 + 5 \times 1}{8}$$

$$= \frac{6 + 4 + 5}{8} = \frac{15}{8} = \underline{1\frac{7}{8}}$$

Example. Add together $2\frac{1}{4} + \frac{5}{8} + 1\frac{5}{32}$.

L.C.M. by inspection is 32.

Add the whole numbers $2 + 1 = 3$.

Now convert the fractions to thirty-seconds.

$$\frac{8 + 20 + 5}{32} = \frac{33}{32} = 1\frac{1}{32}$$

$$\text{Total} = 3 + 1\frac{1}{32} = \underline{4\frac{1}{32}}$$

Example. Add $3\frac{9}{14} + 7\frac{21}{35} + 3\frac{1}{7}$.

L.C.M.: $\quad 7)7 : 14 : 35$

$\qquad \overline{\cdot : 2 : 5} = 7 \times 2 \times 5 = 70.$

Add the whole numbers $3 + 7 + 3 = 13$.

Add the fractions $\frac{9}{14} + \frac{21}{35} + \frac{1}{7}$.

$$\frac{45 + 42 + 10}{70} = \frac{97}{70} = \underline{1\frac{27}{70}}$$

$$\text{Total} = 13 + 1\frac{27}{70} = \underline{14\frac{27}{70}}$$

d together $\frac{2}{10} + \frac{25}{15} + 3\frac{5}{60}$.

ce the fractions to their lowest terms and change to mixed

$$\tfrac{2}{10} = \tfrac{1}{5} \quad \tfrac{25}{15} = 1\tfrac{2}{3} \quad 3\tfrac{5}{60} = 3\tfrac{1}{12}$$

Add the whole numbers $1 + 3 = 4$.

L.C.M.: $\qquad 3)3 : 5 : 12$

$\qquad\qquad\overline{\quad\cdot : 5 : \ 4} = 3 \times 5 \times 4 = 60$

Now add the fractions $\frac{1}{5} + \frac{2}{3} + \frac{1}{12}$.

$$\frac{12 + 40 + 5}{60} = \tfrac{57}{60}$$

$$\text{Total} = 4 + \tfrac{57}{60} = \underline{4\tfrac{19}{20}}$$

Example. Subtract $\frac{5}{12}$ from $\frac{7}{8}$ or $(\frac{7}{8} - \frac{5}{12})$.

L.C.M. by inspection $= 24$.

Now subtract the fractions $\frac{7}{8} - \frac{5}{12}$.

$$\frac{21 - 10}{24} = \underline{\tfrac{11}{24}}$$

Example. Subtract $9\frac{15}{32}$ from $17\frac{9}{16}$ or $(17\frac{9}{16} - 9\frac{15}{32})$.

Subtract the whole numbers $17 - 9 = 8$.

L.C.M. by inspection $= 32$.

Now subtract the fractions $\frac{9}{16} - \frac{15}{32}$.

$$\frac{18 - 15}{32} = \tfrac{3}{32}$$

$$\text{Total} = 8 + \tfrac{3}{32} = \underline{8\tfrac{3}{32}}$$

The fractional part of a mixed number may be greater than the fractional part of the mixed number from which it is to be subtracted.

Example. Subtract $3\frac{3}{4}$ from $5\frac{1}{4}$ or $(5\frac{1}{4} - 3\frac{3}{4})$.

As $\frac{3}{4}$ cannot be subtracted from $\frac{1}{4}$, we take one unit from the whole number 5, and as 1 equals $\frac{4}{4}$, we have:

$$5 - 1 + \tfrac{4}{4} + \tfrac{1}{4} = 4\tfrac{5}{4}$$

Then $4\frac{5}{4} - 3\frac{3}{4} = 4 - 3$ and $\frac{5}{4} - \frac{3}{4}$

$$= 1 \text{ and } \tfrac{2}{4} \text{ or } 1 + \tfrac{1}{2} = \underline{1\tfrac{1}{2}}$$

Problems with Mixed Plus and Minus Signs

In these problems first add together all the numbers with plus (+) signs (remembering that if no sign appears before the first number a plus is understood), then add together all the numbers with a minus (−) sign, subtract the total of those with a minus from those with a plus.

Example. Solve $\frac{3}{4} - \frac{1}{4} + \frac{5}{8} - \frac{5}{16}$

$$= \frac{12 - 4 + 10 - 5}{16}$$

$$= \frac{12 + 10 - (4 + 5)}{16}$$

$$= \frac{22 - 9}{16} = \underline{\frac{13}{16}}$$

Example. Solve $\dfrac{\frac{3}{4} - \frac{3}{5}}{\frac{3}{8} + \frac{3}{16}}$.

$$= (\tfrac{3}{4} - \tfrac{3}{5}) \div (\tfrac{3}{8} + \tfrac{3}{16})$$

$$= \left(\frac{15 - 12}{20}\right) \div \left(\frac{16 + 3}{16}\right)$$

$$= \frac{3}{20} \div \frac{9}{16}$$

$$= \frac{3}{20} \times \frac{16}{9} = \underline{\tfrac{4}{15}} \text{ (by cancelling)}$$

Brackets

As shown in the foregoing examples, brackets are used to enclose two or more expressions in order to simplify the operations of addition, subtraction, and so on. There are several types of bracket in general use and the following examples will show these brackets and the methods of removing them in order to obtain a final answer.

The types of bracket in general use are (round), {curly}, [square], as shown in the expression:

$$6 \times [5 \times \{4 + 9 - 1 + (\tfrac{1}{2} - \tfrac{1}{4})\}]$$

If more than one bracket is used, the round bracket is placed inside, then the curly bracket, then the square bracket outside.

The rules for working out problems with brackets are:
(1) Work out the part inside the bracket, starting with the round
    (inside) bracket first.
(2) Work multiplication and division together.
(3) Work addition and subtraction together.
(4) When an expression is separated by a horizontal line, the part
    above the line has to be divided by the part below the line after
    both have been simplified.

Example. Simplify $6 \times [5 \times \{4 + 9 - 1 + (\frac{1}{2} - \frac{1}{4})\}]$.
(1) Remove and work out round brackets first, $\frac{1}{2} - \frac{1}{4} = \frac{1}{4}$
    $= 6 \times [5 \times \{4 + 9 - 1 + \frac{1}{4}\}]$
(2) Remove and work curly bracket, $4 + 9 - 1 + \frac{1}{4} = 12\frac{1}{4}$
    $= 6 \times [5 \times 12\frac{1}{4}]$
(3) Remove and work square bracket, $5 \times 12\frac{1}{4} = 61\frac{1}{4}$
    $= 6 \times 61\frac{1}{4} = \underline{367\frac{1}{2}}$

When we find a number in the front or the rear of brackets containing
an expression without a sign between the number and the bracket, we
know that the expression must be multiplied by the number.

Example.

$$5(7 - 4) = 5 \times (7 - 4) = 5 \times 3 = \underline{15}$$

Exercise 1

Express as improper fractions:
1. $2\frac{1}{8}$ **2.** $5\frac{3}{4}$ **3.** $3\frac{1}{16}$ **4.** $2\frac{1}{5}$ **5.** $1\frac{5}{12}$ **6.** $4\frac{5}{32}$ **7.** $3\frac{5}{64}$ **8.** $3\frac{1}{7}$
   $(\frac{17}{8})$ $(\frac{23}{4})$ $(\frac{49}{16})$ $(\frac{11}{5})$ $(\frac{17}{12})$ $(\frac{133}{32})$ $(\frac{197}{64})$ $(\frac{22}{7})$

Reduce to whole or mixed numbers:
1. $\frac{163}{4}$ **2.** $\frac{37}{16}$ **3.** $\frac{127}{2}$ **4.** $\frac{12}{4}$ **5.** $\frac{121}{64}$ **6.** $\frac{21}{8}$ **7.** $\frac{23}{7}$ **8.** $\frac{125}{25}$
   $(40\frac{3}{4})$ $(2\frac{5}{16})$ $(63\frac{1}{2})$ (3) $(1\frac{57}{64})$ $(2\frac{5}{8})$ $(3\frac{2}{7})$ (5)

Reduce to their lowest terms:
1. $\frac{12}{64}$ **2.** $\frac{10}{32}$ **3.** $\frac{144}{60}$ **4.** $\frac{12}{48}$ **5.** $\frac{8}{20}$ **6.** $\frac{40}{64}$ **7.** $\frac{24}{144}$ **8.** $\frac{64}{1000}$
   $(\frac{3}{16})$ $(\frac{5}{16})$ $(2\frac{2}{5})$ $(\frac{1}{4})$ $(\frac{2}{5})$ $(\frac{5}{8})$ $(\frac{1}{6})$ $(\frac{8}{125})$

Find the value of the following:
1. $\frac{1}{4} \times 6$ **2.** $\frac{15}{16} \times 8$ **3.** $5 \times \frac{13}{32}$ **4.** $\frac{3}{8} \times \frac{4}{7}$
   $(1\frac{1}{2})$ $(7\frac{1}{2})$ $(2\frac{3}{32})$ $(\frac{3}{14})$

5. $\frac{2}{3} \times \frac{3}{4} \times \frac{5}{8}$ **6.** $\frac{1}{2}$ of $\frac{1}{4}$ **7.** $5 \div 6$
   $(\frac{5}{16})$ $(\frac{1}{8})$ $(\frac{5}{6})$

8. $2 \div \frac{3}{4}$ **9.** $\frac{5}{16} \div \frac{5}{32}$ **10.** $4\frac{2}{3} \div 3\frac{1}{7}$
   $(2\frac{2}{3})$ (2) $(1\frac{16}{33})$

11. $\dfrac{\frac{7}{16}}{\frac{3}{8}}$ $(1\frac{1}{6})$ **12.** $\dfrac{7\frac{1}{2}}{1\frac{5}{8}}$ $(4\frac{8}{13})$

Find the value of the following:

1. $\frac{1}{2} + \frac{1}{8} + \frac{5}{12}$ **2.** $1\frac{1}{3} + \frac{5}{16} + \frac{9}{48}$ **3.** $\frac{2}{3} + \frac{5}{9} + \frac{7}{18}$
    $(1\frac{1}{24})$ $(1\frac{5}{6})$ $(1\frac{11}{18})$

4. $2\frac{1}{4} + 5\frac{3}{8} + 1\frac{13}{16}$ **5.** $\frac{2}{10} + \frac{5}{15} + 4\frac{3}{5}$
    $(9\frac{7}{16})$ $(5\frac{2}{15})$

6. $\frac{2}{3} - \frac{1}{8}$ **7.** $\frac{11}{16} - \frac{9}{32}$ **8.** $4\frac{1}{7} - 3\frac{4}{5}$
   $(\frac{13}{24})$ $(\frac{13}{32})$ $(\frac{12}{35})$

9. $8\frac{1}{8} - 4\frac{3}{16}$ **10.** $4\frac{17}{64} - 2\frac{11}{32}$
   $(3\frac{15}{16})$ $(1\frac{59}{64})$

11. $3\frac{3}{4} + 6\frac{7}{8} - 4\frac{5}{6}$ **12.** $\dfrac{4\frac{1}{2} \times 6\frac{3}{4}}{1\frac{4}{5}}$ $(16\frac{7}{8})$
   $(5\frac{19}{24})$

13. $\frac{7}{8} - \frac{1}{4} + \frac{5}{16} - \frac{3}{32}$ **14.** $5\frac{1}{2} - 2\frac{3}{8} + 1\frac{1}{4} - \frac{9}{32}$
   $(\frac{27}{32})$ $(4\frac{3}{32})$

15. $\frac{65}{100} \times 5\frac{5}{8} \div 4\frac{1}{2}$ **16.** $65\frac{5}{8} - 46\frac{2}{3}$ **17.** $\dfrac{\frac{7}{8} + \frac{3}{16}}{\frac{9}{16} - \frac{7}{32}}$ $(3\frac{1}{11})$
   $(\frac{13}{16})$ $(18\frac{23}{24})$

18. $\left\{\left(\dfrac{25 + 32}{8}\right) \times \left(\dfrac{25 - 22}{8}\right) \div \left(\dfrac{160 - 103}{64}\right)\right\}$
                          (3)

Practical Problems

1. If the load that a vehicle will carry is $2\frac{1}{2}$ tonne and this load is $\frac{5}{9}$ of the vehicle's mass, what is the total mass of the vehicle?

              $(4\frac{1}{2}$ tonne$)$

2. A tank containing 40 litres of oil leaks at the rate of $1\frac{1}{4}$ litres per hour. How many hours will it take to empty the tank?

              $(32$ hours$)$

3. A length of 'silver steel' is 330 mm long. How many pieces each $41\frac{1}{4}$ mm long can be obtained from this rod? (Ignore the width of the saw-cuts).

              (8)

4. A vehicle travels a distance of 507 kilometres and uses $40\frac{1}{2}$ litres of petrol. Calculate the kilometres per litre.

              $(12\frac{14}{27}$ km/litre$)$

2 Decimals

Decimal fractions, or simply **Decimals,** are often used in motor vehicle calculations.

The basis of the decimal system is the division of the fractional part of a number into $\frac{1}{10}$ths, $\frac{1}{100}$ths, $\frac{1}{1000}$ths, and so on. If a number has three figures, say 456, the first figure 4 represents hundreds, the second figure 5 represents tens, and the third figure 6 represents units.

We can continue this system still further to the right; for example, 456·523, making each place represent one-tenth of the place in front of it; thus giving in succession, tenths, hundredths and thousandths.

The figures ·523 are therefore 5 tenths, 2 hundredths and 3 thousandths. The number ·523 is known as a decimal fraction.

The 'dot' (·) in front of the 5 is called the **decimal point**; it is always placed between the units figure and the tenths figure in order to show which are the whole parts and which are the fractional parts of a number. If the number is less than one a 0 is placed to the left of the decimal point, e.g. 0·284, to show that no whole number is present. It is essential to insert this 0 as otherwise errors can easily occur.

We say that the decimal fraction 0·284 is worked out to three 'decimal places'; the 2, immediately to the right of the decimal point being the first decimal place, the next number 8 being the second decimal place, and the next number, the 4, being the third decimal place.

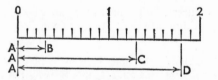

Fig. 2.1

Let us examine the use of decimals in another way. To measure the length of three lines *AB, AC, AD* (Fig. 2.1) we can use a scale which has each unit divided into ten equal divisions. With the help of the scale we can divide each of the three lines into similar equal divisions. Then the distance from A to the first division is $\frac{1}{10}$th or 0·1, and the length of AB is $\frac{3}{10}$ths or 0·3. The length of AC is $1\frac{3}{10}$ths or 1·3, and the length of AD is $1\frac{8}{10}$ths or 1·8.

The reader should understand clearly that

$$0·5 \quad = \frac{5}{10} \quad = 5 \text{ tenths}$$
$$0·05 \quad = \frac{5}{100} \quad = 5 \text{ hundredths}$$
$$0·005 \quad = \frac{5}{1000} \quad = 5 \text{ thousandths}$$
$$0·0005 = \frac{5}{10\,000} = 5 \text{ tenthousandths}$$

Addition and Subtraction of Decimals

To **add** decimals, write down the sum so that the decimal points are under each other and the corresponding figures—the tens, the tenths, the hundredths—are under each other. Add as with whole numbers and place the decimal point in the answer under the decimal points above.

Example. Add together 63·5, 0·25, 8·75, 118·125.

$$
\begin{array}{r}
63·5 \\
0·25 \\
8·75 \\
118·125 \\
\hline
190·625
\end{array}
$$

Example. Add together 241, 33·3, 3·1, 0·3, 0·005.

$$
\begin{array}{r}
241·0 \\
33·3 \\
3·1 \\
0·3 \\
0·005 \\
\hline
277·705
\end{array}
$$

To **subtract decimals,** write down the sum as for the subtraction of whole numbers but with the decimal point under the decimal point.

Example. Subtract 8·375 from 12·496.

$$
\begin{array}{r}
12·496 \\
8·375 \\
\hline
4·121
\end{array}
$$

Example. Subtract 18·4375 from 25·6.

$$
\begin{array}{r}
25·6000 \text{ (noughts added for convenience)} \\
18·4375 \\
\hline
7·1625
\end{array}
$$

Multiplication of Decimals

When multiplying decimals, first ignore the decimal point and proceed as in the multiplication of whole numbers. The decimal point is then placed in the answer as follows:

Count the number of figures appearing after the decimal point in both the multiplicand and the multiplier; mark off this number, starting from the right-hand side of the answer, as shown in the following example.

Example. Multiply 25·4 by 6·5.

$$
\begin{array}{r}
25 \cdot 4 \text{ multiplicand} \\
6 \cdot 5 \text{ multiplier} \\
\hline
1524 \\
1270 \\
\hline
165 \cdot 10
\end{array}
\left.\right\}
\begin{array}{l}
2 \text{ figs. after decimal} \\
\text{point}
\end{array}
$$

165·10 (2 figs. after decimal point)

Example. Multiply 0·232 by 0·002.

$$
\begin{array}{r}
0 \cdot 232 \\
0 \cdot 002 \\
\hline
0 \cdot 000\ 464
\end{array}
\left.\right\}
6 \text{ figs. after decimal point}
$$

In this example, 6 decimal places are required in the answer; thus 3 noughts are placed on the left of 464 in order to give the required 6 places.

Care must be taken when a nought appears in the multiplier; the following example shows the method of working.

Example. Multiply 1·225 by 1·05.

$$
\begin{array}{r}
1 \cdot 225 \\
1 \cdot 05 \\
\hline
1225 \\
0000 \qquad \text{(for the 0 in the multiplier)} \\
6125 \\
\hline
1 \cdot 286\ 25
\end{array}
$$

Multiplying Decimals by 10

A decimal fraction can be multiplied by 10, 100, 1000, and so on, by moving the decimal point to the right by as many places as there are noughts in the multiplier.

Example.   2·735 ×   10 =   27·35, point moved one place.
2·735 ×   100 =   273·5, point moved two places.
2·735 × 1000 = 2735, point moved three places.

Division of Decimals

In the division of decimals, where the divisor is a whole number we proceed as in the division of whole numbers until the last figure before the decimal point is used, i.e. the last whole number, then we place a point in the answer.

Example. Divide 635·2 by 8.

$$8)\overline{635·2}$$
$$\overline{79·4}$$
$$\therefore 635·2 \div 8 = \underline{79·4}$$

Where the divisor is a decimal we proceed thus:

(1) Make the divisor a whole number by moving the decimal point to the right and at the same time move the decimal point in the dividend the same number of places to the right.

(2) Proceed with the division until all the figures are used; at this point add a decimal point to the answer and one nought to the dividend, repeating this until the required number of places is reached.

Example. Divide 326 by 0·24 to one decimal place.

Make divisor a whole number by moving decimal point two places to right. Move decimal point in dividend two places to right by adding two noughts. Then

```
                1358·3
        24·)32 600·
            24
            ──
            86
            72
            ───
            140
            120
            ───
            200
            192
            ───
             80—0 added
             72
             ──
              8—remainder
```

$$\therefore 326 \div 0·24 = \underline{1358·3}$$

Example. Divide 0·0035 by 1·25.

$$
\begin{array}{r}
0·0028 \\
125\overline{)0·350} \\
250 \\
\overline{1000} \\
1000 \\
\overline{\cdots\cdots}
\end{array}
$$

$$\therefore 0·0035 \div 1·25 = \underline{0·0028}$$

Dividing Decimals by 10

A decimal fraction can be divided by 10, 100, 1000, and so on, by moving the decimal point to the left by as many places as there are noughts in the divisor, adding noughts as required.

Example.

2·735 ÷   10 = 0·2735, point moved one place.

2·735 ÷   100 = 0·027 35, point moved two places.

2·735 ÷ 1000 = 0·002 735, point moved three places.

Conversion of Decimals

To convert a decimal to a vulgar fraction, place the figure 1 under the decimal point followed by as many noughts as there are figures after the decimal point, and then reduce the resulting fraction to its lowest terms.

Example. Convert 0·375 to a vulgar fraction.

$$0·375 = \tfrac{375}{1000} = \tfrac{15}{40} = \tfrac{3}{8}$$
$$\therefore 0·375 = \underline{\tfrac{3}{8}}$$

Example. Convert 0·0625 to a vulgar fraction.

$$0·0625 = \tfrac{625}{10\,000} = \tfrac{5}{80} = \tfrac{1}{16}$$
$$\therefore 0·0625 = \underline{\tfrac{1}{16}}$$

To convert a vulgar fraction to a decimal divide the numerator by the denominator. It is usually an advantage first to reduce the fraction to its lowest terms.

Example. Convert $\frac{5}{8}$ to a decimal.

$\frac{5}{8} = 5 \div 8$

$$\begin{array}{r} 8)\overline{5 \cdot 000} \\ \hline 0 \cdot 625 \end{array}$$

$$\therefore \frac{5}{8} = \underline{0 \cdot 625}$$

Example. Convert $\frac{21}{24}$ to a decimal.

$\frac{21}{24} = \frac{7}{8} = 7 \div 8$

$$\begin{array}{r} 8)\overline{7 \cdot 000} \\ \hline 0 \cdot 875 \end{array}$$

$$\therefore \frac{21}{24} = \underline{0 \cdot 875}$$

Example. Convert $\frac{1}{9}$ to a decimal.

$\frac{1}{9} = 1 \div 9$

$$\begin{array}{r} 9)\overline{1 \cdot 0000} \\ \hline 0 \cdot 1111 \end{array}$$

$$\therefore \frac{1}{9} = \underline{0 \cdot 1111}$$

Recurring Decimals

Many vulgar fractions can be converted exactly into a decimal, although the decimal may be a long one. With some vulgar fractions, however, this is not the case. In the example of one-ninth, worked above, the figures in the quotient would never stop; they keep recurring. This kind of decimal is called a **recurring** decimal. Other examples are:

$$\tfrac{1}{3} = 0 \cdot 3333 \qquad \tfrac{2}{3} = 0 \cdot 6666 \qquad \tfrac{1}{7} = 0 \cdot 142\ 857\ 142$$

These are written as $0 \cdot \dot{3}$, $0 \cdot \dot{6}$ and $0 \cdot \dot{1}42\ 85\dot{7}$; dots are placed over the figures which recur. In practice, we seldom carry the result to more than four places, thus for $0 \cdot \dot{3}$ we use $0 \cdot 3333$; for $0 \cdot \dot{6}$ we use $0 \cdot 6667$ and for $0 \cdot \dot{1}42\ 85\dot{7}$ we use $0 \cdot 143$, and so on.

To reduce a recurring decimal to a vulgar fraction we place it over as many nines as there are decimal places, thus:

$$0 \cdot \dot{3} = \tfrac{333}{999} \qquad 0 \cdot \dot{6} = \tfrac{6666}{9999} \qquad 0 \cdot \dot{1}42\ 85\dot{7} = \tfrac{142\text{-}857}{999\text{-}999}$$

Approximations and Rough Checks

The student will have noticed that in the division of decimals a large number of decimal places may be obtained in the answer simply by continuing the division. In practical work this could suggest accuracy far beyond our own ability or the correctness of our instruments— which is absurd. In most motor vehicle calculations four places of decimals are sufficient and usually three places of decimals are 'near enough'.

The rules for finding an answer correct to a certain number of decimal places are:

(1) Take the calculation to one more than the number of places required.

(2) If the last figure is less than 5, omit it; if the last figure is 5 or more, omit it and add 1 to the preceding figure.

Example.

$1·735\ 56 = 1·7356$ correct to four decimal places.

$5·7343\ \ \ = 5·734$ correct to three decimal places.

$0·9375\ \ \ = 0·94$ correct to two decimal places.

When calculating, it is always best to make a rough check in order to get an idea of what the answer should be. If our answer is not somewhere near the rough check result, we shall know that a mistake has been made either in the working or in the placing of the decimal point.

Example. $1·54 \times 9·85$ is about
$1·5\ \ \times 10 = 15$ roughly.

The actual answer $= \underline{15·169}$

During the working of practical problems we can often see, or know roughly, what the answer should be; e.g. when working out the capacity of a petrol tank for a normal car we know the answer should be about 45 litres.

If we obtained 550 litres as a result, we should know that we had made a mistake. On the other hand, a result of 55 litres would be accepted as a reasonable answer.

The Micrometer

The micrometer is a device for measuring in thousandths; 'micro' means small (i.e. small quantities) and 'meter' means measuring device. To be able to use the micrometer with confidence and accuracy, a good knowledge of decimals and fractions is necessary.

For accurate measurement of motor vehicle parts, instruments based on the micrometer principle are used extensively. In this chapter, however, we shall not consider details of their construction but only the basic principle of the micrometer.

Almost all modern micrometers intended to read 1000ths of an inch are made with a screwed spindle of 40 threads per inch of length; thus for one complete revolution of the spindle, the instrument opens or closes $\frac{1}{40}$ in or 0·025 in (25 'thou.'). Fig. 2.2 shows the measuring parts of a micrometer. There are two scales, the horizontal or **sleeve** scale, and the **thimble** scale. The sleeve scale has ten main divisions each representing $\frac{1}{10}$ in or 0·1 in; each of these main divisions is divided into four small divisions. These small divisions show how many revolutions the spindle has made and they are thus equal to $\frac{1}{40}$ in or 0·025 in. The thimble scale is divided into 25 equal divisions, and as the thimble is fixed firmly to the spindle, then one complete revolution of the thimble will show $\frac{1}{40}$ in or 0·025 in; therefore *one* division on the thimble will show $\frac{1}{25}$ of $\frac{1}{40}$ in = 0·001 in (1 'thou.').

In order to read the micrometer we proceed (see Fig. 2.2):

(*a*) Note the number of main divisions showing on the sleeve scale, in Fig. 2.2; these are 3 or 0·3 in.

(*b*) Note the number of small divisions showing on the sleeve scale, in Fig. 2.2; these are 2 or 2(0·025) in.

(*c*) Note the number of small divisions showing on the thimble scale between 0 and the line coinciding with the horizontal line on the sleeve; in Fig. 2.2 these are between 10 and 11, say 10 or 0·010 in.

Fig. 2.2   Fig. 2.3

∴ The reading in Fig. 2.2 = 0·3 + 2(0·025) + 0·010 in
                = 0·36 in

Fig. 2.3 shows a reading of 0·028 in.

It has already been stated that most micrometers intended to measure 1000ths of an inch are made with a screwed spindle having 40 threads per inch of length. While this is convenient and customary, micrometers using other numbers of threads per inch besides 40 will provide accurate measurement also. The number of threads per inch used should divide into a thousand, thus enabling a suitable scale to be used for the sleeve and thimble. For example, 50 threads per inch of spindle length will give a sleeve scale of 5 small divisions per $\frac{1}{10}$ in, i.e. one small division is equal to $\frac{1}{50}$ in or 0·020 in (20 'thou.'). Spindles with 20 and 25 threads per inch of length would be suitable also.

Example. A measuring device of the micrometer type has a spindle cut with 20 threads per inch. Attached to the spindle and revolving with it is a disc engraved with a certain number of equal divisions. How many divisions must there be if the device is to read to one thousandth of an inch?

$$\text{Number of divisions on disc} = \frac{1000}{20}$$

$$= \underline{50 \text{ divisions}}$$

Many micrometers are fitted with a **vernier** scale which is engraved on the sleeve of the micrometer; this vernier scale is read in conjunction with the thimble scale. The vernier scale consists of ten equal divisions which are equal in length to nine divisions on the thimble scale (see (Fig. 2.4). Therefore, the difference in width between a division on the thimble scale and a division on the vernier sleeve scale is one tenth of a thimble division, i.e. $\frac{1}{10}$ of $\frac{1}{1000}$, which equals $\frac{1}{10\,000}$, or 0·0001 in.

Micrometers fitted with a vernier scale are thus accurate to 0·0001 in and the method of reading this type is shown in Fig. 2.4. The reading in tenths, hundredths and thousandths is found to be 0·437 in, but there remains a part of a thimble division unread. In order to read this part accurately we must use the vernier scale: note the line of the vernier scale which coincides exactly with a division line on the thimble scale; in Fig. 2.4 this vernier scale line is shown to be numbered 3. Thus the final reading will be 0·437 plus 0·0003, which equals 0·4373 in. Fig. 2.5 shows a reading of 0·2554 in.

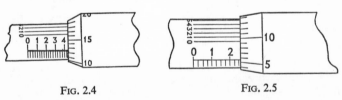

FIG. 2.4   FIG. 2.5

The Vernier

The vernier has an advantage over the micrometer because of its greater range, e.g. a 0 to 12 in vernier is able to take inside and outside measurements up to 12 in, whereas the micrometer is usually made in separate sizes: 0 to 1 in; 1 to 2 in; 2 to 3 in, and so on. A separate instrument, called an 'inside' micrometer, is required to take inside measurements. Modern verniers are capable of giving accurate readings to 0·001 in.

Construction of the Vernier

A vernier which reads to 0·001 in is shown in Fig. 2.6.

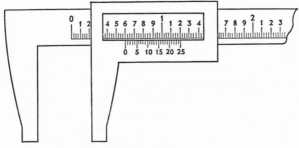

FIG. 2.6

The **main rule** is divided into fortieths of an inch along its whole length and every fourth division is numbered, thus representing 0·1 in. The numbers range from 1 to 9 between each inch. Fitted to the main rule is a **sliding piece** which has 25 equal divisions marked on it, and every five is numbered as shown. The total length of the 25 divisions on the sliding piece is equal in length to 24 divisions on the main rule. Therefore, each division on the sliding piece is shorter than each division on the main rule by $\frac{1}{25}$ of $\frac{1}{40}$ in, which equals $\frac{1}{1000}$ in or 0·001 in.

To Read the Vernier (see Fig. 2.7)

(1) Note the division on the main rule to the left of the mark L; this is 0·5 in.

FIG. 2.7

(2) Look along the sliding piece in order to find a division on it exactly in line with a division on the main rule; in this example the division on the sliding piece is 12. Thus, the mark L is $\frac{12}{1000}$ ths of an inch past the 0·5 in line.

(3) The total reading is 0·5 + 0·012 = 0·512 in.

Verniers are made with 50 divisions to the inch on the main rule and 20 divisions on the sliding piece, and these 20 divisions are equal in length to 19 divisions on the main rule. Each division on the sliding piece is shorter than each division on the main rule by $\frac{1}{20}$ of $\frac{1}{50}$ in, which equals $\frac{1}{1000}$ in or 0·001 in. The method of reading is similar to the first type.

The Metric System

The **metric** system is now used in the United Kingdom as well as on the Continent and in South America and most other countries. This system is used by scientists universally and is based on the decimal system.

There are three principal metric units in general use, for length, volume and mass.

The unit of **length** is the **metre** (m), but for transportation we refer to the **kilometre** (km) which is equal to 1000 metres, and for small lengths the **millimetre** (mm) which is equal to $\frac{1}{1000}$th part of a metre.

The unit of **volume** is the cubic metre (m³) or (cu. m), but for the measurement of liquid the **litre** (l), which is $\frac{1}{10}$th of a metre cubed, is normally used. For small volumes the **millilitre** (ml), which is $\frac{1}{1000}$th part of a litre, is used.

The unit of mass is the **kilogramme** (kg); for a large mass the 'metric ton', now known as the **tonne** (t), is used; it is equivalent to 1000 kg. For a small mass the **gramme** (g), which is $\frac{1}{1000}$th part of a kilogramme, is used.

The metric system contains many multiples and sub-multiples of the basic unit, but it is intended that with time many of these will gradually disappear.

It is useful to remember the following approximations: 1 metre equals 39·37 in (roughly 3 ft $3\frac{1}{3}$ in); 0·5 mm equals 0·020 in (20 thou.); 1 mm equals 0·040 in (40 thou.); 63·5 mm equals 2·5 in; 100 mm equals 4 in; 1 kilometre equals $\frac{5}{8}$ mile; 1 in equals 25 mm; 2·2 lb equals 1 kilogram and 1·76 pints equals 1 litre.

The Metric Micrometer

Metric micrometers are made with a finer thread than those in British units and the screwed spindle has a 'pitch' of 0·5 mm (the distance between the tops of adjacent (next to) threads is called the pitch of the screw). Thus, for one complete revolution of the spindle the instrument opens or closes 0·5 mm.

The sleeve scale is graduated in 0·5 mm divisions (Fig. 2.8); each fifth division is marked 5, 10, 15, 20 and 25, thus corresponding to the British micrometer. The thimble, however, is divided into 50 parts; each fifth division is numbered 0, 5, 10, 15, and so on. Therefore, at each complete revolution of the thimble a $\frac{1}{2}$-mm or 0·5 mm division is uncovered on the sleeve. Movement of the thimble through one thimble division, i.e. $\frac{1}{50}$th of a turn, opens or closes the instrument $\frac{1}{50}$ of $\frac{1}{2}$ mm, which is $\frac{1}{100}$ mm or 0·01 mm.

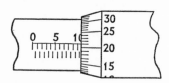

Fig. 2.8

Now 0·01 mm equals 0·000 393 7 or nearly $\frac{4}{10\,000}$ths, which is less than a half-thousandth of an inch. The metric micrometer is therefore a finer measuring instrument than the British micrometer, except those fitted with a vernier scale. For this reason the metric micrometer is used extensively in the United Kingdom both in the manufacture and the repair work of motor vehicles.

Fig. 2.8 shows a reading of 10·71 mm; it should be carefully noted that the thimble revolves *one* complete turn for 0·5 mm and *two* complete turns for 1 mm.

The metric unit of capacity, the **litre,** and the unit of mass, the **gramme,** will be dealt with in Chapter 5 under areas, volumes and mass.

Exercise 2

1. 25·4 + 0·987   **2.** 6·375 + 10·0875   **3.** 51 + 0·075
   (26·387)   (16·4625)   (51·075)

4. 11·7 − 8·07   **5.** 0·01 − 0·001   **6.** 51·1 − 25·579
   (3·63)   (0·009)   (25·521)

7. Multiply: **8.** Divide:

1. 4·5 by 5·6   (25·2)   1. 45 by 0·0015   (30 000)
2. 0·0007 by 0·045   (0·000 031 5)   2. 0·0025 by 1·75   (0·0014)

Multiply			Divide	
3. 25·4 by 91·5	(2324·1)		3. 0·725 by 25	(0·029)
4. 125·3 by 0·000 75	(0·093 975)		4. 0·4 by 0·04	(10)
5. 65 by 0·015	(0·975)		5. 0·555 by 0·0025	(222)
6. 2·735 by 7·707	(21·078 6)		6. 0·0145 by 0·025	(0·58)

9. Express as vulgar fractions:

1. 0·185 $\left(\frac{37}{200}\right)$
2. 0·031 25 $\left(\frac{1}{32}\right)$
3. 0·725 $\left(\frac{29}{40}\right)$
4. 0·425 $\left(\frac{17}{40}\right)$
5. 0·135 $\left(\frac{27}{200}\right)$
6. 0·297 $\left(\frac{297}{1000}\right)$

10. Express as decimals:

1. $\frac{31}{32}$ (0·968 75)
2. $\frac{21}{64}$ (0·328 125)
3. $\frac{7}{32}$ (0·218 75)
4. $\frac{9}{16}$ (0·5625)
5. $\frac{2}{9}$ (0·2222)
6. $\frac{6}{7}$ (0·8571)

Practical Problems

1. A float-chamber which holds one twelfth of a litre is three-quarters full of petrol. What fraction of a litre does the float-chamber contain?
(0·0625)

2. If a litre of petrol has a mass of 0·75 kg, calculate the mass of 2250 litres and express the answer in tonne. (1 tonne = 1000 kg).
(1·6875 tonne)

3. A fitter receives 45p per hour and an apprentice receives 25p per hour. Express the wage of the apprentice as a decimal of the fitter's wage (2 decimal places). (0·55)

4. A certain engine normally develops 32·5 kW; by increasing the compression ratio the power is raised to 37·7 kW. Express as a decimal this increase in power. (0·16)

5. A fuel tank can hold 96 litres of oil, but only contains 18 litres of oil. Express the contents (the oil) as a decimal of the total capacity.
(0·1875)

6. An instrument of the micrometer type has a spindle cut with 25 threads per inch. Attached to the spindle and revolving with it is a disc engraved with a certain number of equal divisions. How many divisions must there be if the instrument is to read to one-thousandth of an inch?

If the spindle is revolved through 17 complete turns and 23 divisions on the disc from its zero position, how far in inches has the spindle been moved from its zero position? (40; 0·703 in) (C. and G.)

7. The bore of an engine cylinder is 3·334 in. Express this in millimetres (1 in = 25·4 mm), (84·68 mm) (U.E.I.)

8. Express a distance of 20 kilometres in miles, given that a yard = 0·914 metre and a mile = 1760 yards.   (12·43 miles)   (E.M.E.U.)

9. Sketch a standard 0–1 in micrometer in good proportion to show a setting of 0·282 in.   (U.E.I.)

10. Express 723 mm in metres and find the corresponding measurement in feet and inches to the nearest sixteenth of an inch.
(1 in = 25·4 mm)   (0·723 metres)   (2 ft $4\frac{7}{16}$ in)

11. Sketch and describe a vernier caliper gauge capable of measuring to 0·01 mm.

Give a diagram of the scales set for a dimension of 40·12 mm.

(E.M.E.U.)

12. Sketch a standard 0–25 mm micrometer in good proportion to show a setting of 8·22 mm.

3

Powers and Roots

Powers

When a number is multiplied by itself, the result is called the **square** or **second power** of the number and the number is said to be squared. Thus, the square or second power of 4 is 4 multiplied by 4, which equals 16. Instead of writing this expression 4 multiplied by 4 or 4×4 in full, we show the power by a small figure placed at the top right-hand side of the number. This number is known as the **index** number. Then $4 \times 4 = 4^2$; in the same way 3^4 means $3 \times 3 \times 3 \times 3$, and it is called 3 to the fourth power.

Now 125 is called the **cube** of 5, or 5 to the third power, i.e. $5 \times 5 \times 5$ or 5^3, and it is called 5 cubed.

A whole number or decimal is raised to any power by multiplying the number by itself as many times as the index number or figure indicates.

Examples.
$$9^3 = 9 \times 9 \times 9 = \underline{729}$$
$$1 \cdot 2^2 = 1 \cdot 2 \times 1 \cdot 2 = \underline{1 \cdot 44}$$
$$0 \cdot 03^2 = 0 \cdot 03 \times 0 \cdot 03 = \underline{0 \cdot 0009}$$

A fraction is raised to any power by multiplying both the numerator and the denominator by themselves as many times as the index or figure indicates.

Examples.
$$\left(\frac{5}{8}\right)^3 = \frac{5 \times 5 \times 5}{8 \times 8 \times 8} = \frac{125}{\underline{512}}$$
$$\left(\frac{3}{4}\right)^2 = \frac{3 \times 3}{4 \times 4} = \frac{9}{\underline{16}}$$

The process of obtaining the power of a whole number, a decimal or a fraction is called **involution**.

Roots

The **root** of a number is that number which, when multiplied by itself a given number of times, produces the original number. The symbol for the root of a number is $\sqrt{}$ and it is called the **radical sign.**

The **square root** of a number is that number which, when multiplied by itself, will equal the original number; thus 2 is the square root of 4, since $2 \times 2 = 4$. In the same way 2 is the **cube root** of 8, since $2 \times 2 \times 2 = 8$. Roots are usually indicated by using the radical sign and the index figure of the root:

$\sqrt[2]{4}$, i.e. the square root of 4 $\sqrt[3]{8}$, i.e. the cube root of 8.

The index figure 2 is usually omitted for square roots, e.g. $\sqrt{4}$ is the square root of 4, but $\sqrt[3]{27}$ indicates the cube root of 27, which is 3, because $3 \times 3 \times 3 = 27$; 3 is the fourth root of 81 because $3 \times 3 \times 3 \times 3 = 81$, or $3 = \sqrt[4]{81}$.

There are few numbers whose root is evident by inspection or can be found by simple calculation. For example, the square root of 12 lies between $\sqrt{9}$ and $\sqrt{16}$, i.e. between 3 and 4. The $\sqrt{12}$ must therefore be 3 plus a fraction, and to find the square root of 12 the following method is used.

(1) Mark off the number into groups of two figures by means of brackets starting at the second figure on either side of the decimal point and moving both to the left and to the right. Noughts are added behind the decimal point in order to form a group, and the word **root** placed:

$$
\begin{array}{l}
\qquad\qquad \textbf{Root} \\
3]\ (12)\cdot(00)\ [3\cdot464 \\
\qquad\ \ 9 \\
\overline{\quad} \\
(a)\quad 64)\overline{300}\text{—attached} \\
64 \times 4 =\ 256 \\
\qquad\quad \overline{686)\cdot4400} \\
686 \times 6 = 4116 \\
\qquad\quad \overline{6924)\cdot28\ 400} \\
6924 \times 4 = 27\ 696 \\
\qquad\qquad \overline{\cdot\cdot704}\ \text{remainder}
\end{array}
$$

(2) Consider the first group 12 on the left of the decimal point. It is necessary to find the greatest number whose square is equal to or less

than 12; this number is 3. Set this 3 in both the root and the left-hand side of the number. Place the square of this 3, i.e. 9, under the first group 12, subtract 9 from 12 and obtain the remainder 3; place a decimal point behind 3 in the root.

(3) Bring down the group 00 and attach these to the remainder 3 as shown. Next multiply the root figure 3 by 2 to give 6; place this 6 on the left of 300 as shown at (*a*). We now require a figure to place next to the 6 at (*a*) so that when 6 and this figure are multiplied by the figure a number under 300 will be obtained. By trial this figure is found to be 4; write 4 in the root and also next to the 6 at (*a*) in order to form a new divisor.

Multiply 64 by 4 to obtain 256 and subtract 256 from 300 to give a remainder of 44.

(4) Add two noughts to the remainder 44, making 4400. (This addition of noughts sometimes puzzles students, but we should remember that 12·000 000 still only equals 12 and the noughts are only used for convenience.) Ignoring the decimal point in the root, we multiply 34 by 2 and place the product of 68 to form the first two figures of the new divisor.

By trial we find the third figure of the new divisor is 6; place this 6 in the root as shown and attach it also to the divisor 68 to give 686. (This figure 6 was obtained in the same way as we obtained the figure 4 in section (3).)

Multiply 686 by the 6 in the root to give 4116 and subtract 4116 from 4400 as shown, to leave a remainder of 284.

(5) Attach two noughts to 284 to give 28 400, which is the new dividend; multiply 346 in the root by 2 and obtain the new divisor 692. By trial we find that the fourth figure of the new divisor is 4; place this 4 in the root as shown and attach it also to the divisor 692 to give 6924. (This figure 4 was obtained as shown in section (3).)

Multiply 6924 by the 4 in the root to give 27 696, and as shown there will be a remainder of 704.

The square root of 12 is therefore 3·46 to two decimal places; when more decimal places are required the operations can be continued.

Example. Find the square root of 234·5 to two decimal places.

In this example we have one figure only in the extreme left-hand group; this figure, however, will represent a group.

Now the square root of 2 must lie between 1 and 2, so we place 1 in the root and 1 to the left as shown at (*a*). We continue the working, as shown in the previous example, to two decimal places.

```
                              Root
        (a)   1](2)(34)·(50)[15·31
                   1
                   ‒‒
              25)134
     25 × 5 =   125
              303)··950
    303 × 3 =     909
              3061) ·4100
   3061 × 1 =      3061
                   1039 remainder
```

The square root of 234·5 = <u>15·31</u>

Example. Find the square root of 0·0125 to three decimal places.

In this example the nought directly behind the decimal point counts as part of the group 01, but we ignore the nought during the working out.

Note that the square root of this decimal 0·0125 has a greater value than the original number; this is not surprising because, for example, $0·2 \times 0·2 = 0·04$, i.e. the square root of 0·04 is 0·2.

```
                         Root
            1]0·(01)(25)[0·1118
   1 × 1 =      1
            21)··25
  21 × 1 =      21
           221) 400
 221 × 1 =      221
          2228)17 900
2228 × 8 =     17 824
               ···76
```

The square root of 0·0125 = <u>0·112</u>

Example. Find the square root of 0·005 76 to three decimal places.

In this example the first group consists of noughts, therefore the first figure of the root will be a nought. The rest of the working is the same as before.

```
                          Root
              7]0·(00)(57)(60)[0·0758
          7 × 7 =    49
                   145)·860
        145 × 5 =    725
                   1508)13 500
       1508 × 8 =      12 064
                        ·1436
```

The square root of $0·005\ 76 = \underline{0·076}$

In order to 'prove' a square root, the result obtained should be multiplied by itself. If this result equals the original number the square root is correct. Where we have a remainder, the square root when multiplied by itself will not equal the original number and the square root is only approximate.

When the square root of a number is multiplied by itself and the result equals the number exactly, this root is **perfect.**

Roots of Fractions

The square root of a fraction is found as follows:

Find the square root of both the numerator and the denominator; if both the numerator and the denominator have perfect squares we can find the roots by inspection.

Where the square root of the numerator or the denominator cannot be found in this way we can convert the fraction to a decimal and find the square root as shown in previous examples.

Example. Find the square root of $\frac{4}{9}$.

$$\sqrt{\frac{4}{9}} = \frac{\sqrt{4}}{\sqrt{9}} = \underline{\frac{2}{3}}$$

Example. Find the square root of $\frac{9}{16}$.

$$\sqrt{\frac{9}{16}} = \frac{\sqrt{9}}{\sqrt{16}} = \underline{\frac{3}{4}}$$

Example. Find the square root of $\frac{3}{8}$.

$$\sqrt{\frac{3}{8}} = \sqrt{0·375} = \underline{0·612\ 36}$$

The process of finding the roots of whole numbers, decimals and fractions is called **evolution.** The finding of other roots, e.g. cubes, by arithmetic is tedious. Evolution and involution by logarithms are described in Part 2 of these books.

Exercise 3

Find the square root of the following:

1. 386	(19·647)	**6.**	Evaluate $5 \cdot 2^3$		(140·608)
2. 25·45	(5·04)	**7.**	,,	$0 \cdot 1^2$	(0·01)
3. 0·09	(0·3)	**8.**	,,	$0 \cdot 2^3$	(0·008)
4. 1·025	(1·01)	**9.**	,,	$0 \cdot 3^3$	(0·027)
5. $\frac{35\,000}{9}$	(62·37)	**10.**	,,	$(\frac{5}{8})^2$	$(\frac{25}{64})$

Averages, Ratio, Proportion and Percentages

Most students will understand the idea of an **average** or **mean** as it is sometimes called.

The average distance covered by a vehicle can be expressed in kilometres per day, per week, per month, and so on. These averages are obtained by dividing the total distance covered by the number of days, weeks, etc., as shown in the example below. 'Per' means 'for every' or 'in each', e.g. 'for every day', 'in each week', and so on.

Example. A delivery van covers 80 km on Monday; 112 on Tuesday; 130 on Wednesday; 140 on Thursday; 64 on Friday and 32 on Saturday. Calculate the average distance per day.

Total distance $= 80 + 112 + 130 + 140 + 64 + 32 = 558$ km

$$\text{Average distance per day} = \frac{\text{Total distance}}{\text{Number of days}}$$

$$= \frac{558}{6} = \underline{93 \text{ km per day}}$$

Example. A vehicle travels equal distances at 60 km/h and 90 km/h. What is its average speed?

In problems of this kind we must be careful; the average speed is *not* $\dfrac{60 + 90}{2} = 75$ km/h, as it is stated that the vehicle travels equal distances. The average speed is obtained as follows:

$$60 \text{ km/h} = 1 \text{ km in } 1 \text{ minute, and}$$
$$90 \text{ km/h} = 1 \text{ km in } \tfrac{2}{3} \text{ minute}$$

Then 2 km are covered in $1 + \tfrac{2}{3} = 1\tfrac{2}{3} = \tfrac{5}{3}$ min.

$\therefore$ 1 km will be covered in $\tfrac{5}{3} \div 2 = \tfrac{5}{6}$ minute

As the vehicle takes $\tfrac{5}{6}$ minutes to travel 1 km, then:

In 1 minute the distance will be $1 \div \tfrac{5}{6} = 1 \times \tfrac{6}{5} = 1\cdot2$ km

∴ In 1 hour (60 min) the vehicle will travel 60 × 1·2 = 72 km.
∴ Average speed = 72 km/h.

Example. The average speed of a vehicle for $2\frac{1}{2}$ hours is 40 km/h and 64 km/h for $1\frac{3}{4}$ hours; calculate the total distance travelled.

$$\text{Total distance at 40 km/h} = 40 \times 2\tfrac{1}{2} = 100 \text{ km}$$
$$\text{,,} \quad \text{,,} \quad \text{,,} \; 64 \text{ km/h} = 64 \times 1\tfrac{3}{4} = 112 \text{ km}$$
$$\text{Total} \; = 212 \text{ km}$$

Ratio

When the magnitude (size) of two quantities of the same kinds are compared, the relation which one quantity bears to the other is called **a ratio.** Such a comparison is often expressed as a fraction with one quantity as the numerator and the other quantity as the denominator. For example, if one quantity is 10 and the other is 5, then the ratio between these quantities can be expressed in three ways:

$$\tfrac{10}{5}; \; 10 \div 5 \text{ or } 10{:}5$$

The figures in a ratio or ratios can and do refer to definite things, such as metres, millimetres, litres, and so on; but it should be realized that a ratio, in itself, is only a number.

When comparing the magnitude of quantities it is necessary to write those quantities in the same units, e.g. the ratio of 90 mm to 2 metres is obtained by converting the 2 metres into mm, i.e. 2 metres equals 2000 mm and the ratio is therefore $\frac{90}{2000}$ or 9: 200.

When we want to divide a given number into a ratio, we add together the terms of the ratio in order to obtain a common denominator and take each number in turn as a numerator.

Example. Divide 35 metres into the ratio of 2:5.

The denominator is 2 + 5 equals 7 and the required lengths are:

$$35 \times \tfrac{2}{7} = 10 \text{ m}$$
$$35 \times \tfrac{5}{7} = 25 \text{ m}$$

When we require to divide a number in the ratio of two or more fractions, we must express the fractions with a common denominator, and if we cancel out the common denominators, we need only consider the numerators.

Example. Divide 48 litres in the ratio of $\frac{1}{3}$ to $\frac{1}{5}$.

This does *not* mean $\frac{1}{3}$ of 48 and $\frac{1}{5}$ of 48, and we must express the fractions with a common denominator: $\frac{1}{3} = \frac{5}{15}$ and $\frac{1}{5} = \frac{3}{15}$, the common denominator 15 cancels out to leave 5 and 3. Then it is only necessary to divide 48 into the ratios of the numerators 5 and 3; the new denominator will be $5 + 3 = 8$ and the required amounts are:

$$\tfrac{5}{8} \text{ of } 48 = \underline{30 \text{ litres}}$$
$$\tfrac{3}{8} \text{ of } 48 = \underline{18 \text{ litres}}$$

We can prove the working correct by adding together the amounts obtained which should, of course, equal the original quantity. In this example, $18 + 30$ equals 48 litres, the original quantity.

Example. Two vehicles travel 480 km in 8 hours and 10 hours respectively. Calculate the ratio of the two speeds of the vehicles.

As the distance 480 km is common to both vehicles, we can ignore it. Then:

$$\text{the ratio of the two speeds} = \tfrac{10}{8} = \tfrac{5}{4} = \underline{5{:}4}$$

This type of ratio is often expressed as 'so much' to 'one', i.e. the first figure of the ratio is divided by the last figure as shown in the following.

Using the last worked example:

$$\tfrac{5}{4} = 1{\cdot}25 \text{ to } 1 \text{ or } 1{\cdot}25{:}1$$

We are able to say that the first vehicle is $1{\cdot}25$ times faster than the second vehicle.

In motor vehicle calculations, most of the ratios are given as 'so much' to 'one', e.g. the compression ratio of a certain engine could be expressed as, say, 9 to 1 and the rear axle ratio as 5 to 1. The calculation of these and other ratios is described in the second part of this book.

Proportion

Four quantities are said to be **in proportion** or are proportional when the ratio of the first quantity to the second is equal to the ratio of the third quantity to the fourth, i.e. 2 is to 4 as 6 is to 12 or $\tfrac{2}{4}$ equals $\tfrac{6}{12}$.

Take a simple example. If one vehicle of a fleet uses 120 litres of petrol per day, how much petrol is used by six vehicles operating under the same conditions?

Now, if one vehicle uses 120 litres of petrol per day, then six vehicles will use 6 times as much. The ratios are therefore equal or proportional i.e. 1 is to 120 as 6 is to (6×120), equals 720, or $\tfrac{1}{120}$ equals $\tfrac{6}{720}$.

The answer to the foregoing example was obvious because the working out started with unity, i.e. one vehicle. In examples which do not start with unity it is essential as a first step to reduce one of the quantities to unity. This method is called the **unitary** method and the following example illustrates its working.

If four vehicles of a fleet use 480 litres of petrol per day, how much petrol will be used by twelve vehicles operating under the same conditions?

4 vehicles use 480 litres per day.

Then 1 vehicle will use $\frac{480}{4}$ litres per day.

Therefore 12 vehicles will use $\frac{480}{4} \times 12$ litres per day or 1440 litres.

Both the foregoing examples are known as **simple proportions** because they include only two quantities, i.e. vehicles and litres of petrol, the 'day' is common to both ratios and therefore cancels out.

Compound Proportion

Problems with more than two quantities are also worked out by means of the unitary method.

Example. If five fitters take 21 days to overhaul six vehicles, how long will it take seven fitters to overhaul eight vehicles? (Assuming that each vehicle takes the same amount of time to overhaul.)

This type of problem is made easier by using numbered steps:

(1) 5 fitters overhaul 6 vehicles in 21 days, therefore

(2) 1 fitter will overhaul 6 vehicles in 21×5 days (5 times longer) and

(3) 1 fitter will overhaul 1 vehicle in $\dfrac{21 \times 5}{6}$ days (6 times shorter), now

(4) 7 fitters will overhaul 1 vehicle in $\dfrac{21 \times 5}{6 \quad 7}$ days (7 times shorter), therefore

(5) 7 fitters will overhaul 8 vehicles in $\dfrac{21 \times 5 \times 8}{6 \quad 7}$ (8 times longer) or 20 days.

In the foregoing example the following should be noted:

Quantities of the same kind as the answer required (days) are placed last.

In the step (3) the first two quantities are reduced to unity, i.e. one fitter and one vehicle.

Example. A vehicle worth £500 can be insured for 2 years at a cost of £25. How much would it cost to insure a vehicle worth £800 for 1 year and 3 months at the same rate?

£500 vehicle, 2 years' insurance	£25
£1 vehicle, 2 years' insurance	$£\dfrac{25}{500}$
£1 vehicle, 1 year's insurance	$£\dfrac{25}{500}\dfrac{\times 1}{2}$
£800 vehicle, 1 year's insurance	$£\dfrac{25 \times 800}{500 \quad 2}$
£800 vehicle, $1\frac{1}{4}$ year's insurance	$£\dfrac{25 \times 800}{500 \quad 2} \times 1\frac{1}{4}$
	$= \underline{£25}$

Inverse Proportion

Students are often puzzled by the term **inversely** proportional, or what is meant when one quantity is said to vary inversely as another quantity. These terms mean that an increase in the value of one quantity will produce a corresponding decrease in the value of the other quantity. That is to say, if the first quantity is doubled, the other quantity will be halved and so on, e.g. if one pump fills a fuel tank in 12 minutes, then two pumps will *halve* the time taken, not double it.

Example. If two pumps take 30 minutes to fill a tank, how long will six similar pumps take to fill this tank?

As 2 pumps take 30 min to fill the tank
then   1 pump will take 30 × 2 min
Therefore   6 pumps will take $\dfrac{30 \times 2 \text{ min}}{6}$

$$= \underline{10 \text{ minutes}}$$

The last example is really a simple proportion; the next example, however, includes both inverse and compound proportion.

Example. A storage tank has two inlet pipes, one capable of filling the tank in 3 hours and the other in 4 hours. The outlet pipe is capable of emptying the tank in 5 hours. How long will it take to fill an empty tank if all are turned on?

No. 1 inlet takes 3 h to fill tank, thus it fills $\frac{1}{3}$ in 1 h

No. 2 inlet takes 4 h to fill tank, thus it fills $\frac{1}{4}$ in 1 h

The outlet takes 5 h to empty tank, thus it empties $\frac{1}{5}$ in 1 h

If all are working, then they fill $\frac{1}{3} + \frac{1}{4} - \frac{1}{5} = \dfrac{20 + 15 - 12}{60}$

$$= \tfrac{23}{60} \text{ of the tank in 1 h}$$

$\therefore \frac{1}{60}$ of tank will be filled in $\frac{1}{23}$ of 1 h

$\therefore \frac{60}{60}$ of tank will be filled in $\frac{1}{23}$ of 1 h $\times$ 60

$\therefore$ Time taken to fill tank $= \frac{1}{23} \times 1 \times 60 = \underline{\mathbf{2 \cdot 6 \text{ hours}}}$

Proportional Parts

The division of quantities into parts proportional to certain numbers is often necessary in practice, and the following examples will show the method of solving these problems.

Example. Water has the chemical formula H_2O, which means that each molecule of water contains 2 atoms of hydrogen and 1 atom of oxygen. If the oxygen atom has a mass 16 times as much as the hydrogen atom, what are the proportions of oxygen and hydrogen in 1 kg of water? Then parts by mass of water are:

$$\text{Oxygen} \quad \frac{16}{2} = 8$$

$$\text{Hydrogen} \ \frac{1}{1} = 1$$

Total number of parts $= 8 + 1 = 9$

$\therefore \frac{8}{9}$ parts are oxygen $= \underline{\frac{8}{9} \text{ kg of oxygen}}$

$\frac{1}{9}$ part is hydrogen $= \underline{\frac{1}{9} \text{ kg of hydrogen}}$

Example. A certain hydrocarbon fuel has the formula C_6H_{14}. This means that each molecule of the fuel contains 6 atoms of carbon and 14 atoms of hydrogen. If the carbon atom has a mass 12 times as much as the hydrogen atom, what are the proportions of hydrogen and carbon in 1 kg of the fuel?

Parts of carbon by mass $= 6 \times 12 = 72$

Parts of hydrogen by mass $= 14$

Total number of parts $= 72 + 14 = 86$

$\therefore$ Mass of carbon $= \frac{72}{86}$ or $\frac{36}{43}$ kg $= \underline{0 \cdot 8372 \text{ kg}}$

Mass of hydrogen $= \frac{14}{86}$ or $\frac{7}{43}$ kg $= \underline{0 \cdot 1628 \text{ kg}}$

Percentages

The percentage system is the most satisfactory method of comparing one quantity with another or comparing two or more results. The term **per cent** means 'for every hundred' or 'in each hundred'. Thus, 25 per cent means 25 for every hundred, and is the same numerically as $\frac{25}{100}$ or $\frac{1}{4}$. It can be said, therefore, that a percentage is really a fraction whose denominator is 100; this denominator, however, is not written down and is replaced by the symbol %. Then $\frac{25}{100}$ can be written 25%.

The most practical method of solving problems containing percentages is by thinking of each percentage as a fraction.

Thus:
$$1\% = \tfrac{1}{100}$$
$$5\% = \tfrac{5}{100} \text{ or } \tfrac{1}{20}$$
$$12\% = \tfrac{12}{100} \text{ or } \tfrac{3}{25}, \text{ and so on.}$$

Example. Express as fractions: $2\frac{1}{2}\%$; $1\frac{1}{4}\%$; 35%; 75%.

$$2\tfrac{1}{2}\% = \frac{2\frac{1}{2}}{100} = \frac{5}{2} \times \frac{1}{100} = \tfrac{1}{40}$$

$$1\tfrac{1}{4}\% = \frac{1\frac{1}{4}}{100} = \frac{5}{4} \times \frac{1}{100} = \tfrac{1}{80}$$

$$35\% = \frac{35}{100} = \tfrac{7}{20}$$

$$75\% = \frac{75}{100} = \tfrac{3}{4}$$

Example. Express as a percentage: $\frac{2}{3}$; $\frac{1}{6}$; $\frac{1}{5}$; $\frac{1}{70}$.

$$\tfrac{2}{3} = 100 \times \tfrac{2}{3} = 66\tfrac{2}{3}\%$$
$$\tfrac{1}{6} = 100 \times \tfrac{1}{6} = 16\tfrac{2}{3}\%$$
$$\tfrac{1}{5} = 100 \times \tfrac{1}{5} = 20\%$$
$$\tfrac{1}{70} = 100 \times \tfrac{1}{70} = 1\tfrac{3}{7}\%$$

In order to find the value of a percentage of any quantity we multiply the quantity by the percentage and divide the product by 100.

Example. What length is 5% of 1 kilometre?

$$1 \text{ km} = 1000 \text{ m}$$

$$5\% \text{ of } 1000 \text{ m} = \frac{1000 \times 5}{100} = \underline{50 \text{ metres}}$$

Example. What is the value of $2\frac{1}{2}\%$ of £25?

$$2\frac{1}{2}\% \text{ of £25} = \frac{25 \times 2\frac{1}{2}}{100} = \frac{25}{100} \times \frac{5}{2} = \text{£}\frac{5}{8} = \underline{62\frac{1}{2}\text{p}} = \text{£0·62}\frac{1}{2}$$

In order to express one number as the percentage of another number we multiply the number by 100 and divide this product by the other number.

Example. What percentage of 70 is 2?

$$2 \times 100 = 200; \frac{200}{70} = 2\cdot85$$

$$\therefore 2 \text{ is } \underline{2\cdot85\%} \text{ of } 70$$

Example. What percentage of 1 is 0·5?

$$0\cdot5 \times 100 = 50; \frac{50}{1} = \underline{50\%}$$

The following example shows the method of solving problems which deal with mass and percentages of materials in alloys.

Example. A casting consists of 5·28 kg of copper; 1·06 kg of zinc; 0·84 kg of lead and 0·82 kg of dross. What percentage of the casting is (*a*) copper; (*b*) lead?

In problems of this kind, first find what 1 kg represents.

$$\begin{aligned}
\text{Copper} &= 5\cdot28 \text{ kg} \\
\text{Zinc} &= 1\cdot06 \text{ ,,} \\
\text{Lead} &= 0\cdot84 \text{ ,,} \\
\text{Dross} &= 0\cdot82 \text{ ,,} \\
\text{Total mass} &= 8\cdot00 \text{ kg}
\end{aligned}$$

Now the total mass of the casting = 8 kg.

$$\therefore 8 \text{ kg will be equal to } 100\%.$$

$$8 \text{ kg} = 100\%$$

$$\therefore 1 \text{ kg} = \frac{100}{8}\%$$

$$\therefore \text{Copper} = \frac{100}{8} \times 5\cdot28 = \underline{66\% \text{ of copper}}$$

and

$$\text{Lead} = \frac{100}{8} \times 0\cdot84 = \underline{10\cdot5\% \text{ of lead}}$$

Example. A certain solder consists of 35 per cent tin and 65 per cent lead. What mass in kg of each of these metals will be found in 28 kg of the solder?

In problems of this kind, first find what 1% represents.

Now $35\% + 65\%$ or $100\% = 28$ kg of the solder

$$\therefore\ 1\% = \frac{28}{100} \text{ kg of solder}$$

$$\therefore\ 35\% = \frac{28}{100} \times 35 \text{ kg of tin} = \underline{9\cdot8 \text{ kg of tin}}$$

$$\therefore\ 65\% = \frac{28}{100} \times 65 \text{ kg of lead} = \underline{18\cdot2 \text{ kg of lead}}$$

In order to find by what percentage one quantity is greater or less than another quantity we proceed as follows.

Subtract the smaller from the larger quantity and convert this difference to a percentage of the larger or smaller quantity as the case may be, i.e.

Increase or **decrease** multiplied by 100, divided by the original quantity, or

$$\frac{\text{Increase or Decrease} \times 100}{\text{Original quantity}}$$

Example. A vehicle uses 20 litres of petrol per day when travelling at an average speed of 25 km/h; after a 'top' overhaul, the consumption falls to 18 litres per day. Calculate the percentage saving.

$$\text{Percentage saving} = \frac{\text{Decrease in consumption} \times 100}{\text{Original consumption}}\%$$

Decrease in consumption per day = $20 - 18 = 2$ litres
Original consumption per day = 20 litres

$$\therefore\ \text{Percentage saving} = \frac{2}{20} \times 100 = \underline{10\%}$$

Example. A heavy goods vehicle used 20 litres of fuel oil per day when travelling at an average speed of 25 km/h and 25 litres per day when travelling at 30 km/h. Calculate the percentage increase in consumption in order to get the extra speed.

At 25 km/h the fuel consumption = 20 litres
*At 1 km/h the fuel consumption = $\frac{1}{25}$ of 20 = $\frac{4}{5}$ litres

* In actual practice, of course, this would not be the fact.

At 30 km/h the fuel consumption = 25 litres

At 1 km/h the fuel consumption = $\frac{1}{30}$ of 25 = $\frac{5}{6}$ litre

∴ Extra fuel oil used per day = $\frac{5}{6} - \frac{4}{5} = \frac{1}{30}$ litre

$$\therefore \text{Percentage increase} = \frac{\text{Increase}}{\text{Original}} \times 100\%$$

$$= \tfrac{1}{30} \div \tfrac{4}{5} \times 100 = \underline{4 \cdot 16\%}$$

Exercise 4

1. The total petrol consumption of a car on four different journeys each of 200 km was: 29·5, 32·25, 30·35, 31·65 litres.

(*a*) What was the average consumption (1) per journey, (2) per km?

(*b*) Express the maximum consumption as a percentage of the average.

((*a*) (1) 30·9375 litres; (*a*) (2) 0·1547 litres; (*b*) 104·3 per cent)

(E.M.E.U.)

2. The exhaust gases from an engine contain 76% of nitrogen by mass. How many kg of nitrogen are there in $27\frac{1}{2}$ kg of the gases?

(20·9 kg) (E.M.E.U.)

3. What percentage increase in the price of petrol is represented by a change from $6\frac{1}{2}$p to 7p per litre? (7·69 per cent)

4. A soft solder is composed of 30 per cent tin and 70 per cent lead. Assuming that 60 kg of tin are available, what mass of solder could be manufactured? (200 kg)

5. Having given that the percentage composition of phosphor-bronze is: copper 80·5, lead 9·5, tin 10·0, what will be the mass in kg of each of these metals in 25 kg of the alloy?

(20·125 kg of copper; 2·375 kg of lead; 2·5 kg of tin) (C. and G.)

6. A motor fuel consists of 16 per cent hydrogen and 84 per cent carbon; 1 kg of hydrogen requires 34·8 kg of air for complete combustion and 1 kg of carbon requires 11·6 kg. Calculate the mass of air required for complete combustion of 1 kg of the fuel.

(15·312 kg) (C. and G.)

7. In the first 12 minutes of a journey a car travelled 12 km and in the next 20 minutes 24 km. It then continued at 65 km per hour for 18 minutes. (*a*) How far did it travel altogether? (*b*) What was its average speed? ((*a*) 55·5 km; (*b*) 66·6 km/h) (E.M.E.U.)

8. A vehicle is driven at 50 km/h for 2 hours and then at 65 km/h for ½ hour. Find its average speed for the whole journey.

(53 km/h)

9. In an electrical machine it is found that a tungsten steel magnet of mass 5 kg can be replaced by an aluminium-nickel alloy magnet of mass 1 kg. If the tungsten steel costs 3p per kg and the aluminium-nickel alloy costs 14p per kg; how does the cost of the two magnets compare? (The tungsten steel magnet costs 1p more.) (C. and G.)

10. If the difference in the cost price of two kinds of car battery, selling for the same amount, the one at 25% profit and the other at 20% profit, is 25p, find the cost prices and the selling price.

(£6; £6·25; £7·50) (I.M.I.)

11. The speedometer of a car is 10% fast. A man drives the car at a steady pace for a measured km and completes the journey in 1 minute 40 seconds. What did the speedometer register? Give the true speed in km per hour. (39·6 km/h; 36 km/h) (I.M.I.)

12. If a car is marked for sale at 25% above cost price, and 5% discount is allowed for cash payment, what is the actual profit on a car, the cost price of which is £700? (£131·25) (I.M.I.)

5   Areas, Volumes, Capacity and Mass

The area of a surface, known as a **plane** figure, is the number of square units and parts of square units contained in that surface. A plane figure is a figure with a flat surface.

Examples of square units in common use are:

(1) A square millimetre, denoted by mm²

(2) A square metre, denoted by m²

Areas of Squares and Rectangles

In Fig. 5.1, which represents one square metre, thus the square formed in this way has sides which will represent one metre in length.

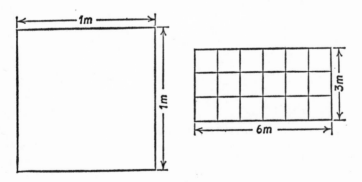

FIG. 5.1   FIG. 5.2

The area is $1^2 = 1 \times 1 = 1 \text{ m}^2$

Thus, the area of any square can be found by squaring the length of one side.

A **rectangle,** Fig. 5.2 is a plane figure with four sides. The adjacent (next to) sides are unequal and the opposite sides are equal in length; all corners are square, so the opposite sides are parallel.

The area of a rectangle is found by multiplying the length by the breadth.

Area = length × breadth

In Fig. 5.2 the length of 6 metres multiplied by the breadth of 3 metres gives an area of 18 square metres, which is the same as the number of squares in the diagram.

Areas of Triangles

The **triangle** is a three-sided plane figure enclosed by straight lines. In Fig. 5.3 the side of 4 metres is called the base and the dimension of 3 metres is called the vertical height. The area of this or any triangle is found:

$$\text{Area} = \frac{\text{base} \times \text{vertical height}}{2}$$

$$= \frac{4 \times 3}{2} = 6 \text{ m}^2$$

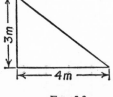

FIG. 5.3

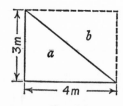

FIG. 5.4

This can be proved:

The triangle, Fig. 5.3, can be converted to a rectangle by the addition of two dotted lines, as shown in Fig. 5.4, and the area of this rectangle will be 4 metres multiplied by 3 metres which equals 12 square metres. It will, however, be evident that the area of the triangle *a* is equal to the area of the triangle *b*, i.e.

$$\text{Area of } a = \frac{4 \times 3}{2} = \underline{\underline{6 \text{ m}^2}}$$

$$\text{Area of } b = \frac{4 \times 3}{2} = \underline{\underline{6 \text{ m}^2}}$$

Example. Find the area of the triangle shown in Fig. 5.5.

$$\text{Area} = \frac{5 \times 4}{2} = \underline{\underline{10 \text{ m}^2}}$$

Fig. 5.6 shows that the area of the triangles $a + b$ equals the area of the triangles $c + d$, i.e. $(a + b) = (c + d)$.

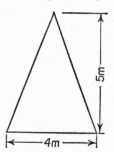

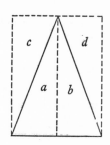

FIG. 5.5

FIG. 5.6

Example. Find the area of the triangle shown in Fig. 5.7.

$$\text{Area} = \frac{3 \times 2}{2} = \underline{\underline{3 \text{ m}^2}}$$

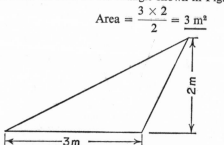

FIG. 5.7

Fig. 5.8 shows that the area of the triangle a is equal to the area of the triangle c minus the area of the triangle b, i.e. $a = (c - b)$.

Area of Trapezium

The **trapezium** is a four-sided plane figure with only two sides parallel and its area is found:

$$\text{Area} = \frac{\text{sum of parallel sides} \times \text{vertical height between them}}{2}$$

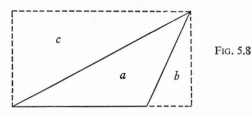

FIG. 5.8

In Fig. 5.9

$$\text{Area} = \frac{(7 + 5) \times 3}{2} = \underline{18 \text{ m}^2}$$

Fig. 5.9 shows that a straight line drawn across the figure will give the two triangles *a* and *b*.

$$\text{The area of one triangle} = \frac{7 \times 3}{2} = 10 \cdot 5 \text{ m}^2$$

$$\text{The area of the other triangle} = \frac{5 \times 3}{2} = 7 \cdot 5 \text{ m}^2$$

$$\therefore \text{Total area} = 10 \cdot 5 + 7 \cdot 5 = \underline{18 \text{ m}^2}$$

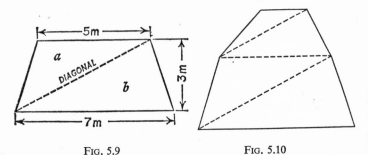

FIG. 5.9   FIG. 5.10

The area of any plane figure enclosed by straight lines can be found by dividing the figure into triangles and then finding their areas separately. The total area of the figure will be the sum of the areas of the triangles. Fig. 5.10 shows a plane figure divided into triangles.

The Circle
The **circle** is a plane figure enclosed by a curved line which at all points is equally distant from an internal point called the **centre,** Fig. 5.11. The total distance round the circle is called the **circumference.** A straight line

drawn through the centre and finished at each end by the circumference is called the **diameter.** A straight line drawn from the centre to the circumference is called the **radius** and it is equal in length to one half the diameter. A **chord** is a straight line joining any two points on the circumference.

An **arc** of a circle is any part of the circumference, Fig. 5.12. A semicircle is one of the two equal parts into which a diameter divides a circle, Fig. 5.12, or simply half a circle. A **segment** of a circle is the space included between a chord and an arc, Fig. 5.13. A **sector** of a circle is the space enclosed by two **radii** (plural of radius) and an arc, Fig. 5.13.

To find the circumference of a circle when the diameter is known we

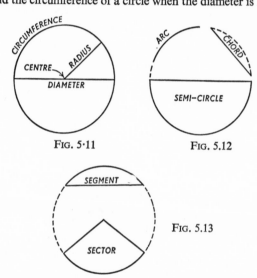

FIG. 5·11   FIG. 5.12

FIG. 5.13

multiply the diameter of the circle by 3·141 59, which is usually denoted by the Greek letter π (pronounced 'pi'). For the number 3·141 59 we often use $3\frac{1}{7}$ or $\frac{22}{7}$ or 3·142, which is sufficiently accurate for most calculations.

$$\text{Circumference} = \text{Diameter} \times \pi$$

or

$$\frac{\text{Circumference}}{\pi} = \text{Diameter}$$

or

$$\frac{\text{Circumference}}{\text{Diameter}} = \pi$$

In the same way, the radius of a circle is equal to the circumference divided by $2 \times 3\frac{1}{7}$ or 2π:

$$\frac{\text{Circumference}}{2\pi} = \text{Radius}$$

Example. Find the circumference and radius of a circle whose diameter is 14 metres.

$$\text{Circumference} = \text{Diameter} \times \pi = 14 \times \frac{22}{7} = \underline{44 \text{ m}}$$

$$\text{Radius} \qquad = \frac{\text{Diameter}}{2} \qquad = \frac{14}{2} \qquad = \underline{7 \text{ m}}$$

The Area of a Circle

The area of a circle is found by multiplying the radius of the circle by itself, i.e. squaring the radius, and then multiplying this square by π:

$$\text{Area} = \pi \times \text{radius} \times \text{radius}$$
$$= \pi \times r^2 \text{ where } r = \text{the radius}$$

Example. Find the area of a circle whose diameter is 35 mm.

$$\text{Area} = \pi \times r^2 \qquad\qquad r = 35 \div 2 = 17 \cdot 5 \text{ mm}$$

$$= \frac{22}{7} \times \frac{35}{2} \times \frac{35}{2} = \frac{1925}{2} = \underline{962 \cdot 5 \text{ mm}^2}$$

Example. Find the area of a circle whose diameter is 63 mm.

$$\text{Area} = \pi \times r^2$$

$$= \frac{22}{7} \times \frac{63}{2} \times \frac{63}{2} = \frac{6237}{2} = \underline{3118 \cdot 5 \text{ mm}^2}$$

Note, in some examples where the radius is an awkward number it is an advantage to modify the foregoing to

$$\text{Area} = \frac{\pi}{4} \times d^2, \text{ i.e. } \left(\pi \times \frac{d}{2} \times \frac{d}{2} \right)$$

where d is the diameter of the circle.

The Area of a Sector

The area of a sector (Fig. 5.13) when given the radius and the length of arc is found by:

Multiplying the length of arc by the radius and dividing this product by two.

Example. Find the area of a sector whose radius and length of arc are 6 metres and 4 metres respectively.

$$\text{Area} = \frac{\text{Radius} \times \text{arc}}{2} = \frac{6 \times 4}{2} = \underline{12 \text{ m}^2}$$

The Ellipse

Fig. 5.14 shows an ellipse. The line AB is called the major axis and the line CD the minor axis.

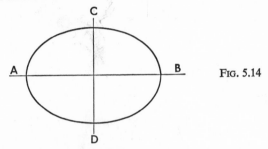

Fig. 5.14

The area of an ellipse is found by:

$$\text{Area} = \frac{\text{Major axis}}{2} \times \frac{\text{Minor axis}}{2} \times \pi$$

Example. Find the area of an ellipse whose major axis is 8 metres and minor axis 6 metres.

$$\text{Area} = \frac{8}{2} \times \frac{6}{2} \times \frac{22}{7} = \underline{37 \cdot 7 \text{ m}^2}$$

The Annulus (Flat Circular Ring)

The area of a flat circular ring (Fig. 5.15) is found by subtracting the area of the smaller circle from the area of the larger circle.

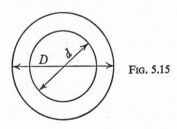

Fig. 5.15

$$\text{Area} = \frac{\pi}{4} \times (D^2 - d^2)$$

where $\qquad$ D = diameter of the large circle

d = diameter of the small circle.

In this case it is convenient to use the diameters instead of the radii, so we must divide by 4, otherwise the answer would be four times too great.

Example. Find the area of a ring whose diameters are 4 metres and 3 metres respectively.

$$\text{Area} = \frac{\pi}{4} \times (D^2 - d^2)$$

$$= \frac{22}{7} \times \frac{1}{4} \times (16 - 9) = \frac{22}{7} \times \frac{1}{4} \times 7 = \underline{5 \cdot 5 \text{ m}^2}$$

Irregular Figures

Two methods are used in finding the areas of irregular-shaped figures:

(1) **The Mid-Ordinate Rule.** This method of finding the area of an irregular-shaped figure is reasonably easy:

$\quad$ (*a*) Draw a base line XY (Fig. 5.16) and divide the figure along its $\qquad$ length into a convenient number of equal strips.

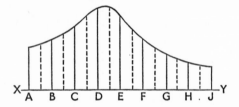

Fig. 5.16

$\quad$ (*b*) Draw vertical lines A, B, C, D, etc., as shown. In the centre of $\qquad$ each strip obtained, draw other vertical lines, shown dotted; $\qquad$ these are called **ordinates.**

$\quad$ (*c*) Measure the length of each ordinate, add these lengths together $\qquad$ and divide this sum by the total number of the ordinates. The $\qquad$ result is the average or mean height of the ordinates.

$\quad$ (*d*) Multiply this mean height by the length AJ of the base line XY. $\qquad$ The product is the approximate area of the figure.

Example. The dimensioned cross-section of a combustion chamber for a side-valve engine is shown in Fig. 5.17. Calculate the area of the cross-section.

Ordinate (1) = 6·5 mm
,,   (2) = 12·0 mm
,,   (3) = 20·0 mm
,,   (4) = 10·0 mm
,,   (5) = 1·5 mm
Total   = 50·0 mm

Mean height of ordinates = $\frac{50}{5}$ mm

= 10 mm

Length of combustion chamber section = 125 mm

∴ Area of combustion chamber section = 10 × 125 = 1250 mm²

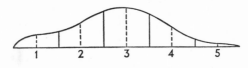

Fig. 5.17

(2) **Simpson's rule** is more accurate than the mid-ordinate method and it is often used for finding the areas of irregular-shaped figures (see Fig. 5.18). The method of using Simpson's rule is:

(*a*) Divide the base of the figure into an even number of equal strips

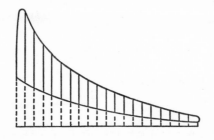

Fig. 5.18

and draw vertical lines, called **ordinates,** to obtain an odd number of ordinates. Measure the length of each ordinate and proceed:

(*b*) Let *A* denote the sum of the end ordinates; *B* the sum of the even ordinates and *C* the sum of the odd ordinates but not the first or the last ordinate.

Let *S* denote the common distance between the ordinates.

Then the area of the figure will be:

$$\text{Area} = \frac{S}{3}[A + (4 \times B) + (2 \times C)]$$

Example. Using Fig. 5.19, we divide the base into eight equal strips and by measurement we find that the lengths of the nine ordinates are:

No. 1 = 6·5 mm	No. 6 = 11·0 mm
,, 2 = 6·8 mm	,, 7 = 3·0 mm
,, 3 = 7·5 mm	,, 8 = 1·5 mm
,, 4 = 17·5 mm	,, 9 = 1·5 mm
,, 5 = 20·0 mm	

Fig. 5.19

Now $S = 15\cdot5$ mm (since base length = 124 mm)

$A = 6\cdot5 + 1\cdot5 = 8$ mm

$B = 6\cdot8 + 17\cdot5 + 11 + 1\cdot5 = 36\cdot8$ mm

$C = 7\cdot5 + 20 + 3 = 30\cdot5$ mm

$$\therefore \text{Area} = \frac{15\cdot5}{3} \times [8 + (4 \times 36\cdot8) + (2 \times 30\cdot5)]$$

$$= \frac{15\cdot5}{3} \times [8 + 147\cdot2 + 61] \text{ mm}^2$$

$$= \frac{31}{6} \times \frac{2162}{10} = \frac{33\ 511}{30} = \underline{\underline{1117 \text{ mm}^2}}$$

Note, the expression was converted to fractions because $\dfrac{15\cdot5}{3}$ is a recurring decimal and $\dfrac{31}{6}$ makes the calculation easier.

The answers obtained in the foregoing example by the two methods can be shown to differ by 133 mm². That obtained by Simpson's rule is the more accurate.

Simpson's rule may be used to find the area of any plane figure. The figure need not have any straight lines or it can have a mixture of curved and straight lines.

In both methods, however, the greater the number of ordinates used the more accurate will be the result.

Volumes

All solid objects or simple solids have three dimensions: length, breadth and thickness.

The volume of a regular solid is the product of these three dimensions.

Volume = length × breadth × thickness

Fig. 5.20 shows a simple solid, the **cube**, which has three perpendicular edges all equal in length. If each edge is 1 metre long, then the amount of space the cube occupies (or its volume) is called one **cubic metre.** The cubic metre and the cubic millimetre are common units of volume.

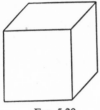

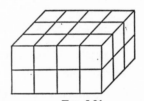

Fig. 5.20   Fig. 5.21

Fig. 5.21 shows a rectangular block; the ends are rectangles and the sides of the block are parallel. The volume of this block is the product of the length, the breadth and the thickness:

Volume = $4 \times 3 \times 2 = \underline{24 \text{ m}^3}$

Example. Find the volume of a rectangular block which has the following dimensions: length = 0·16 m; breadth = 0·09 m, and thickness = 7·5 mm.

In examples of this type it is essential to bring all the dimensions to the same units before multiplication, i.e. mm multiplied by mm, metres multiplied by metres, and so on.

Now 0·16 m = 160 mm and 0·09 m = 90 mm
∴ Volume of block = 160 × 90 × 7·5 mm³
= $\underline{108\ 000 \text{ mm}^3 \text{ or } 0\cdot000\ 108 \text{ m}^3}$

The **American gallon** and the **litre** are used as units of capacity. The American gallon equals 3·68 litres.

Volume and Surface Area of a Cylinder

Fig. 5.22 shows a **cylinder**. Now a cylinder has the same diameter at all points along its length (or **height**) and the **volume of a cylinder** is equal

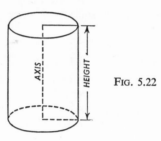

Fig. 5.22

to its height multiplied by the area of one circular end or the height multiplied by the area of the base. This volume can be expressed simply as

$$\pi \times r^2 \times h$$

where r = the radius and h = the height of the cylinder.

Example. Find the volume of a cylinder whose diameter is 40 mm and whose height is 70 mm.

$$\begin{aligned}
\text{Volume} &= \pi \times r^2 \times h \\
&= \frac{22}{7} \times \frac{40}{2} \times \frac{40}{2} \times 70 \text{ mm} \\
&= \underline{88\ 000 \text{ mm}^3}
\end{aligned}$$

The **surface area of a cylinder** consists of two parts: (*a*) the **flat surface** which consists of the two circular ends and (*b*) the **curved surface**.

(*a*) The area of the flat surface is $2(\pi \times r^2)$.

(*b*) The curved surface, if it could be 'peeled-off' and laid flat, would form a rectangle whose length is the height of the cylinder and whose breadth is equal to the circumference of one circular end, i.e. $\pi \times$ diameter.

The area of the curved surface is therefore $\pi \times$ diameter $\times$ height, and as the area of the two circular ends is $2(\pi \times r^2)$, then the total surface area of the cylinder is the sum of the area of the circular ends and the curved area.

Example. Find the volume and total surface area of a cylinder 0·35 m diameter and 0·6 m high.

Volume $= \pi \times r^2 \times h$, where r = radius and h = height

$$= \frac{22}{7} \times \frac{0 \cdot 7}{4} \times \frac{0 \cdot 7}{4} \times 0 \cdot 6 = \underline{0 \cdot 05775 \text{ m}^3}$$

Surface area $= (\pi \times d \times h) + 2(\pi \times r^2)$, where d = diameter

$$= \left(\frac{22}{7} \times \frac{0 \cdot 7}{2} \times 0 \cdot 6\right) + 2\left(\frac{22}{7} \times \frac{0 \cdot 7}{4} \times \frac{0 \cdot 7}{4}\right) = \underline{0 \cdot 8525 \text{ m}^2}$$

Many motor vehicle problems containing volumes are concerned with the **piston-swept** volume of a cylinder, i.e. the volume through which the piston passes when it moves from the bottom of its stroke (b.d.c.) to the top of its stroke (t.d.c.) or vice versa. The piston-swept volume is calculated in the same way as for a solid cylinder, i.e. $\pi \times r^2 \times h$, where r is the radius of the cylinder or radius of the **bore** and h is the distance travelled by the piston during one stroke; h is usually called the **stroke**.

Example. Find the piston-swept volume of a single-cylinder engine having a bore of 75 mm and a stroke of 80 mm.

Piston-swept volume $= \pi \times r^2 \times h$

$$= \frac{22}{7} \times \frac{75}{2} \times \frac{75}{2} \times 80 \text{ mm}^3$$

$$= 353\ 570 \text{ mm}^3 \text{ or}$$
$$\underline{0 \cdot 3536 \text{ litres}}$$

Volume of a Hollow Cylinder or Tube

The calculation of this volume is similar to that of a solid cylinder, i.e. area of base multiplied by height.

Let R and r denote the radii (see Fig. 5.23) of the outer and inner circles respectively, then:

$$\text{Area of base} = (\pi \times R^2) - (\pi \times r^2)$$
$$= \pi \times (R^2 - r^2)$$
$$\therefore \text{Volume of cylinder} = \pi \times (R^2 - r^2) \times h$$

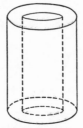

Fig. 5.23

Example. Find the volume of a hollow cylinder with an outside diameter of 4 m and an inside diameter of 3·5 m; its height is 8 m.

$$\text{Volume} = \pi \times (R^2 - r^2) \times h$$
$$= \frac{22}{7} \times \left(2^2 - \frac{7^2}{4}\right) \times 8 \text{ m}^3$$
$$= \frac{22}{7} \times \left(4 - \frac{49}{16}\right) \times 8 \text{ m}^3$$
$$= \frac{22}{7} \times \frac{15}{16} \times 8 = \underline{23 \cdot 57 \text{ m}^3}$$

The Volume and Surface Area of a Cone

The **cone** is a solid which has a circular base connected by a curved surface to the **apex** (see Fig. 5.24).

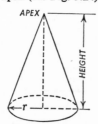

Fig. 5.24

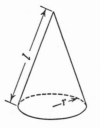

Fig. 5.25

The volume of a cone is

$$\tfrac{1}{3} \times \pi \times r^2 \times h$$

where r is the radius of the base and h is the height of the cone.

The volume of a cone can also be considered as one third of the volume of a cylinder which has the same diameter base and the same height.

The curved surface area of a cone is

$$\pi \times r \times l$$

where l is the **slant** height of the cone (see Fig. 5.25). The slant height l can be found from

$$l = \sqrt{(h^2 + r^2)}$$

where h is the height and r the radius of the cone.

The total surface area of the cone is the sum of the curved surface area and the area of the base, i.e.

$$(\pi \times r \times l) + (\pi \times r^2)$$

Example. Find the volume and surface area of a cone whose height is 5 m and base 4 m diameter.

$$\text{Volume of cone} = \tfrac{1}{3} \times \pi \times r^2 \times h$$

$$= \frac{1}{3} \times \frac{22}{7} \times 2^2 \times 5 = \underline{20{\cdot}95 \text{ m}^3}$$

$$\text{Surface area of cone} = (\pi \times r \times l) + (\pi \times r^2)$$

$$= \left(\frac{22}{7} \times 2 \times l\right) + \left(\frac{22}{7} \times 2^2\right)$$

$$\text{Now } l = \sqrt{(h^2 + r^2)}$$
$$= \sqrt{25 + 4} \text{ m}$$
$$= 5{\cdot}39 \text{ m}$$

$$\therefore \text{ Surface area of cone} = \left(\frac{22}{7} \times 2 \times 5{\cdot}39\right) + \left(\frac{22}{7} \times 2^2\right)$$

$$= \underline{46{\cdot}45 \text{ m}^2}$$

The Volume and Surface Area of a Sphere

A **sphere** is a solid in the shape of a ball and its volume is

$$\tfrac{4}{3} \times \pi \times r^3$$

where r is the radius of the sphere, which is the distance from an internal point called a centre to any point on the surface (see Fig. 5.26).

Fig. 5.26

The surface area of a sphere is
$$4 \times \pi \times r^2$$
The diameter of a sphere is its radius multiplied by two.

Example. Find the volume and surface area of a sphere whose diameter is 3 metres.

$$\text{Volume} = \frac{4}{3} \times \pi \times r^3$$

$$= \frac{4}{3} \times \frac{22}{7} \times \left(\frac{3}{2}\right)^3 = \underline{14 \cdot 14 \text{ m}^3}$$

$$\text{Surface area} = 4 \times \pi \times r^2$$

$$4 \times \frac{22}{7} \times \left(\frac{3}{2}\right)^2 = \underline{28 \cdot 28 \text{ m}^2}$$

A **hemisphere** is one half of a sphere and its volume is found by finding the volume of the sphere and dividing it by two.

Example. Find the volume of a hemisphere with a diameter of 4 m

$$\text{Volume of sphere} = \frac{4}{3} \times \pi \times r^3$$

$$= \frac{4}{3} \times \frac{22}{7} \times 2^3 = 33 \cdot 52 \text{ m}^3$$

$$\therefore \text{Volume of hemisphere} = \frac{33 \cdot 52}{2} = \underline{16 \cdot 76 \text{ m}^3}$$

Finding the volume of a hemisphere would normally require one step only and not two as shown in the example,

$$\text{i.e.} \frac{4}{3} \times \frac{22}{7} \times \frac{(2)^3}{2} = \underline{16 \cdot 76 \text{ m}^3}$$

The Volume of Irregular Shapes

A useful method of finding the volume of an irregular-shaped solid is to divide the mass of the solid by the mass of one cubic millimetre of the same material. The result will give the number of cubic millimetres in the solid.

Example. An irregular-shaped piece of cast iron has a mass of 7000 grammes. The mass of one cubic millimetre of cast iron is 0·0078 grammes. Calculate the volume of the casting in cubic millimetres.

$$\text{Volume of cast iron} = \frac{\text{Total mass}}{\text{Mass of 1 mm}^3}$$

$$= \frac{7000}{0\cdot0078} = \underline{897\ 743\ \text{mm}^3}$$

Volumes of Tanks

We are often concerned with the volumes of tanks containing petrol or fuel oil. These tanks are usually parallel along their length, and and have varying shaped ends. The volume of these tanks if the ends are parallel is found by multiplying the area of one end by the length of the tank. The areas of the various shapes likely to be met have been dealt with earlier in this chapter.

Example. Find the volume of a tank with square ends of 0·3 m and length 1·2 m.

$$\text{Volume} = \text{Area} \times \text{length}$$
$$= 0\cdot3 \times 0\cdot3 \times 1\cdot2\ \text{m}^3$$
$$= \underline{0\cdot108\ \text{m}^3}$$

Example. Find the volume of a tank with rectangular ends of 0·2 m by 0·3 m and length 1·0 m.

$$\text{Volume} = \text{Area} \times \text{length}$$
$$= 0\cdot2 \times 0\cdot3 \times 1\cdot0 = \underline{0\cdot06\ \text{m}^3}$$

Example. Find the volume of a tank with trapezium-shaped ends; the parallel sides are 0·3 m and 0·5 m respectively and the depth between the parallel sides is 0·3 m. The length is 1·0 m.

$$\text{Volume} = \frac{\text{Sum of parallel sides} \times \text{depth} \times \text{length}}{2}$$

$$= \frac{(0\cdot3 + 0\cdot5) \times 0\cdot3 \times 1\cdot0}{2}$$

$$= \frac{0\cdot8 \times 0\cdot3}{2} = \underline{0\cdot12\ \text{m}^3}$$

Example. Find the volume of a tank with triangular-shaped ends of base 0·32 m, vertical height 0·45 m and the length is 1·10 m.

$$\text{Volume} = \frac{\text{Base} \times \text{vertical height} \times \text{length}}{2}$$

$$= \frac{0\cdot32 \times 0\cdot45 \times 1\cdot10 \text{ m}^3}{2}$$

$$= \underline{0\cdot0792 \text{m}^3}$$

Example. Find the volume of a tank with circular ends of 0·3 m diameter and length of 1·12 m.

$$\text{Volume} = \pi \times r^2 \times \text{length}$$

$$r = \frac{0\cdot30}{2} = 0\cdot15 \text{ m}$$

$$\therefore \text{Volume} = \frac{22}{7} \times 0\cdot15 \times 0\cdot15 \times 1\cdot12 = \underline{0\cdot0792 \text{ m}^3}$$

Example. Find the volume of a tank with elliptical ends whose major and minor axes (plural for axis) are: 0·3 m and 0·21 m. Length of tank is 1·2 m.

$$\text{Volume} = \frac{\text{Major axis}}{2} \times \frac{\text{Minor axis}}{2} \times \pi \times \text{length}$$

$$= \frac{0\cdot3}{2} \times \frac{0\cdot21}{2} \times \frac{22}{7} \times 1\cdot2 = \underline{0\cdot0594 \text{ m}^3}$$

Example. Find the volume of a tank with half-spherical ends of diameter 0·3 m and total length 1·2 m.

Total volume = Volume of sphere + volume of cylindrical part

$$= \frac{4}{3} \quad \pi \times r^3 + (\pi \times r^2 \times \text{length of cylindrical part})$$

$$= \left\{ \frac{4}{3} \times \frac{22}{7} \times \left(0\cdot15 \right)^3 \right\} + \left\{ \frac{22}{7} \times \left(0\cdot15 \right)^2 \times (1\cdot2 - 0\cdot3) \right\}$$

$$= \underline{0\cdot077\ 786 \text{ m}^3}$$

In this example the length of the cylindrical part is found:
Total length minus diameter equals 1·2 m minus 0·3 m which is

0·9 m. The half-spherical ends, when added together, form a complete sphere whose diameter is 0·3 m and the radius is thus 0·15 m.

Tank Capacity

When we find the volume of liquid in a tank the unit used is the litre and one litre is equal to 1000 millilitres or 0·001 m³.

Example. The volume of a tank is 0·095 m³. How many litres of petrol will be required to fill the tank?

$$\text{Capacity of tank} = \frac{0·095}{0·001}\left(\frac{m^3}{m^3}\right)$$

$$= \underline{95 \text{ litres}}$$

It is general practice to calibrate petrol tank gauges in litres.

Mass, Specific Gravity or Relative Density and Density

The **mass** of a body depends on the number of particles or the amount of matter it contains, and will not alter unless some of the particles are removed or added.

Mass must not be confused with volume, because, when its temperature changes so will its volume, but its mass does not alter.

The standard unit of mass is the **kilogramme,** and when a force of one **newton** is applied, the mass will accelerate at one **metre** per second per second.

It will be seen that a coherent unit thus exists, unit mass, unit force and unit acceleration, completely **independent** of the force of gravity. Expressed as Force (N) = Mass (kg) × Acceleration (m/s²). It will be seen that no additional numerical factors are present, and this coherence will be found to extend to all SI units.

Another unit of mass is the **gramme** (g) and the gramme is taken to equal the mass of 1 millilitre (ml) of water. One kilogramme (kg) equals 1000 grammes and 1000 kg equals 1 tonne.

The American **short ton** is 2000 lb. i.e. 907·1 kg.

Specific Gravity or Relative Density

The term specific gravity will gradually disappear as the SI units come into everyday use, and the term **Relative Density** (d) will take its place. Density is already used for many problems and since the sp. gr. of a substance has the same value as the density value in grammes of one cubic centimetre of the same substance, no clear definition has been previously used. For this reason we have in these text books used both terms, but the reader must realize that in the future the term sp. gr. will disappear.

When we take hydrometer readings of the electrolyte (acid) used in a battery, we are really testing the **specific gravity** of this electrolyte. What do we mean by this?

The specific gravity of a substance, liquid or solid, is the **ratio** of the mass of any volume of the substance to the mass of an equal volume of water. (Note, *equal* volumes!) This statement can be conveniently expressed:

$$\text{Specific gravity} = \frac{\text{Mass of any volume of a substance}}{\text{Mass of an equal volume of water}}$$

The specific gravity of water is 1.

Let us examine further the relationship between hydrometer readings and specific gravity. For convenience, hydrometer readings show four figures without a decimal point, e.g. 1285. However, only the figure 1 is considered to be a whole number; thus, should the hydrometer in the electrolyte show a reading of 1300, this will indicate a specific gravity of 1·3. If water is used in place of the electrolyte the hydrometer will show a reading of 1000, because the specific gravity of the water is 1.

It is well known that a litre of water has a mass of 1 kg. A litre of electrolyte whose specific gravity is 1·3 has a mass of 1·3 kg

Most liquids, however, are lighter than water, e.g. the specific gravity of a certain petrol is 0·75, therefore a litre of this petrol will have a mass of 0·75 kg.

From what has already been stated it should be clear that if we are given the specific gravity of any liquid, then its mass per litre can easily be found. This fact is useful to vehicle operators, enabling them to choose suitable 'tankers' when dealing with the haulage of liquids in bulk.

A list giving the specific gravities of some common liquids and solids will be found at the end of this chapter.

When dealing with solids, which are usually heavier than water, the unit generally used is the kilogramme (kg) which is equal to the mass of 0·001 m^3 or 1 litre of water, therefore the mass in kilogrammes of 1 litre of any substance, e.g. a mass of 1 litre of lead, is 11·3 kilogrammes and 11·3 is known to be the specific gravity of lead.

Density

If we take an equal mass of different metals, e.g. lead and aluminium, it will be found that the volume of lead will be much smaller than the volume of aluminium and we say that lead is more **dense** or the **density** of lead is greater than the density of aluminium.

The density of water is 1 gramme per millilitre (1 g/ml).

To calculate the mass of any given volume of a substance in any units or to calculate the volume of a given mass of a substance in any units, the specific gravity or density of the substance must be known.

Example. If the specific gravity of a certain Diesel oil is 0·84, what is the mass of 2000 litres of this oil in tonne?

$$\text{Mass of oil} = \text{Specific gravity} \times \text{volume (litres)}$$

$$= \frac{0 \cdot 84 \times 2000}{1000} = \underline{1 \cdot 68 \text{ tonne}}$$

Example. Calculate the mass of 1000 litres of undiluted sulphuric acid whose specific gravity is 1·8.

$$\text{Mass of acid} = \frac{1 \cdot 8 \times 1000}{1000} \underline{= 1 \cdot 8 \text{ tonne}}$$

Example. A solid gudgeon pin is 14 mm diameter and 75 mm long. Calculate its mass. The material is mild steel having a specific gravity of 7·85.

$$\text{Volume of pin} = \pi \times r^2 \times \text{length}$$

$$= \frac{22}{7} \times \frac{14}{2} \times \frac{14}{2} \times 75 \text{ mm}^3$$

$$\text{Mass of pin} = \text{Volume} \times \text{specific gravity}$$

$$= \frac{22}{7} \times \frac{14}{2} \times \frac{14}{2} \times \frac{75}{1000} \times \frac{785}{100} \text{ grammes}$$

$$= \underline{90 \cdot 67 \text{ grammes}}$$

This method of 'doing the sum all in one line' is to be recommended as it is easier and gives a more accurate result.

Example. Calculate the mass of 3 metres of copper bar, 14 mm diameter. Specific gravity of copper is 8·9

Volume of copper $= \pi \times r^2 \times$ length

$$= \frac{22}{7} \times \frac{14}{2} \times \frac{14}{2} \times 3000 \text{ mm}^3$$

Mass of copper $= \dfrac{22}{7} \times \dfrac{14}{2} \times \dfrac{14}{2} \times \dfrac{3000}{1\,000\,000} \times \dfrac{89}{10} \text{ kg}$

$= \underline{4 \cdot 1 \text{ kg}}$

A list of the specific gravities of the common materials used in motor vehicles are given below:

Petrol	.	.	. 0·75	White metal	.	. 7·5
Alcohol	.	.	0·8	Cast-iron	.	. 7·8
Benzol	.	.	0·89	Brass	.	. 8·2
Water	.	.	1·00	Phosphor-bronze	.	8·4
Battery 'acid'	.	.	1·285	Copper	.	. 8·7
Aluminium	.	.	2·6	Lead	.	. 11·4
Mild steel	.	.	7·3	Mercury	.	. 13·6

Exercise 5

1. A 4-cylinder engine has a cylinder bore of 60 mm and a stroke of 95 mm. What is the total capacity of the engine in millilitres?

(1075 millilitres)   (C. and G.)

2. A cylindrical drum contains 36 kg of petrol when it is $\frac{3}{4}$ full. How many litres does it hold when it is full? (A litre of petrol has a mass of 0·72 kg)   (66·6 litres)   (E.M.E.U.)

3. The bore and stroke of an engine are given as 61 mm × 85 mm. Calculate the swept volume of the cylinder in litres.

(0·25 litres)   (C. and G.)

4. A petrol tank is of rectangular section 1000 mm long, 300 mm wide and 250 mm deep. Given that 1 litre of petrol has a mass of 0·75 kg, calculate the number of litres and the mass of fuel the tank will hold.   (75 litres; 56·25 kg) (C. and G.)

5. The section of a petrol tank is such that the top and bottom faces are horizontal and the depth between them 0·3 m. The front face is vertical but the rear face slopes so that the top is 0·3 m wide and the bottom 0·45 m. The length of the tank is 1·0 m with flat vertical ends. How many litres will be required to fill the tank to a depth of 0·2 m?

(80 litres)   (C. and G.)

6. A casting has a mass of 14·8 kg. What is the mass of an exactly similar casting whose length, breadth and thickness are all double those of the first? (118·4 kg) (E.M.E.U.)

7. A copper wire is wound with 56 parallel turns on a reel, the diameter of which is 0·49 m. If the wire mass is 35g to the metre what is the mass of wire on the reel? (Omit the diameter of the wire from your calculations.) (3·02 kg) (I.M.I.)

8. Find the depth in metres of a hemispherical bowl that will hold 12·75 kg of water.

(0·1826 m) (I.M.I.)

9. A cylindrical storage tank is 1 m in diameter and 1·4 m long. It is being filled with petrol at the rate of 1 litre per second. How long does it take to fill the tank?

(18·3 min) (I.M.I.)

10. A cylindrical tank when full holds 1·2 cubic metres of water. The area of the surface of the water is 0·8 m². How deep is the tank and what mass of petrol would it hold? (Sp. gr. of petrol is to be taken as 0·72.) (1·5 m; 864 kg) (I.M.I.)

11. Two tonne of metal are melted down and cast into solid cylinders, each of which is 0·1 m in diameter and 0·7 m long. If only 38 such cylinders are obtained, what percentage of the metal is wasted?
(Sp. gr of metal 8·8) (8·05 per cent) (I.M.I.)

12. A roll of wire has a mass of 1·24 kilogrammes. From the roll is cut a piece 0·037 m long and this is found to have a mass of 2·93 g. What is the length of wire in the roll? (15·658 m)

13. A four-cylinder 'square' engine has a bore and stroke of 86 mm. Calculate the cubic capacity of the engine in litres.

(1·998 litres)

14. A vee-4 'oversquare' engine has a bore of 94 mm and stroke of 60 mm. Calculate the cubic capacity of the engine in litres.

(1·666 litres)

15. A fuel tank of rectangular section 0·25 m by 0·4 m is 0·85 m long.
(*a*) How many litres of fuel will it hold?
(*b*) Calculate the mass of this amount of fuel if its specific gravity is 0·8.

((*a*) 85 litres: (*b*) 68 kg) (E.M.E.U.)

16. A bronze gudgeon pin bush is 35 mm long and has an outside diameter of 42 mm and an inside diameter of 35 mm. Calculate the volume of bronze in the bush.

Why are gudgeon pins usually made hollow?

(14 822·5 mm³)   (E.M.E.U.)

6   Algebra

Algebra is that section of mathematics where **quantities** are represented by letters and figures.

Terms used in Algebra

When a figure and a letter are joined together by a sign they form what is known as a **term.** For example, 5 multiplied by a, or $5a$, is a term; the figure 5 is called a **coefficient.** Terms fall into two classes, **like** and **unlike** terms. Like terms must have the same letters but they may have the same or different coefficients, e.g. $2xy$ and $5xy$ are like terms. Unlike terms may have the same or different coefficients but their letters will always be different, e.g. $2xy^2$ and $2xy$ are unlike terms because one term contains y^2 and the other term y. Note that in the term $2xy^2$ only the y is squared, but in the term $2x^2y^2$ both the x *and* the y are squared.

Plus Signs and Minus Signs

In Chapter 1 we dealt with plus and minus signs in arithmetic; we added all the figures with plus signs together and all the figures with minus signs together and then subtracted those with the minus signs from the figures with the plus signs. The figures with the plus signs were always the greater and the result was always **positive.** In algebra we must get used to the idea of a **minus quantity,** i.e. a quantity less than 0. For example, in certain parts of the world a thermometer may register so many degrees below freezing point (0°C), and we indicate this by writing the temperature as, say, minus 5°C (-5°C), minus 10°C (-10°C), and so on.

Example. A fitter's mate has the misfortune to lose his pay packet during the afternoon of pay day (Friday). He draws a 'sub.' of £3 to carry him over the week-end. During Sunday the mate falls sick and he does not return to work during the whole week. On the following Monday week he has no wages due to him and he owes £3 or is minus £3.

Addition

The sum of letters of the same kind is found by adding their coefficients:

$$4x + x = 5x \quad \text{or} \quad 4x + 1x = 5x$$

It is important to remember that x is the same as $1x$; a is the same as $1a$, and so on.

Example.
      (a) $y + y + y + y = 4y$.
      (b) $a + 2a + 3a + 4a = 10a$.

The sum of letters of different kinds is shown by leaving the plus sign between them:

$$5x + 2y + 3y = 5x + 5y$$

In some examples we may find mixed plus and minus quantities, and what is called the **algebraical sum** of the quantities is obtained as follows:

(1) Add all the plus coefficients of each kind together.
(2) Add all the minus coefficients of each kind together.
(3) Take the difference between these two sums.
(4) Give to this difference the sign of whichever is the greater figure.

Example. Find the sum of $2x - 4x - 6x + 5x + 7x$.

(1) $2x + 5x + 7x \quad\quad = + 14x$ or $14x$
(2) $(-4x) + (-6x) = -10x$
(3) $14x - 10x \quad\quad = 4x$
(4) The plus is the greater

$$\therefore \text{ the answer is } \underline{4x}$$

Example. Find the sum of $-8x + 4x - 5x + 2x$.

(1) $4x + 2x \quad\quad\quad = 6x$
(2) $(-8x) + (-5x) = -13x$
(3) $-13x + 6x \quad\quad = -7x$
(4) The minus is the greater

$$\therefore \text{ the answer is } -\underline{7x}$$

The Addition of Expressions containing Two or More Terms

When several terms have to be added together we proceed:

(1) Arrange the letters in alphabetical order and place them in columns.
(2) Add the plus coefficients.
(3) Add the minus coefficients.
(4) Subtract the smaller coefficient from the larger coefficient.
(5) Give the plus or minus sign of the greater coefficient.

Example. Add together $7x + 7y$; $4x - 2y$; $x + 5y$.

$$7x + 7y$$
$$4x - 2y$$
$$x + 5y$$
$$\overline{}$$
$$12x + 10y$$

In the left-hand column we have all plus terms which give $12x$.

In the other column the plus terms are greater, thus giving $12y - 2y$ which equals $10y$.

$$\therefore (7x + 7y) + (4x - 2y) + (x + 5y) = \underline{12x + 10y}$$

Example. Add together $4x - 3y$; $6x + 4y$; $-5x - 5y$.

$$4x - 3y$$
$$6x + 4y$$
$$-5x - 5y$$
$$\overline{}$$
$$5x - 4y$$

In the left-hand column the plus terms are greater, thus giving $10x - 5x$ which equals $5x$.

In the other column the minus terms are greater, thus giving $4y - 8y$ which equals $-4y$.

$$\therefore (4x - 3y) + (6x + 4y) + (-5x - 5y) = \underline{5x - 4y}$$

Subtraction

The process of **algebraic subtraction** is carried out as follows:

Change the sign of the term to be subtracted and then add this term to the other term.

Example.   Subtract $7x$ from $15x$.

$$15x + (-7x) = \underline{8x}$$

Example.   Subtract $15x$ from $7x$.

$$7x - (+15x) = 7x - 15x = -\underline{8x}$$

Example.   Subtract $-7x$ from $15x$.

$$15x - (-7x) = 15x + 7x = \underline{22x}$$

In this example an important fact arises: 'Two **minuses** make a plus'.

The Subtraction of Expressions containing Two or More Terms

When several terms have to be subtracted we proceed:

(1) Arrange the terms as in addition.

(2) Change the signs of all the terms to be subtracted.

(3) Add the terms, whose signs have been changed, to the other expression.

Example. Subtract $2x^2 + 5y$ from $5x^2 - 2y$.

$$5x^2 - 2y$$
$$\underline{-2x^2 - 5y}\qquad \text{signs changed from } + 2x^2 \text{ and } + 5y.$$
$$3x^2 - 7y$$

$$\therefore (5x^2 - 2y) - (2x^2 + 5y) = \underline{3x^2 - 7y}$$

It is, however, not usual to write down the change of signs; the process should be carried out mentally.

Example. Subtract $2x^2 - 3y$ from $-4x^2 + 3y$.

$$-4x^2 + 3y$$
$$\underline{2x^2 - 3y}\qquad \text{change the signs mentally}$$
$$-6x^2 + 6y$$

$$\therefore (-4x^2 + 3y) - (2x^2 - 3y) = -\underline{6x^2 + 6y}$$

Example. Subtract $-10x - 5y$ from $15x + 9y$.

$$15x + 9y$$
$$\underline{-10x - 5y}\qquad \text{change the signs mentally}$$
$$25x + 14y$$

$$\therefore (15x + 9y) - (-10x - 5y) = \underline{25x + 14y}$$

Multiplication

The process of **algebraic multiplication** is carried out as follows:

(1) Multiply the coefficients.

(2) Add the indices of like quantities or terms.

We have seen previously that $4 \times 4 = 4^2$ and $5 \times 5 \times 5 = 5^3$; we can write letters in the same way with the index figure placed: $x \times x = x^1 \times x^1 = x^{1+1} = x^2$. Note that the index figure **one** is not usually shown.

Then $\qquad\qquad\qquad x \times x \times x \times x = x^4$

and $\qquad\qquad\qquad x^2 \times x^2 = x^{2+2} = x^4$

Example. Find the value of $4x^4 \times 2x^2$.

(1) $4 \times 2 = 8$.

(2) $x^4 \times x^2 = x^{4+2} = x^6$.

$$\therefore 4x^4 \times 2x^2 = \underline{8x^6}$$

In the example the sign of both terms was plus; now let us see the method of multiplying terms that are not all plus or positive.

$$4x \times (-2x) = -8x^2$$
$$(-4x) \times 2x = -8x^2$$
$$(-4x) \times (-2x) = +8x^2 \text{ or } 8x^2$$

i.e. two minuses multiplied together make plus.

These results give a definite rule called the **Rule of Signs,** which can be defined:

In the multiplication of two terms, two like signs (plus or minus) will give the product a plus sign but the multiplication of two unlike signs will give the product a minus sign.

Example. Find the value of $(ab - cd)(b^2 - ad)$ when $a = 1$; $b = 3$; $c = 4$; $d = 0$.

Now $(ab - cd)(b^2 - ad) = \{(1 \times 3) - (4 \times 0)\}\{(3^2) - (1 \times 0)\}$
$$= (3 - 0)(9 - 0)$$
$$= 3 \times 9 = \underline{27}$$

Note carefully that the multiplication of any term or figure by 0 will give 0 as the answer.

The Multiplication of Expressions containing Two or More Terms

(1) Write down the two expressions, one under the other, as shown in the following example.

(2) Begin at the left-hand side and multiply each term of the first expression, in turn, by each term of the second expression.

(3) Keep like terms under each other and add these terms together to obtain the product.

The following example shows the method in use.

Example. Multiply $x + 4$ by $x + 7$.

$$x + 4$$
$$x + 7$$

$x^2 + 4x$	(here we have multiplied $x + 4$ by x)
$\quad\;\; 7x + 28$	(here we have multiplied $x + 4$ by 7)
$x^2 + 11x + 28$	(like terms added)

$$\therefore (x + 4)(x + 7) = \underline{x^2 + 11x + 28}$$

Example. Multiply $x + y$ by $x - y$.

$$x + y$$
$$x - y$$
$$\overline{x^2 + xy}$$
$$\underline{ - xy - y^2}$$
$$\overline{x^2 - y^2} \qquad \text{the } xy\text{'s cancel out.}$$
$$\therefore (x + y)(x - y) = \underline{x^2 - y^2}$$

Difference of Two Squares

It has been shown that $(x + y)(x - y) = x^2 - y^2$; this result is important because it expresses a useful rule which we can apply to practical problems. This rule is:

The sum of any two quantities, e.g. $(x + y)$, when multiplied by the difference between the two quantities, i.e. $(x - y)$, will give the difference of the squares of the two quantities $(x^2 - y^2)$.

Example. Suppose the two quantities to be the numbers 5 and 3, now using the foregoing expression $(x + y)(x - y) = x^2 - y^2$. Let $x = 5$ and $y = 3$, then,

$$(5 + 3)(5 - 3) = 8 \times 2 = \underline{16} \qquad \text{or} \qquad 5^2 - 3^2 = 25 - 9 = \underline{16}$$

The method of applying this to a practical problem is as follows.

We have seen in Chapter 5, that the area of a flat ring was found by the formula $\frac{\pi}{4}(D^2 - d^2)$ where D = the outside diameter and d = the inside diameter of the ring. By using our rule we can write down the formula in a simpler form:

$$\frac{\pi}{4}(D + d)(D - d)$$

which in most problems will simplify the calculation.

We shall now consider how the foregoing rule will help us to factorize in arithmetic.

In the expression $(x + y)(x - y)$ let $y = 1$, then

$$(x + 1)(x - 1) = x^2 - 1^2 \qquad \text{or} \qquad x^2 - 1$$

Thus, if we have a number which is one less than a square, then this number can be factorized.

Example. Find the factors of 288.

Now, $289 = 17^2$

$$\therefore 288 = 289 - 1 = 17^2 - 1^2 = (17 + 1)(17 - 1) = 18 \times 16$$
$$\therefore \text{the factors of } 288 = \underline{18 \text{ and } 16}$$

Division

The process of **algebraic division** is carried out:

(1) Divide the coefficients.

(2) Subtract the indices of like quantities or terms.

Example. Find the value of $4x^4 \div 2x^2$.

(1) $4 \div 2 = 2$

(2) $x^{4-2} = x^2$

By collecting the terms from each stage we shall get $2x^2$

$$\therefore 4x^4 \div 2x^2 = \underline{2x^2}$$

Example. Find the value of $8x^6y^4z^5 \div 4x^4y^3z^2$.

Working in stages we get:

(1) Whole numbers first, $8 \div 4 = 2$

(2) $x^6 \div x^4 = x^{6-4} = x^2$

(3) $y^4 \div y^3 = y^{4-3} = y$

(4) $z^5 \div z^2 = z^{5-2} = z^3$

By collecting the terms from each stage we shall get

$$2 \times x^2 \times y \times z^3$$
$$\therefore 8x^6y^4z^5 \div 4x^4y^3z^2 = \underline{2x^2yz^3}$$

Factors

In order to deal successfully with certain types of algebraic expressions and to help us to **factorize** in arithmetic also, some knowledge of **factors** must be obtained.

We have seen already that an expression can be obtained by multiplying together two or more quantities or terms. Each of these separate quantities or terms can be said to be a factor of the product. For example, if we multiply $x + 4$ by $x + 7$ the result is $x^2 + 11x + 28$, and we say that the two quantities $x + 4$ and $x + 7$ are the factors of the expression.

$$x^2 + 11x + 28$$

The following factors are important because they occur frequently in algebra. They are explained below and should be carefully memorized.

(1) $(x + y)(x - y) = x^2 - y^2$

(2) $(x + y)(x + y) = (x + y)^2 = x^2 + 2xy + y^2$

In examples where the difference between the number to be factorized and a square is more than one, we can find the factors by using

$(x + y)(x - y) = x^2 - y^2$ as before, always provided the difference between the number and the square is itself a square.

Example. Find the factors of 187.

Now the nearest whole square number is 196 or 14^2.

Let $196 = x^2$ and, since $196 - 187 = 9$, then we shall have $187 = x^2 - 9$; $\sqrt{9} = 3$ and $\sqrt{196} = 14$.

Thus,
$$(x + 3)(x - 3) = 187$$
$$(14 + 3)(14 - 3) = 17 \times 11$$
$$\therefore \text{ the factors of } 187 = \underline{17 \text{ and } 11}$$

Exercise 6

1. Add $2x + 3y$, $3x - 5y$ and $2x - y$ and multiply the result by $x + y$. $\hfill (7x^2 + 4xy - 3y^2)$

2. Multiply the square of $(x - y)$ by $5x$. $\hfill (5x^3 - 10x^2y + 5xy^2)$

3. Add $2x + 3y - 4z$, $3x + 2y - 5z$, $4x - 8y + 7z$, $9x - 4y + 6z$ and $5x + 7y - 9z$. $\hfill (23x - 5z)$

4. Subtract $6x^2 + y - 2z + 3$ from $12x^2 - 3y + z - 1$. $\hfill (6x^2 - 4y + 3z - 4)$

5. Divide $x^2 - y^2$ by $x + y$. $\hfill (x - y)$

6. Simplify $\dfrac{\dfrac{d^5}{d^4} \times \dfrac{d^3}{d}}{\dfrac{a}{a^3} \times \dfrac{a^9}{a^7}}.$ $\hfill (d^3) \quad \text{(U.E.I.)}$

7. Express in its simplest form each of the following:

$$(1) \; \frac{c^3 \times c^{10}}{c^6 \times c^5} \qquad (2) \; \frac{(ab)^3}{a^2b^2}$$

$\hfill ((1) \; c^2 \quad (2) \; ab) \quad \text{(N.C.T.E.C.)}$

8. Factorize $x^2 + 16x - 36$. $\hfill ((x + 18)(x - 2)) \quad \text{(U.L.C.I.)}$

9. If $A = 2b$; $B = 2b^2 - bc$, find the value of $2B \div A$. $\hfill (2b - c) \quad \text{(U.L.C.I.)}$

10. Find the value of $(98\,695)^2 - (98\,690)^2$. $\hfill (986\,925) \quad \text{(U.L.C.I.)}$

11. Resolve into factors $x^2 - 9y^2$. $\hfill ((x + 3y)(x - 3y)) \quad \text{(U.L.C.I.)}$

12. Simplify:

$$\frac{x}{x^2 - x - 6} + \frac{x}{x^2 - 4x + 3} - \frac{2x}{x^2 + x - 2} \quad \text{(I.M.I.)}$$

What does the result become when $x = 4$?

$$\left(\frac{7x}{(x-3)(x+2)(x-1)}; \ 1\tfrac{5}{9} \right)$$

13. The sides of a rectangle are as shown in the figure. Find the area of the rectangle. (207) (I.M.I.)

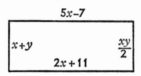

14. Find the mass of a steel propeller shaft, 72·5 mm outside diameter, 3·175 mm thick and 1200 mm long. The specific gravity of the steel is 7·2. (5·977 kg)

15. A piece of brass piping 300 mm long has an outside diameter of 38 mm and an inside diameter of 25 mm. If the specific gravity of the brass is 8·9, what is the mass of the piping?

(1·718 kg)

7

Equations

Formulae (singular **formula**) are used to find the value of an unknown quantity from the known values of other quantities. Now what do we mean by a formula? A formula is a simple and abbreviated way of expressing a rule in order to avoid long written descriptions.

Symbols, usually letters, represent the various quantities used in stating the rule. The following example shows the method using a formula.

We have seen in Chapter 5 that the rule for calculating the area of a circle is: square the radius of the circle and multiply this square by the value of π, i.e. $3\frac{1}{7}$.

Let us represent the area by the letter A and the radius of the circle by r, then we may write down the following:

$$A = \pi \times r^2 \qquad \text{or} \qquad A = \pi r^2$$

It is usual to leave out the multiplication sign when dealing with letters in a formula. When dealing with figures, however, the multiplication sign must be used in order to avoid confusion.

A formula consists of two parts, separated by an equals sign, which gives what is called an **equation** or an equality. Thus, $A = \pi r^2$ is an equation, i.e. both sides are equal or an equality exists between the two sides. This point cannot be too highly stressed because many students go astray in their calculations by not realizing that where an equals sign exists then both sides of the equation must be equal.

It is usual to place the symbol or letter representing the unknown quantity, or simply the 'unknown', i.e. the quantity or value to be found, alone on the left-hand side of the equals sign and all the other symbols or letters or figures on the right-hand side of the equals sign.

Example. We are told, in the formula $\text{hp} = \dfrac{D^2 N}{1614}$, used at one time by the Treasury for finding the horsepower of an engine, the following:

Horsepower equals the square of the diameter of the cylinder bore, in mm (symbol D); multiplied by the number of engine cylinders (symbol N); divided by 1614 (a constant). Now if we consider hp to be the unknown in the equation and we know that $D = 89$ mm and $N = 4$, then we can write down:

$$\text{hp} = \frac{(89)^2 \times 4}{1614} = \frac{31\ 684}{1614} = 19\cdot63$$

Finding the value of the unknown is often called 'solving' the equation.

The value of an equation remains unchanged, i.e. both sides will still be equal when:

(1) Equal quantities are added to each side of the equation.
(2) Equal quantities are subtracted from each side of the equation.
(3) Each side of an equation is multiplied by equal quantities.
(4) Each side of an equation is divided by equal quantities.
(5) The square, or any, root of each side of the equation is taken.
(6) Both sides of the equation are completely raised to any power.

The application of these operations is shown in the following examples:

Example. Calculate the value of x in the following equation:
$$7x - 7 = 2x + 5$$

The unknown x is present, together with known quantities, on both sides of the equation. In order to enable x to appear on one side only (left) we can proceed as follows.

Using operation (2), we can remove $2x$ from the right-hand side by subtracting $2x$ from each side:
$$(7x - 2x) - 7 = (2x - 2x) + 5$$
$$5x - 7 = 5$$

Using operation (1), we can remove -7 by adding 7 to each side:
$$5x(-7 + 7) = 5 + 7$$
i.e. $$5x = 12$$
(The 7's cancel out on the left-hand side.)

Using operation (4), we can remove 5 on the left-hand side by dividing each side by 5:
$$\frac{5x}{5} = \frac{12}{5}$$

(The 5's on the left-hand side cancel out.)

$$\therefore x = \frac{12}{5} = \underline{2\cdot4}$$

Example. Calculate the value of C in the following equation:

$$5 = \frac{35 + C}{C}$$

Using operation (3), we can transfer or **transpose**, as it is called, C from the bottom of the right-hand side to the top of the left-hand side by multiplying each side by C:

$$5 \times C = \frac{(35 + C)}{C} \times C$$

i.e. $\qquad\qquad 5C = 35 + C$

(The last C on the top line, right hand, and the C on the bottom line, right hand, cancel out.)

Using operation (2), we can remove C on the right-hand side by subtracting C from each side:

$$5C - C = 35 + C - C$$

i.e. $\qquad\qquad 4C = 35$

(The last two C's on the right-hand side cancel out, and as C is the same as $1C$, then $5C - 1C = 4C$.)

Using operation (4), we can remove 4 from the left-hand side by dividing each side by 4:

$$\frac{4C}{4} = \frac{35}{4}$$

(The 4's on the left-hand side cancel out)

i.e. $\qquad\qquad C = \frac{35}{4} = \underline{8 \cdot 75}$

Example. Calculate the value of x in the following:

$$x^2 = 64$$

Using operation (5), we take the square root of each side:

$$x = \sqrt{64} = \underline{8}$$

The foregoing is the usual method of solving equations; another and more simple method is:

Using the example $5 = \dfrac{35 + C}{C}$,

(1) Transfer C from the bottom right-hand side to the top left-hand side, giving $5C = 35 + C$.

(2) Transfer the other C from the top right-hand side to the top left-hand side. This C will now become a minus quantity and it is thus subtracted from $5C$:

$5C - C = 4C$. (We must remember that C is the same as $1C$.)

(3) Transfer the figure 4 from the top left-hand side to the bottom right-hand side, and by dividing 35 by 4, i.e. $\frac{35}{4}$, we obtain $\underline{8\cdot75}$

as before.

This method is called the **cross** method, and the following points concerning it should be noted.

(*a*) Any symbol or figure or a collection of symbols and figures can be transferred diagonally, see Fig. 7.1, i.e. from the bottom of one side to the top of the other side, or vice versa (the other way round). Should the 'quantity' on one side, however, consist of more than one symbol or figure separated by a plus or minus sign, then *all* the 'quantity' must be transferred. This operation is usually carried out first, thus simplifying the remaining operations.

(*b*) Any symbol or figure can be transferred 'straight' from one side to the other side, see Fig. 7.2; if positive, the symbol or figure then

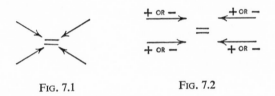

FIG. 7.1   FIG. 7.2

becomes negative, and if they are negative the symbol or figure becomes positive.

Take, for example, $7\cdot5 = \dfrac{x}{x-10}$, then:

$$7\cdot5(x-10) = x;$$

this means that both x *and* -10 are to be multiplied by $7\cdot5$.

$$\therefore 7\cdot5x - (10 \times 7\cdot5) = x$$

or

$$7\cdot5x - 75 = x$$

$$\therefore 7\cdot5x - x = 75$$

(The transferred plus x becomes minus and the transferred minus 75 becomes plus.)

$$\therefore 6\cdot5x = 75$$

$$x = \underline{11\cdot53}$$

A simple method of 'proving' an equation is to substitute the answer obtained in place of the unknown or unknowns in the equation. If both sides of the equation are then equal, the answer to the solved equation is correct.

For example, take the equation, $x = \dfrac{10}{2}$, i.e. $x = 5$.

Substituting in the equation:

$$5 = \frac{10}{2}, \text{ i.e. } 5 = 5 \text{ or } 5 \times 2 = 10$$

and the equation is proved.

With practice the student will be able to transpose and bring a simple equation to its final stage in one step. Many problems in motor vehicle calculations and science require the use of equations and it is essential for the student to understand the methods of solving because the application of equations to practical problems occur many times in the following chapters.

Problems are sometimes given where the unknown is to be made the subject of the formula or the formula rearranged in terms of the unknown. This simply means that the unknown is to be isolated or placed alone on the left-hand side of the equation.

Take, for example, the formula $G = \dfrac{1 + 1 \cdot 98}{C}$; we are required to rearrange the formula in order to make C the subject:

$$G = \frac{1 + 1 \cdot 98}{C}$$

Multiplying both sides by C and dividing by G gives

$$C = \frac{1 + 1 \cdot 98}{G}$$

Example. Rearrange the formula $V = \dfrac{bh^2}{l}(s + 3)$ to find b.

Calculate b when $V = 5$; $h = 7$; $l = 6$ and $s = 2$.

Now
$$V = \frac{bh^2}{l}(s + 3)$$

then
$$Vl = bh^2(s + 3)$$

and
$$\frac{Vl}{h^2(s + 3)} = b$$

$$\therefore b = \frac{Vl}{h^2(s + 3)}$$

Substituting the values we have:

$$b = \frac{5 \times 6}{(7 \times 7)(2 + 3)} = \frac{6}{49} = \underline{0\cdot122}$$

Some of the problems we meet have no ready-made or obvious formula and, in order to find the unknown quantity, we use a letter or symbol and fit it into an equation together with the other known quantities. In other words we make up our own formula and choose our own letter or symbol for the unknown quantity, e.g. x; y; z, and so on. This letter or symbol may be used more than once in an equation as we shall see in the following examples.

Example. Find three consecutive numbers whose sum is 84.

Let
$$x = \text{the 1st number}$$
$$x + 1 = \text{the 2nd number}$$
$$x + 2 = \text{the 3rd number}$$
then:
$$x + (x + 1) + (x + 2) = 84$$
$$3x + 3 = 84$$
$$3x = 84 - 3$$
$$3x = 81$$
$$x = 81 \div 3$$
$$x = 27.$$
∴ the three numbers are: <u>27, 28 and 29</u>

Example. When loaded into 6-tonne vehicles a quantity of sand needs 18 less vehicles than if loaded into 2-tonne vehicles. Find the number of 6-tonne vehicles and the quantity of the sand.

Let x = the number of 6-tonne vehicles, then:
$$x \times 6 = 2(x + 18)$$
$$6x = 2x + 36$$
$$6x - 2x = 36$$
$$x = 9.$$
∴ the number of 6-tonne vehicles = <u>9</u>

and the quantity of sand = $6 \times 9 = $ <u>54 tonne</u>

Example. A certain cylinder has a volume of 572 000 mm³ and its length is 1·5 times its diameter. Calculate the length and diameter of the cylinder.

Let d = diameter of the cylinder, then the length = $1\cdot5d$

Then
$$\frac{\pi d^2}{4} \times 1\cdot5d = 572\,000 \text{ mm}^3$$

$$\frac{22}{7} \times \frac{1}{4} \times d^2 \times 1{\cdot}5d = 572\ 000 \text{ mm}^3$$

$$\therefore \frac{22}{7} \times \frac{1}{4} \times \frac{3d^3}{2} = 572\ 000 \text{ mm}^3 \text{, because } d^2 \times \frac{3d}{2} = \frac{3d^3}{2}$$

Transposing
$$d^3 = \frac{572\ 000 \times 7 \times 4 \times 2}{22 \times 3}$$

$$d^3 = 485\ 000$$

$$d = \sqrt[3]{485\ 000}$$

$$\therefore d = \underline{78{\cdot}56 \text{ mm}}$$

$$\therefore \text{length} = \overline{1{\cdot}5 \times 78{\cdot}56} = \underline{117{\cdot}84 \text{ mm}}$$

Simultaneous Equations

We shall now consider equations which contain two unknown quantities; these equations cannot be solved by the same methods as were those met earlier in this chapter. To solve problems containing two unknowns we must first have two definite and separate equations which are worked out at the same time. The dictionary defines simultaneous as 'done at the same time', hence the term **simultaneous** equations. If we have three unknowns in a problem, then three distinct equations are used; in this chapter, however, we shall only consider problems containing two unknown quantities.

The equations
$$\left.\begin{array}{r} 5x - 2y = 7 \\ 3x + 4y = 12 \end{array}\right\}$$

are examples of simultaneous equations and we have to find values for both x and y which will **satisfy** each equation.

Two **methods of solving** simultaneous equations by calculation are as follows:

(1) By **eliminating** one of the unknowns.

This method makes the coefficients of x or y equal in both equations; this is shown in the following example.

Example. Solve the equations (1) $5x - 2y = 7$.

$$\text{(2) } 3x + 4y = 12.$$

(*a*) To eliminate y we multiply $5x - 2y = 7$ throughout by 2 in order to make the coefficients of y equal but of opposite sign, this will give $10x - 4y = 14$, i.e. $2(5x - 2y) = 7$.

(*b*) We add equation (2) to the product of (*a*), thus:

$$10x - 4y = 14$$
$$3x + 4y = 12$$
$$\overline{13x \qquad = 26} \qquad \therefore x = 2$$

(*c*) We substitute this value of x in either of the original equations; let us use equation (2).

Then
$$(3 \times 2) + 4y = 12$$
$$6 + 4y = 12$$
$$4y = 12 - 6$$
$$y = 6 \div 4 = 1\tfrac{1}{2}$$

Check by using $x = 2$ in equation (1).

$$(10 \times 2) - 4y = 14$$
$$20 - 4y = 14$$
$$20 - 14 = 4y$$
$$6 \div 4 = y$$
$$1\tfrac{1}{2} = y$$
$$\therefore x = \underline{2}; y = \underline{1\tfrac{1}{2}}$$

(2) By substitution

$$\text{Equation (1)} \quad 5x - 2y = 7$$
$$\text{Equation (2)} \quad 3x + 4y = 12$$

From equation (1) $\quad -2y = (7 - 5x) \qquad$ or $\qquad 2y = (5x - 7)$

$$\therefore y = \frac{5}{2}x - \frac{7}{2}$$

Substituting $\dfrac{5}{2}x - \dfrac{7}{2}$ for y in equation (2), then:

$$3x + 4\left(\frac{5}{2}x - \frac{7}{2}\right) = 12$$

$$3x + \frac{20}{2}x - \frac{28}{2} = 12$$

$$3x + 10x - 14 = 12$$
$$13x = 12 + 14$$
$$13x = 26$$
$$x = 2$$

$$\therefore y = \left(\frac{5}{2} \times 2\right) - \frac{7}{2}$$

$$= 5 - \frac{7}{2} = 1\tfrac{1}{2}$$

Both the equations (1) and (2) are therefore satisfied by the answers $x = \underline{2}$; $y = \underline{1\frac{1}{2}}$.

In order to find the value of the unknown quantities in a problem we must construct our own equations and the following examples will show the method of solving practical problems.

Example. A traveller calls at a garage and pays £3·05 for 40 litres of petrol and a litre of oil. Later he buys 30 litres of petrol and 2 litres of oil of the same respective brands at a cost of £2·60.

What price per litre does he pay for petrol and oil respectively?

Let x = the price of petrol per litre.

y = the price of oil per litre.

Then

$$(1) \; 40x + y = 305p$$
$$(2) \; 30x + 2y = 260p$$

Multiply equation (1) by 2 in order to eliminate y.

$$(1) \; 80x + 2y = 610p$$
$$\underline{(2) \; 30x + 2y = 260p}$$
$$50x = 350p \text{ by subtraction,}$$
$$\therefore \quad x = 350p \div 50 = 7p$$

Now substituting 7p in equation (1), then:

$$40 \times 7 + y = 305p$$
$$y = 305 - (40 \times 7)p$$
$$y = 305 - 280p$$
$$y = 25p$$

$\therefore$ Price of petrol = $\underline{7p}$ per litre.

$\therefore$ Price of oil = $\underline{\underline{25p}}$ per litre.

Quadratic Equations

An equation which contains the second (but no higher) power or square of the unknown quantity is known as a **quadratic equation**. Now these equations have two solutions or **roots** as they are usually called. In the solution of a quadratic equation it is possible that only one of the roots has any practical application to a particular problem, thus the other root can be ignored.

We shall now see the build-up of a formula which will enable us to solve any quadratic equation.

Any quadratic equation can be expressed in the following form:

$$ax^2 + bx + c = 0$$

where x, a, b and c are given values.

Using the basic equation $ax^2 + bx + c = 0$, we proceed:

Divide the equation throughout by a:

$$x^2 + \frac{bx}{a} + \frac{c}{a} = 0$$

Then $$x^2 + \frac{bx}{a} = -\frac{c}{a}$$

Complete the square on the left-hand side by adding $\left(\frac{b}{2a}\right)^2$ to each side of the equation, then:

$$x^2 + \frac{bx}{a} + \frac{b^2}{4a^2} = \frac{b^2}{4a^2} - \frac{c}{a}$$

$$\left(x + \frac{b}{2a}\right)^2 = \frac{b^2 - 4ac}{4a^2}$$

Take the square root of each side of the equation, then:

$$x + \frac{b}{2a} = \pm\sqrt{\frac{b^2 - 4ac}{4a^2}}$$

$$x + \frac{b}{2a} = \frac{\pm\sqrt{b^2 - 4ac}}{2a}$$

and $$x = \frac{\pm\sqrt{b^2 - 4ac}}{2a} - \frac{b}{2a}$$

$$\therefore x = \frac{-b \pm \sqrt{b^2 - 4ac}}{2a}$$

The above formula can now be used to solve any quadratic equation.

Example. Solve the equation $x^2 - 4x = -3$.

$$x^2 - 4x = -3$$

$$\therefore x^2 - 4x + 3 = 0$$

Using the formula $x = \dfrac{-b \pm \sqrt{b^2 - 4ac}}{2a}$

we have $a = 1$, $b = -4$ and $c = 3$

$$\therefore x = \frac{-(-4) \pm \sqrt{-4^2 - 4 \times 1 \times 3}}{2 \times 1}$$

$$= \frac{4 \pm \sqrt{16 - 12}}{2}$$

$$= \frac{4 \pm \sqrt{4}}{2}$$

$$= \frac{4 \pm 2}{2}$$

$$= \frac{6}{2} \text{ or } \frac{2}{2}$$

$$= \underline{3 \text{ or } 1}$$

Check: $x^2 - 4x + 3 = 0$, then using the 3,

$$9 - 12 + 3 = 0$$

$$\therefore 12 = 12$$

Using the 1, $1 - 4 + 3 = 0$

$$\therefore 4 = 4$$

The roots of the equation $x^2 - 4x = -3$ are $\underline{3 \text{ or } 1}$

Example. The circumference of the front wheel of a tractor is 1 m shorter than the rear wheel. The front wheel makes 10 revolutions more than the rear wheel while the tractor travels 120 metres. Find the circumference of the two wheels.

Let x = circum. of front wheel, in m, then:

$$x + 1 = \text{circum. of rear wheel, in m.}$$

Thus
$$\frac{120}{x} - \frac{120}{x + 1} = 10$$

Multiplying throughout by $x(x + 1)$

$$120(x + 1) - 120x = 10x(x + 1)$$

Then
$$120x + 120 - 120x = 10x(x + 1)$$

Since the 120x's cancel out,
$$120 = 10x(x + 1)$$

Dividing each side by 10, we have
$$12 = x(x + 1)$$
$$\text{or} \quad 12 = x^2 + x$$

Transposing, $x^2 + x - 12 = 0$

Using the formula $x = \dfrac{-b \pm \sqrt{b^2 - 4ac}}{2a}$,

Then $x = \dfrac{-1 \pm \sqrt{1^2 - 4 \times 1 \times (-12)}}{2 \times 1}$

$$= \frac{-1 \pm \sqrt{1^2 + 48}}{2}$$

$$= \frac{-1 \pm \sqrt{49}}{2}$$

$$= \frac{-1 \pm 7}{2} = \frac{6}{2} \text{ or } \frac{8}{2}$$

$$\therefore x = 3 \text{ or } 4$$

Circum. of front wheel $= \underline{3 \text{ m}}$

Circum. of rear wheel $= \underline{4 \text{ m}}$

Two further methods of solving quadratic equations are as follows:

(1) Solution by factors.

(2) Solution by 'completing the square'.

The following examples illustrate the two methods:

(1) Solution by factors

Example. Solve the equation $x^2 - 9x = 36$.

(*a*) Reduce one side of the equation to zero by bringing all the terms to one side:

$$x^2 - 9x - 36 = 0$$

(*b*) Obtain the factors of the left-hand side of the equation:

$$(x - 12)(x + 3) = 0$$

(*c*) Equate each factor obtained to zero and thus obtain the roots of the equation:

$$x - 12 = 0, \text{ thus } x = 12$$
$$x + 3 = 0, \text{ thus } x = -3$$

(*d*) Check the roots:

Substituting 12 in the same equation $x^2 - 9x = 36$, then:

$$12^2 - (9 \times 12) = 36, \text{ i.e. } 36 = 36$$

Substituting -3 in the equation, then:

$$(-3 \times -3) + (9 \times 3) = 36, \text{ i.e. } 36 = 36$$

∴ The roots of the equation $x^2 - 9x = 36$ are 12 or -3

(2) Solution by completing the square

Example. Solve the equation $x^2 - 12x + 35 = 0$

(*a*) Rearrange the equation:

$$x^2 - 12x = -35$$

(*b*) Square half the coefficient of x and add this figure to each side of the equation, thus completing the square.

$$\frac{12}{2} = 6 \text{ and } (6)^2 = 36$$

then $\qquad x^2 - 12x + 36 = -35 + 36$

(*c*) Simplify throughout:

$$(x - 6)(x - 6) = 1$$

or $\qquad (x - 6)^2 = 1$

(*d*) Take the square of each side of the equation:

$$x - 6 = \pm 1$$

(*e*) Use the $\pm$ as in the formula method previously described, then:

$$x = 6 + 1 = 7$$

and $\qquad x = 6 - 1 = 5$

∴ The roots of the equation $x^2 - 12x + 35 = 0$ are 7 or 5

Note: The formula method of solving quadratic equations is, however, recommended for general use.

Exercise 7

1. The power required to drive a car which exerts a downward force of N newtons having a frontal area of A m² at a speed of V km/h up an incline of 1 in n is given by:

$$P \text{ (kW)} = \frac{V}{810}\left(\frac{N}{270} + CAV^2 + 0 \cdot 225\,\frac{N}{n}\right)$$

where C is the coefficient depending upon the shape of the body. If $C = 0.0076$; $A = 1.5$; $V = 70$; $N = 13\,500$, and $n = 20$, calculate the power required. (22·27 kW)   (C. and G.)

2. A formula used for the rating of a petrol engine is
$$\text{power (W)} = 0.231d^2(r + 1)$$
where d = diameter of piston in mm, r = bore to stroke ratio. If the power = 47 74 W, calculate d when $r = 1$.

(101·6 mm)   (N.C.T.E.C.)

3. In the formula $F = \dfrac{0.0396F_1V^2}{D}$, F is the braking force in newtons (N); F_1 is the downward force of the vehicle in newtons; V is the speed in km/h and D is the stopping distance in metres (m). If $F = 3\,600$ N; $F_1 = 10\,000$ N; and $V = 35$ km/h, find the distance D in metres.

(134·75 m)   (N.T.C.E.C.)

4. (*a*) Rearrange the formula $H = \dfrac{G - S}{G - 1}W$ to make W the subject.
Calculate the value of W when $H = 12\,400$; $G = 1.4$ and $S = 1.24$.
(*b*) What must be the value of G if $W = 30\,000$; $H = 14\,000$ and $S = 1.24$?   ((*a*) 31 000; (*b*) 1·45)   (E.M.E.U.)

5. Solve the equation:
$$\frac{x}{2} + \frac{x}{3} - \frac{5x}{12} = \frac{x}{6} + 36$$
(144)   (E.M.E.U.)

6. If $H = 0.197d(d - 1)(r + 2)$, find r when $d = 3.21$ and $H = 5.54$.
(1·967)   (U.E.I..

7. In the formula $D = d + \dfrac{1.299}{N}$ used in connection with American threads, calculate d when $D = 0.875$ and $N = 9$.   (0·731)   (U.E.I.)

8. The power transmitted by a belt over a pulley is given by
$$\text{Power} = \frac{(T_1 - T_2)V}{60}$$
Find the value of the power when $T_1 = 980$ N, $T_2 = 80$ N, and $V = 200$.   (3000 W)   (I.M.I.)

9. The volume of a wedge is given by $V = \dfrac{bh}{6}(2l + e)$. Where b and h are the dimensions of the rectangular base, e is the length of the edge and l is the height of the wedge. Find the value of l when $e = 350$ mm; $b = 80$ mm; $h = 130$ mm and $V = 1\,127\,000$ mm^3.

(150 mm)   (I.M.I.)

10. Solve the equation $\dfrac{x + 4}{x - 2} = \dfrac{5}{8}$. $\qquad (- 14)$ (U.L.C.I.)

11. (*a*) Rearrange the following formula to find *C*.
$$A^2 = CA + CB$$
(*b*) In the above formula, given that $C = \frac{1}{2}$ and $A = B$, find the value of *A*.

$$\left((a)\ \ C = \frac{A^2}{A + B};\ \ (b)\ 1 \right)$$ (U.L.C.I.)

12. Find the value of *x* in the equation:
$$7(2x - 3) = 3(x + 4) \qquad\qquad (3)$$

13. A garage account for four sparking plugs and one inner tube at list prices amounts to £2·35. A similar account for one sparking plug and three inner tubes is £4·08.

Calculate the respective prices of sparking plug and inner tube.

$\qquad\qquad$ (£0·27; £1·27) (U.E.I.)

14. A cooling medium for machine tools was made of 3 litres of water and 5 litres of special oil; the total mass of the solution was 7 kg. Another mixture was made with 9 litres of water and 7 litres of the special oil, and had a mass of 14·6 kg.

Calculate the mass of 8 litres of the special oil.

$\qquad\qquad$ (6·4 kg) (U.E.I.)

15. If a speed of one m per second is the same as $\frac{1}{2}(3S - 8 \cdot 8)$ km per hour, what is the value of *S*? $\qquad\qquad$ (3·6) (U.E.I.)

16. The total cost per hour *X* of running a machine is represented by the formula $X = a + bN^2$, *N* being the speed of the machine in rev/min. By experiment it was found that when
$$N = 100;\ X = 15 \cdot 25\ \text{p}$$
$$N = 150;\ X = 21 \cdot 5\ \text{p}$$
Choosing your own method, find the values of *a* and *b*.

$\qquad\qquad$ ((*a*) 10·25; (*b*) 0·0005) (U.E.I.)

17. The effort *E*, which must be exerted to lift a load *W* by means of a small crane, is given by the equation: $E = aW + b$.

If *E* is 9 N when *W* is 100 N, and *E* is 30 N when *W* is 800 N, determine the values of *a* and *b*.

$\qquad\qquad$ ($a = 0 \cdot 03$; $b = 6$) (E.M.E.U.)

18. Solve the following simultaneous equation:
$$9 - x = 4y;\quad 8 - 3y = 2x.$$

$\qquad\qquad$ ($x = 1$; $y = 2$)

19. A can has a mass of 3·6 kg when full of petrol and a mass of 2·7 kg when two-thirds full. Find the mass of the can when empty.

(0·9 kg)

20. A lorry and a sports car travelled a distance of 21 km. The difference in their times was 70 minutes. If the speed of the sports car was six times that of the lorry, find the speed of each.

(15 km/h; 90 km/h)

21. In a workshop the wage bill for four fitters and two mates was £96. If a fitter earns $1\frac{1}{2}$ times as much as a mate, find the wage of each.

(£18; £12)

22. The difference of the squares of two consecutive numbers is 49. Find the two numbers. (24; 25)

23. Nuts of 6 mm diameter at 3p per dozen and others of 8 mm diameter at 4p per dozen cost 66p. If the nuts of 6 mm diameter had cost 4p per dozen and those of 8 mm diameter had cost 5p per dozen, the cost would have been 19p more.

How many nuts of each size were bought?

(6 mm, 10 doz; 8 mm, 9 doz)

24. A racing track 6·1 km long is triangular in shape. Let *A, B, C,* be turning points.

BC is $\frac{5}{6}$ of *AB* and 0·3 km longer than *CA*.

What are the lengths of the sides? (2·4; 2 and 1·7 km)

25. The cost of manufacturing water-pump impellers and casings consists of the initial cost plus a fixed sum for each part.

If the impellers cost £14 per dozen or £80 per gross and the casings cost £27 per dozen or £192 per gross, find:

(*a*) The initial cost of the impeller.
(*b*) The selling cost of one impeller.
(*c*) The initial cost of the casing.
(*d*) The selling cost of one casing.

((*a*) £8; (*b*) £0·50; (*c*) £12; (*d*) £1·25

26. Solve the equations:

(*a*) $3x + 6y = 39$
$4x - 3y = 8$.

(*b*) $\dfrac{7a + 6}{3} = \dfrac{12a - 7}{2}$.

((*a*) $x = 5$; $y = 4$; (*b*) $a = 1·5$) (E.M.E.U.)

27. The circumference of one wheel is 20 mm longer than that of another wheel. The product of the two circumferences is 144 300 mm. Calculate the lengths of the two circumferences. (370 mm; 390 mm)

28. The area of a rectangular sheet of metal is 24000 mm². The length is 10 mm greater than the width. Calculate the length and width.

(160 mm; 150 mm)

29. A solid propeller shaft 100 mm diameter has to be replaced by a hollow shaft so that the internal diameter is 75 mm and the cross-sectional area of the hollow shaft must be the same as that of the solid shaft. Calculate the outside diameter of the hollow shaft.

(125 mm)

30. Solve the following equation:
$$\tfrac{1}{4}x^2 + 1\tfrac{1}{4}x + 1\tfrac{1}{2} = 0$$

(− 3 and − 2)   (I.M.I.)

8

Graphs

Drawings of motor vehicle parts are usually made smaller than 'full' size, and in order to do this we use a **scale,** i.e. a certain length (say 1 mm) on the drawing is made equivalent to 10 mm on the part. A drawing made in this way will be one tenth full size and the scale is, 1 mm equals 10 mm.

The foregoing applies only to the measurement of length, but we can extend the idea and represent *any* quantity by means of the length of a line drawn to a suitable scale; such a line is known as a **scalar quantity.** For example, we can prepare a scale in which 1 mm (or any other length) represents a mass of 1 kilogramme, 1 tonne, or a period of time (say 1 minute or 1 hour), and so on. These and similar scales are used in the production of **graphs.**

Where quantities are related to each other so that a change in the value of one quantity produces a change in the value of the other quantity, it is often convenient to represent the effect of these changes by means of a line diagram called a graph. By the use of graphs we can obtain answers to problems without further calculation; experimental results can be shown and, as already stated, the effect on one quantity by varying the other quantity can be observed. In short, it reduces work and conveys information quickly!

The following points concerning graphs should be noted.

(1) Graphs are usually **plotted** (drawn) on squared paper. This paper is ruled with both vertical and horizontal lines drawn at equal distances apart, usually 2 mm; these lines are subdivisions of 20 mm squares which are indicated by bolder lines, as shown in Fig. 8.1. Plain paper, however, can be used, but it is not so convenient.

(2) The vertical line OY (Fig. 8.1.) is called the vertical axis or **ordinate.** The horizontal line OX is called the horizontal axis or **abscissa,** and as it is easier to remember 'vertical' and 'horizontal' we shall use these terms. The point O is called the **origin.**

(3) One or more of the squares measured along the line OX is taken

as the unit of measurement for the quantity whose values are selected. In the same way one or more of the squares measured along the line OY is taken as the unit of measurement for the quantity whose values are calculated.

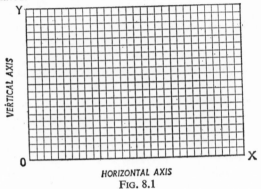

Fig. 8.1

(4) In order to make a graph easier to understand, the further following instructions should be obeyed:

(*a*) Write a title or heading above the graph.

(*b*) At the side of each axis OX and OY write what the axis represents and the unit, e.g. time in seconds, distance in mm or m, and so on.

(*c*) Graduate each axis clearly with the correct unit and scale.

(*d*) Choose as large a scale as the size of the paper will allow, but always use a scale which makes plotting and reading easy.

(*e*) If more than one graph appears on the same paper, label each clearly.

Plotting Graphs

From note (3) it will be seen that for any pair of quantities two points are obtained, one on OX and the other on OY. If a horizontal line is drawn on the squared paper from the point on OY and a vertical line is drawn from the point on OX, then the two lines will intersect (meet). Thus, by plotting several pairs of quantities a series of points are obtained on the squared paper. These points are usually marked or plotted by means of a small circle, a cross or a dot, and the graph is completed by joining the points with a thin line called a **curve**. In practice the horizontal and the vertical lines are assumed and not drawn; the circle or cross, however, indicates the point at which these lines would intersect.

The line joining the points may form a regular curve, but if it is irregular a uniform curve lying fairly between the points should be drawn; thus representing an average of the results. Any irregularity is usually caused by slight mistakes in experiment, in observation or in calculation. The term 'curve' denotes any plotted line, straight or otherwise. In some graphs the points may lie nearly on a straight line; here a straight line lying evenly among the points should be drawn.

The following examples will show the methods used.

Example. To determine the number of inches in a given number of millimetres by means of a graph.

From Chapter 2 we know that 1 in = 25·4 mm, thus the corresponding values of inches and millimetres can be tabulated in two columns:

Point	Inches	Millimetres
a	1	25·4
b	2	50·8
c	3	76·2
d	4	101·6
e	5	127·0

Use the vertical axis OY to denote millimetres because these are the calculated values and the horizontal axis OX to denote inches (Fig. 8.2.). Proceed by reading off 25·4 on the vertical axis and 1 on the horizontal axis, thus obtaining the first point which can be represented by *a*. The second point *b* is obtained by reading off 50·8 on the

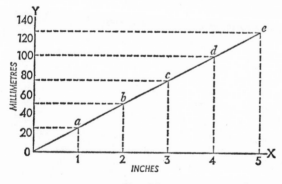

Fig. 8.2

vertical axis and 2 on the horizontal axis. In the same way points *c*, *d* and *e* are obtained and the graph is completed by drawing a fine line evenly through the points. Any intermediate value can now be obtained e.g. 2·5 inches is equivalent to 63·5 millimetres and 88·9 millimetres is equivalent to 3·5 inches. These intermediate values are found by inspecting the curve.

In order to find the inch equivalent between 0 and 1 inch or the millimetre equivalent between 0 and 25·4 millimetres, the curve can be continued until it reaches the origin O and at this point we shall find that 0 inches = 0 millimetres!

Always remember, the purpose of graphs is to convey information quickly.

Example. A vehicle leaves its garage at 9 a.m.; the distance recorded by the speedometer, originally set at zero is:

Time a.m.	9.10	9.20	9.25	9.30	9.40	9.50	10.0	10.10	10.20
Kilometres	2	5	9	12	16	19	24	31	37

Find from a graph:

(1) the readings at 9.26, 9.54, and 10.15 a.m.

(2) the distance travelled between 9.35 a.m. and 10.5 a.m.

(3) the time when the distance travelled is 14 km, 21 km, and 33 km.

The answers are given with Fig. 8.3.

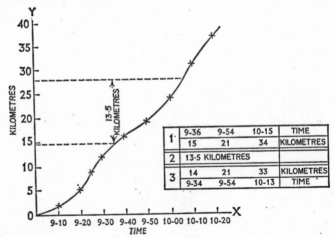

1 ·	9-36	9-54	10-15	TIME
	15	21	34	KILOMETRES
2	13·5 KILOMETRES			
3	14	21	33	KILOMETRES
	9-34	9-54	10-13	TIME

FIG. 8.3

Valve Lift Curves

A typical valve lift against crankshaft movement curve is shown in Fig. 8.4. It will be seen from the curve that the total lift and fall is divided into periods; with this type of curve there is minimum dwell when the valve is fully open.

Valve acceleration is very high and it is almost constant during the period it continues. The deceleration is much lower; thus only a comparatively small spring force is required to avoid valve 'bounce'.

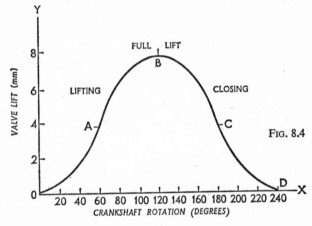

FIG. 8.4

Example. Measurements of crankshaft angles in degrees and valve lift in mm gave the following figures:

Crankshaft rotation (degrees)	Valve lift (mm)
0	0
20	0·5
40	1·7
60	4·0
80	6·6
100	7·6
120	7·8
140	7·6
160	6·6
180	4·0
200	1·7
220	0·5
240	0

To construct the lift curve use the OX axis to a scale of 10 mm = 20° of crank rotation and the OY axis to a scale of 10 mm = 1 mm of valve lift. An inspection of the curve will show that the total lift and fall is divided into periods. Identify these periods and state what is happening to the valve during each period.

Fig. 8.4 shows the completed curve, and the identity of the periods is: Accelerating O—A and B—C. Decelerating A—B and C—D.

Piston and Crank Movement

In any engine the piston travels further and faster in the first half than in the second half of the crank movement from t.d.c. (top dead centre) to b.d.c. (bottom dead centre). The following will show why this is so.

The connecting rod is often about twice the length of the stroke and the figures used are based on this assumption.

Let the distance between the centres of the connecting rod bearings be 200 mm, and the engine stroke 100 mm. Draw the crankpin circle to a scale of half full size. Divide the circle into 12 equal parts as shown in Fig. 8.5. To a scale of half full size draw the connecting

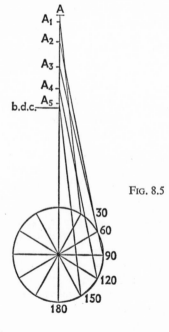

Fig. 8.5

rod for each position of the crank. The points A1, A2, A3, A4, and A5 indicate the position of the piston from t.d.c., point A.

For example, when the crankpin is at O, Fig. 8.5, the piston is at t.d.c., point A. When the crankpin has turned through 30° the piston is at A1, when the crank is at 90° the piston is at A3, and so on.

If we draw a base line BC, Fig. 8.6 to represent crank rotation and divide the line into 6 equal parts so as to correspond to the crank angles 30°, 60°, 90°, 120°, 150°, and 180° of Fig. 8.5, then we can show

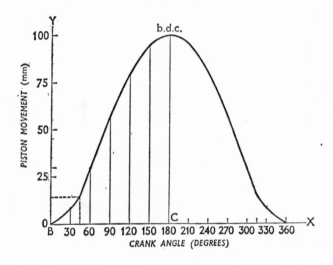

FIG. 8.6

on the vertical axis the piston movement on an angle basis. From each of the foregoing points draw ordinates to represent the distance the piston is from t.d.c., point A, i.e. the ordinate for 30° will be equal to length A to A1, from A to A2, and so on. Join these points with a smooth curve as shown in Fig. 8.6, and the ordinates of the curve will represent piston movement for given crank angles from t.d.c. to b.d.c., i.e. half a revolution. The other half of the revolution, b.d.c. to t.d.c., can be constructed in a similar way.

The following table gives the correct distances of the piston from t.d.c. for the given angles:

Angle of crank from t.d.c. (°)	Distance of piston from t.d.c. (mm)
0	0·0
30	8·3
60	29·8
90	56·4
120	79·8
150	94·9
180	100
Stroke = 100 mm	Connecting rod length = 200 mm

The piston position for any crank angle not given can be obtained from the graph by drawing a suitable ordinate. For example, to find the position of the piston for a crank angle of 45°, see Fig. 8.6; this distance will be 14·3 mm from t.d.c.

Graphs and Equations

The solving of certain equations by algebraic means is both lengthy and involved, so graphical methods are often used, since *any* equation can be solved by means of a graph. It should be realized, however, that the greatest accuracy is obtained by using the largest possible scale.

Graphical Solution of Simultaneous Equations

The axes for this type of graph are drawn in the form of a cross, Fig. 8.7. The horizontal axis gives positive values of x when measured from the origin 0 towards the right and negative values of x when measured towards the left. The vertical axis gives positive values of y above the origin and negative values of y below the origin. The following example shows the method used.

Example. Solve the equations:

$$(1)\ 5x - 2y = 7$$
$$(2)\ 3x + 4y = 12$$

To solve these equations graphically we must plot the graph of each equation.

$$(1)\ 5x - 2y = 7$$

(*a*) Rearrange the equation so that *y* is on the left-hand side and all the other terms are on the right-hand side of the equation.

$$5x - 2y = 7$$
$$-2y = -5x + 7$$
$$2y = 5x - 7$$
$$\therefore \quad y = \frac{5x - 7}{2}$$

(*b*) Determine the values of *y* by substituting values for *x* from 0 to 3:

when $x = 0$, then $y = \dfrac{(5 \times 0) - 7}{2} = -3\frac{1}{2}$

when $x = 1$, then $y = \dfrac{(5 \times 1) - 7}{2} = -1$

when $x = 2$, then $y = \dfrac{(5 \times 2) - 7}{2} = 1\frac{1}{2}$

when $x = 3$, then $y = \dfrac{(5 \times 3) - 7}{2} = 4$

$$(2) \quad 3x + 4y = 12$$

(*a*) Rearrange the equation as before, then:

$$y = -\frac{3x + 12}{4}$$

(*b*) Determine the values of *y* as before:

when $x = 0 \quad 1 \quad 2 \quad 3$
$y = 3 \quad 2\frac{1}{4} \quad 1\frac{1}{2} \quad \frac{3}{4}$

The values of *x* and the calculated values of *y*, for both equations, are plotted on the same graph, Fig. 8.8. The point at which the lines intersect gives the solution of the equations.

$$(1) \quad 5x - 2y = 7$$
$$(2) \quad 3x + 4y = 12$$
$$\text{i.e.} \quad x = \underline{2} \text{ and } y = \underline{1\frac{1}{2}}$$

Check: (i) $\quad (5 \times 2) - (2 \times 1\frac{1}{2}) = 7$
$$10 \quad - \quad 3 \quad\quad = 7, 7 = 7.$$

(ii) $\quad (3 \times 2) + (4 \times 1\frac{1}{2}) = 12$
$$6 \quad + \quad 6 \quad\quad = 12, 12 = 12$$

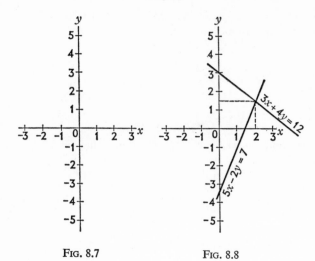

Fig. 8.7   Fig. 8.8

Example. Calculate the respective costs of two jobs *A* and *B* from the following:

Half the cost of *B* equals the cost of *A* plus £9. If *B* cost £14 more, it would cost four times as much as *A*.

$$(1)\ \tfrac{1}{2}B = A + 9$$
$$(2)\ B + 14 = 4A$$

Rearranging,
$$(1)\ \tfrac{1}{2}B = A + 9$$
$$(2)\ \ B = 4A - 14$$

Multiplying (1) by 2,

$$(1)\ B = 2A + 18$$
$$(2)\ B = 4A - 14$$

Only three points are required for plotting from each equation.

Equation (1)   If $A =$ 0   2   4

                    $B =$ 18   22   26

Equation (2)   If $A =$ 0   2   4

                    $B =$ -14 -6 2

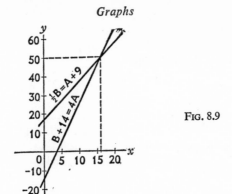

FIG. 8.9

Fig. 8.9 shows both equations plotted on the same graph. The x axis is used for values of A and the y axis for values of B. The points of intersection are 16 and 50. Thus A costs £16 and B £50.

Graphical Solution of Quadratic Equations

Fig. 8.10 shows the graph of the quadratic expression $y = x^2$. The curve shown is called a **parabola**; it is also known as the **curve of squares**, because, in order to obtain the value of y, x has to be squared as shown

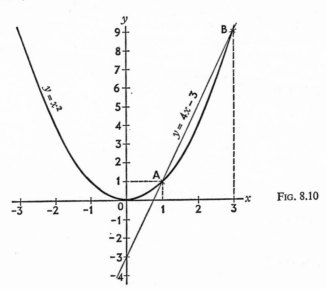

FIG. 8.10

in the following table. The plotted points are obtained by taking values of x from 0 to $+4$ and from 0 to -4. The corresponding values of y are then taken from the table.

x	-4	-3	-2	-1	0	1	2	3	4
$y = x^2$	16	9	4	1	0	1	4	9	16

In Fig. 8.10 it should be noted that in drawing the curve different scales have been used on the two axes. This is because the values of y increase much more rapidly than those of x and the graph so plotted is much easier to read.

Example. Solve the quadratic equation $x^2 - 4x + 3 = 0$.

(*a*) Rearrange the equation as $x^2 = 4x - 3$.

(*b*) Rearrange $x^2 = 4x - 3$ as two equations, then $y = x^2$ and $y = 4x - 3$.

(*c*) Plot and draw the graph of $y = x^2$; this has already been shown to be a parabola in Fig. 8.10.

(*d*) Solve the equation $y = 4x - 3$.

$$\text{If } x = \quad 0 \qquad x = 1 \qquad x = 2$$
$$y = -3 \qquad y = 1 \qquad y = 5$$

Plot and draw these points, which give a straight line across the parabola, Fig. 8.10.

(*e*) The solution of the quadratic equation $x^2 - 4x + 3 = 0$ will be found at the points A and B where the two lines intersect in Fig. 8.10. The values of x at A and B are 1 and 3.

(*f*) Check: $1^2 - 4 + 3 = 0, \quad -3 + 3 = 0$
$\qquad\qquad 9 - 12 + 3 = 0, \quad -3 + 3 = 0$

The solution of the quadratic equation $x^2 - 4x + 3 = 0$ is: 1 or 3.

Example. Solve the quadratic equation $2x^2 + 2 \cdot 2x - 5 = 0$.

(*a*) Divide throughout by 2, then:

$$x^2 + 1 \cdot 1x - 2 \cdot 5 = 0$$
$$\therefore x^2 = 2 \cdot 5 - 1 \cdot 1x$$

(*b*) Plot the parabola $y = x^2$ and the straight line graph $y = 2 \cdot 5 - 1 \cdot 1x$.

(*c*) Fig. 8.11. shows the completed graph. The values at *A* and *B* where the curves intersect provide the solution of the equation $2x^2 + 2\cdot2x - 5 = 0$. The values of *x* at A and B are $-2\cdot25$ and $1\cdot1$.

Fig. 8.12. shows an alternative graphical method of solving the equation $2x^2 + 2\cdot2x - 5 = 0$. Where the curve cuts the *x* axis we get an answer of the same value as before, i.e. $-2\cdot25$ and $1\cdot1$.

The Area Under a Graph (See Chapter 5)

In Chapter 12 of this book we see that work done is the product of the applied force and the distance through which it moves. In doing this, we have considered only the work done by a force of constant magnitude In many problems, however, the magnitude of the force is not constant but may vary throughout the distance moved by the force. To determine a reasonably accurate value of the work done, graphs are used as shown in the following examples.

Example. A force of 8 N acting on an object produces motion, the force reaching a maximum of 10 N when the object has moved through a distance of 10 metres. Determine the energy in joules.

Fig. 8.13. shows the completed graph. The value of the energy is determined by the area under the graph. In this example, the area is bounded by the curve, the horizontal axis and the vertical axis up to 8.3. Using the mid-ordinate rule,

Average Force =

$$\frac{8\cdot3 + 9 + 9\cdot6 + 6\cdot6 + 5\cdot4 + 4\cdot6 + 3\cdot2 + 0\cdot6 + 0\cdot3 + 0\cdot1}{10}$$

$$= 4\cdot77 \text{ N}$$

Total energy = Average force × total distance moved

$$= 4\cdot77 \times 10$$

$$= 47\cdot7 \text{ J}$$

Example. The following values of draw-bar pull (*F*) in N and the corresponding times (*t*) in seconds were obtained for a commercial vehicle during a series of road tests:

t	0	2	4	6	8	10	12	14	16
F	1300	1280	1250	1200	1120	1000	850	750	700

Assume a constant tractive resistance of 500 N.

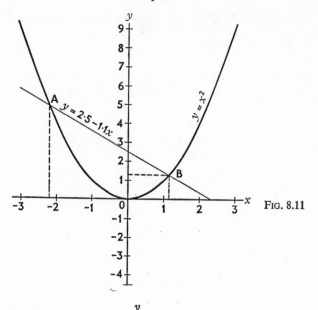

Fig. 8.11

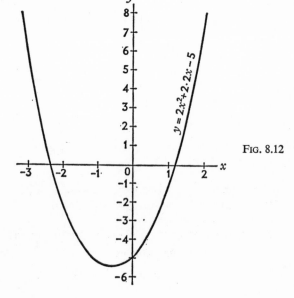

Fig. 8.12

Select scales to make the best use of the graph paper available and plot a graph of net tractive effort to a base *t*.

Determine the average value of the net tractive effort during the 16 second period.

Fig. 8.14. shows the completed graph. Note that the constant tractive resistance of 500 N must first be overcome before the vehicle can move away from rest.

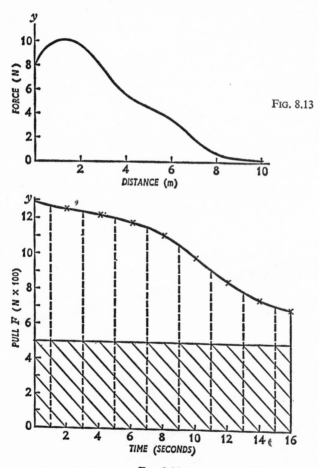

Fig. 8.13

Fig. 8.14

Using the mid-ordinate rule, the total tractive effort applied will be,

Total tractive effort =

$$\frac{1290 + 1270 + 1230 + 1162 + 1070 + 930 + 800 + 720}{8}$$

$$= 1059 \text{ N}$$

Since the tractive resistance is constant at 500 N, the net tractive effort will be:

Total tractive effort − Constant tractive resistance

∴ Net tractive effort = 1059 − 500 N

$$= \underline{559 \text{ N}}$$

Exercise 8

1. On the square paper provided, construct a graph showing the relation between degrees Fahrenheit and degrees Celsius to cover the range between the freezing and boiling points of water. Use the graph to find the Fahrenheit equivalent of 85°C.

(185°F)   (C. and G.)

2. The figures given in the table are the distances D, in km, run from the start by a racing car in accelerating to a speed S km per hour. Plot these figures and draw the graph showing the relation between distance and speed. Scales: for D, 1 km per 20 mm horizontally; for S, 50 km per hour to the 20 mm vertically.

D	1	2	3	4	5	6
S	150	205	240	265	280	290

Determine from the graph the distance the car must run to reach a speed of 225 km per hour. (2·5 km)   (E.M.E.U.)

3. Boyle's Law states that the absolute pressure of a gas varies inversely as the volume, provided that the temperature remains constant. A certain mass of gas has a volume of 0·4 m³ when the pressure is 105 kN/m² absolute. On the squared paper provided, draw a graph showing the change of pressure as the gas is compressed at constant temperature to a volume of 0·1 m³. From the graph find the volume when the pressure is 280 kN/m² (0·15 m³·)   (C. and G.)

4. The following table gives the resistance to motion of a motor vehicle at certain speeds. Plot a graph of resistance on a base of speed and use the graph to find (*a*) the speed when the resistance is least; (*b*) the resistance at 30 km per hour.

| Resistance (N) | 130 | 75 | 64 | 65 | 70 | 78 | 100 | 128 | 207 |
| Speed (km per hour) | 0 | 5 | 10 | 20 | 30 | 40 | 50 | 60 | |

((*a*) 15 km/h (*b*) 85 N) (U.E.I.)

5. The following table gives the values of the available torque at various car speeds. Plot a graph of 'available torque' on a base of 'car speed' and use the graph to determine (*a*) the maximum available torque, (*b*) the car speed at which this value occurs.

| Car speed (km/h) | 10 | 20 | 30 | 40 | 50 | 60 | 70 |
| Available torque (N m) | 360 | 415 | 440 | 445 | 430 | 375 | 275 |

((*a*) 446 N m; (*b*) 38 km/h) (U.E.I.)

6. The following table gives the figures showing how the efficiency of a petrol engine varies with the compression ratio:

| Compression ratio | 4 | 5 | 6 | 7 | 8 | 9 |
| Efficiency (per cent) | 27·9 | 31·4 | 34 | 36·1 | 37·8 | 39·2 |

Plot these figures on squared paper to scales of 1 to the 20 mm horizontally for compression ratio, and 1 per cent to the 10 mm vertically for efficiency. Draw the efficiency curve and determine from it the efficiency for a compression ratio of 7·5

(36·85 per cent) (E.M.E.U.)

7. A certain engine has a stroke of 89 mm and the connecting rod is 178 mm long between the centres of its bearings.

Determine the distance moved by the piston for the following crank angles from the t.d.c. position, 25°, 45°, 75° and 90°.

(5·5 mm; 16·0 mm; 38·5 mm; 50·5 mm)

8. Make a careful freehand drawing of a typical valve-lift curve on a base representing degrees of crankshaft rotation. Each phase in the opening and closing of the valve should be shown with its approximate duration and the shape of the curve during each period should be clearly indicated.

(C. and G.)

9. Measurements of crankshaft angle in degrees and valve lift in mm gave the following figures.

Crankshaft rotation (degrees)	Valve lift (mm)
0	0
10	0·45
20	1·00
30	2·00
40	3·25
50	4·50

60	5·70
70	6·40
80	6·90
90	7·30
100	7·55
110	7·80
120	7·94
130	7·80
140	7·55
150	7·30
160	6·90
170	6·40
180	5·70
190	4·50
200	3·25
210	2·00
220	1·00
230	0·45
240	0

Draw the lift curve to a scale of 20 mm = 40° of crank rotation and 10 mm = 1·0 mm of valve lift. It will be seen from the curve that the total lift and fall is divided into periods. Identify these periods from an inspection of the curve, state what is happening to the valve and estimate when each period begins and ends.   (C. and G.)

10. Solve the following simultaneous equations by graphical means:
$$3x + y = 3, 5x - y = 7$$
$$(x = 1\tfrac{1}{4} \quad y = -\tfrac{3}{4})$$

11. Find the value of x which satisfies simultaneously both of the following equations, by constructing the graph of each equation on the same axes and to the same scale.

Check your answers by an algebraic method:
$$y = 0·8x + 2$$
$$y = 1·7x - 2 \quad (x = 4·444) \quad (U.L.C.I.)$$

12. Using the same axes, plot the two graphs $y = x^2$ and $y = 3x + 8$ from $x = -3$ to $x = +5$. Use the graphs to solve the equation $x^2 - 3x - 8 = 0$. $(-1·7 \text{ or } 4·7)$ (U.E.I.)

13. If a car travelled 5 km/h faster it would cover 60 km in 10 minutes less. Calculate the speed of the car.   (40 km/h)

14. The hypotenuse of a right-angled triangle is 130 mm long and the sum of the other two sides is 170 mm. Calculate the lengths of the two sides.   (120 mm;   50 mm)

15. A car covers a distance of 72 km at a certain speed. If the car had travelled at 6 km/h slower the journey would have taken one hour longer. Calculate the speed of the car.   (24 km/h)

16. On the same axes and to the same scales, graph the functions 3·5 sin x and (2·5 − cos x), taking values of x from 0° to 180°. Then, using your diagrams, solve the equation:

$$3.5 \sin x + \cos x = 2.5 \qquad (27°) \quad \text{(U.E.I.)}$$

17. The final velocity v of an object moving with a constant acceleration a is given by the formula:

$v = u + at$, where u is the initial velocity.

Plot the values of v, for intervals up to 24 seconds, where:

(1) $u = 8$ m/s, $a = 2$ m/s^2

(2) $u = 88$ m/s, $a = -2$ m/s^2 (i.e. retardation)

From your graph find at what instant the velocities are identical, reading off its value. Check by solving the two equations.

             ($t = 20$ seconds)   U.E.I.)

18. A consumer has the following choice with regard to payment for electrical energy:

(*a*) An initial charge of £5 plus $\frac{1}{2}$p per unit consumed.

(*b*) A charge of 4p per unit for lighting and 0·34p per unit for power.

What would be the total cost under each rate if 500, 1000, 1500 and 2000 units respectively were consumed in a certain period, 200 of these being lighting units in each case? Plot two graphs to the same scale, showing total cost in pence against units used with the two systems of payment. When is the total cost of each rate the same?

      (When the number of units = 1450)   (U.E.I.)

19. The air pressure acting on the front of a car at different speeds is as follows:

Speed (km/h)	16	32	48	64	80	88
Pressure (kN/m²)	0·29 × 10³	1·19 × 10³	2·38 × 10³			
	4·77 × 10³	7·45 × 10³	9·3 × 10³			

From these values plot a graph, with speed horizontal, and from it find (*a*) the air pressure at 72 km/h, (*b*) the speed at which the air pressure is 2·9 × 10³ kN/m².

      ((*a*) 6 × 10³ kN/m²;   (*b*) 52 km/h)   (E.M.E.U.)

20. The following values of P give the pressure in N/mm² during the expansion stroke of an internal combustion engine at corresponding distances S mm from the beginning of the stroke. Plot these values and from the graph determine the average pressure and the work done in joules during the stroke. Diameter of cylinder in 100 mm.

S	0	25	50	75	100	125	150
P	4·82	2·83	1·89	1·20	0·69	0·31	0·10

($1·51$ N/mm²; $1778·9$J) (C. and G.)

9

Angles and Trigonometry

Angles

If two lines OA and OB, see Fig. 9.1, meet at a point O, the opening between these two lines is called the **angle AOB** or simply the angle O. The two lines are called the **sides** and their point of meeting is called the **vertex.** Note that the length of the sides does not affect the angle.

Students will know from their drawing class experience that several forms of angle exist:

When a line OA is perpendicular to another line BC, see Fig. 9.1, the angles AOB and AOC are said to be **right angles.**

Fig. 9.1 shows an **acute** angle DOB which is less than one right angle.

Fig. 9.1 shows an **obtuse** angle EOB which is greater than one right angle and less than two right angles.

Fig. 9.1 shows a **reflex** angle BOF which is greater than two right angles.

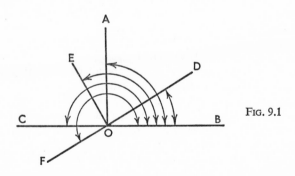

Fig. 9.1

Measurement of Angles

The unit of measurement for angles in general use is the **degree.** The degree is obtained by dividing the circumference of a circle of any radius into 360 equal parts; when two adjacent points are joined by lines to the centre, see Fig. 9.2(a), the opening between these lines is said to be an angle of one degree. Note: the length of the arc AB will vary with the diameter of the circle, but the angle AOB will always be one degree.

Each degree is divided into 60 equal parts, called **minutes,** and each minute is divided into 60 equal parts called **seconds.** Symbols are used to denote these measurements:

degrees °;   minutes ′;   seconds ″

and we write 15 degrees, 14 minutes, 50 seconds as 15° 14′ 50″.

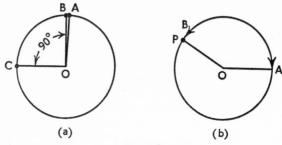

Fig. 9.2

In the circle, Fig. 9.2(a), two radii OC and OB are drawn at right angles to each other thereby enclosing a quarter of the circle, i.e. 360 divided by 4, or 90 degrees. Thus, a right angle consists of 90 degrees. Most students will already know that angles less or greater than a right angle are measured by means of a protractor when drawing and by means of a combination-set in the workshop.

Consider the circle, Fig. 9.2(b). When the point **P** is rotated through one complete revolution, then the distance moved through by **P** will be the length of the circumference of the circle. This length can be expressed in **linear** or **angular** measurement, i.e. in kilometres, metres and millimetres, or in degrees. Now, in a circle of any diameter the length of the circumference will always be equal to 360 degrees. Thus for any one circle we are able to express degrees in linear measurement and linear measurement in degrees.

If the point **P** is moved through only part of a turn, say from A to B, Fig. 9.2 (b) then the length AB can be expressed in linear measurement or in degrees as shown in the following examples:

Example. The diameter of a certain circle is 350 millimetres.

(*a*) What will be the length in mm of one degree as measured on the circumference of the circle?

(*b*) What will be the measurement in degrees of one mm as measured on the circumference of the circle?

(*a*) Circumference of circle $= \pi d = \dfrac{22}{7} \times 350 = 1100$ mm

Then
$$360° = 1100 \text{ mm}$$
$$\therefore 1° = 1100 \div 360 \text{ mm} = \underline{3·05 \text{ mm}}$$
$$1100 \text{ mm} = 360 \text{ degrees}$$
$$\therefore 1 \text{ mm} = 360 \div 1100 \text{ degrees} = \underline{0·327°}$$

The Radian

Another unit used for the measurement of angles is the **radian.** Fig. 9.3 shows a circle which can be of any radius. The length of the arc AB, measured round the circumference of the circle is equal in length

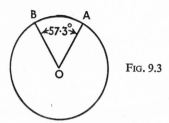

Fig. 9.3

to each of the radii OA and OB. The angle between OA and OB, i.e. the angle AOB, is then one radian.

Now the length of the circumference $= 360°$
$$\therefore \pi d = 360°$$
$$\therefore 2\pi r = 360°$$
$$\therefore r = \frac{360°}{2\pi} = 57·3° \text{ approx.}$$

$\therefore$ 1 radian (the angle opposite an arc of 1 radius) $= 57·3°$.

The radian is generally used to calculate the work done when a torque moves through an angle. For example, in Chapter 11, we calculated the work done in rotation by using the formula $T \times 2\pi$ rev/min and T = torque in Nm.

We must carefully memorize that 2π radians not only equal 360 degrees but also equals the angular distance moved in one revolution. When 2π is multiplied by rev/min we get the angular distance moved. The calculations concerning torque become complicated if degrees are used.

It is sometimes necessary to convert radians to degrees and vice versa. We can do this:

To convert radians to degrees. Multiply by 360 and divide by 2π.

To convert degrees to radians. Multiply by 2π and divide by 360.

Example.

(a) Express in radians 180°.

$$180 \times \frac{2\pi}{360} = \underline{3 \cdot 142} \qquad \text{or} \qquad \pi \text{ radians}$$

(b) Express in degrees 2·5 radians.

$$\frac{2 \cdot 5 \times 360}{2\pi} = \underline{143 \cdot 2^\circ}$$

Example. The radius of a road curve is 150 m. Find the angle turned through in 1 second in radians and degrees by a vehicle travelling at 72 km/h.

$$1 \text{ radian} = \text{arc of } 150 \text{ m}$$

$$72 \text{ km/h} = 20 \text{ m/s}$$

$$\therefore \text{ In 1 second vehicle travels } \frac{20}{150} = \underline{0 \cdot 1333} \text{ radian}$$

$$\therefore \text{ Angle} = 0 \cdot 1333 \times 57 \cdot 3 = \underline{7 \cdot 64^\circ}$$

Engine Timing

We can now apply our theoretical knowledge of angles and angular measurement to set or check valve, ignition and injection timings. We shall also be able to read and understand a valve timing diagram.

Valve Timing

Fig. 9.4(a) shows a typical valve timing diagram. Note, the circle represents the flywheel of the engine viewed from the 'driving-end' or front of the engine. The vertical centre line is marked **t.d.c.** at the top of the circle and **b.d.c.** at the bottom of the circle; t.d.c. corresponds to the position of the crankpin when the piston is at the top dead centre position and b.d.c. corresponds to the position of the crankpin when the piston is at the bottom dead centre position.

The valve opening and closing positions are represented by lines (radii) drawn from the centre to the circumference of the circle. Fig. 9.4(a) shows that the inlet valve opens 10 degrees before the crankpin reaches t.d.c. (note, the crankpin, not the piston), and the inlet valve closes when the crankpin has moved 45 degrees past the b.d.c. position. The exhaust valve, however, opens at 45 degrees before b.d.c. and it closes 10 degrees after the t.d.c. position.

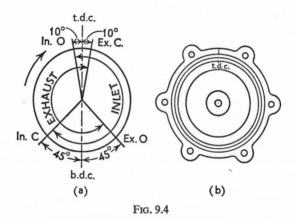

Fig. 9.4

If we are given the diameter of the flywheel and the number of degrees the valves open or close before or after a dead centre position then we shall be able to solve valve timing problems.

Example. On a certain engine the diameter of the flywheel is 350 mm. What distance does 40 degrees represent as measured around the rim of the flywheel?

Circumference of the flywheel $= \dfrac{22}{7} \times 350 = 1100$ mm

Then $\qquad 360° = 1100$ mm

$\qquad \therefore 1° = 1100 \div 360$ mm

$\qquad \therefore 40° = (1100 \div 360)\ 40$ mm $= \underline{122 \cdot 2 \text{ mm}}$

In the following examples, which are practical problems, the opening and closing positions of the valves are taken from what is known as the **datum** mark or point. This mark is a fixed mark or pointer which is fitted to the engine or chassis frame (see (Fig. 9.4(b)). This mark or pointer is generally used to indicate the t.d.c. position and it coincides with a mark, usually a scribed line, on the rim of the flywheel.

Example. On a certain engine the diameter of the flywheel is 350 mm. The inlet valve opens when the flywheel has still 37·5 mm, as measured on the rim of the flywheel, to go before reaching t.d.c. Express this measurement of 37·5 mm to the nearest whole degree.

Circumference of flywheel $= \dfrac{22}{7} \times 350 = 1100$ mm

Then $\qquad$ 1100 mm $= 360°$

$\qquad \therefore$ 1 mm $= 360 \div 1100°$

$\qquad \therefore$ 37·5 mm $= (360 \div 1100)\ 37·5° = \underline{12°}$

Example. When a flywheel 420 mm diameter is rotated it is found that a particular valve opens when the datum mark has travelled a distance of 420 mm past t.d.c. measured around the circumference. The same valve closes when the flywheel mark has moved 40 mm past t.d.c. Calculate these opening and closing positions in degrees of crank movement and state whether it refers to an inlet or an exhaust valve.

Circumference of flywheel $= \dfrac{22}{7} \times 420 = 1320$ mm

Then $\qquad$ 1320 mm $= 360°$

$\qquad \therefore$ 1 mm $= 360 \div 1320°$

$\qquad \therefore$ 420 mm $= (360 \div 1320)\ 420°$

$\qquad\qquad\qquad = \underline{114·5°}$

$\qquad \therefore$ 40 mm $= (360 \div 1320)\ 40° = \underline{10·9°}$

The valve is an exhaust valve, because it opens $180 - 114·5°$, i.e. 65·5° before b.d.c. and closes 10·9° after t.d.c.

Ignition Timing

Most students will have received instruction in ignition timing control and they will know the necessity for timing the spark to occur before t.d.c. The following examples show the type of problem likely to be encountered concerning ignition timing.

Example. The ignition advance of a certain engine is 24 degrees.

(*a*) What distance does this angle represent when measured on the rim of a flywheel 350 mm diameter?

(*b*) What interval of time would this angle represent if the engine were running at 2400 rev/min?

(*a*) Circumference of flywheel $= \dfrac{22}{7} \times 350 = 1100$ mm

Then
$$360° = 1100 \text{ mm}$$
$$\therefore 1° = 1100 \div 360 \text{ mm}$$
$$\therefore 24° = (1100 \div 360)\,24\text{mm} = \underline{73 \cdot 3 \text{ mm}}$$

(*b*) 2400 rev/min $= 2400 \div 60 = 40$ rev/s

Now degrees travelled in 1 second $= 40 \times 360°$

$\therefore$ Time taken to travel 1° $\quad = \dfrac{1}{40 \times 360}$ s

$\therefore$ Time taken to travel 24° $\quad = \dfrac{24}{40 \times 360} = \dfrac{1}{600} = \underline{0 \cdot 0016 \text{ s}}$

Injection Timing

The injection timing for c.i. engines is arranged to take place before t.d.c. and the method of calculating the injection timing is similar to the calculation of ignition timing as shown in the foregoing examples.

Example. On a certain c.i. engine the injection of fuel is timed to begin at 27 degrees before t.d.c. The flywheel diameter is 490 mm.

(*a*) Express this measurement in mm as measured on the rim of the flywheel.

(*b*) If the injection period ceases at 11 degrees after t.d.c., how long does the injection last when the engine speed is 1800 rev/min?

(*a*) Circumference of flywheel $= \dfrac{22}{7} \times 490 = 1540$ mm

Then
$$360° = 1540 \text{ mm}$$
$$\therefore 1° = 1540 \div 360 \text{ mm}$$
$$\therefore 27° = (1540 \div 360)\,27 \text{ mm} = \underline{102 \cdot 6 \text{ mm}}$$

(*b*) Total injection period = 27 + 11 = 38°

Now, 1800 rev/min = 1800 ÷ 60 = 30 rev/s

∴ The number of degrees travelled in 1 second = 30 × 360°

∴ The time taken to travel 1° $= \dfrac{1}{30 \times 360}$ s

∴ The time taken to travel 38° $= \dfrac{38}{30 \times 360}$ s

$= \underline{0 \cdot 0035}$ s

Triangles

Triangles can be considered in two general ways:

(1) According to the lengths of the three sides.

(2) According to the angles formed by the three sides.

Let us consider the sides first.

(*a*) Fig. 9.5(a) shows an **equilateral** triangle and, as its name denotes, the three sides are all equal in length.

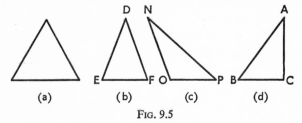

FIG. 9.5

(*b*) Fig. 9.5(b) shows an **isosceles** triangle which has two sides ED and DF equal in length.

(*c*) Fig. 9.5(c) shows a **scalene** triangle which has all its sides of unequal length.

Now let us consider the angles.

(*a*) Figs. 9.5(a) and (b) show acute-angled triangles, each of whose angles are less than 90 degrees.

(*b*) Fig. 9.5(c) shows an obtuse-angled triangle. NOP, the angle at O is obtuse because it is greater than 90 degrees.

(*c*) Fig. 9.5(d) shows a **right-angled** triangle. ABC, the angle at C is a right angle (90°) and the side AB opposite the right angle C is called the **hypotenuse.**

In any triangle the sum of the three angles is always equal to 180 degrees.

The Right-Angled Triangle

This triangle is used to solve practical workshop problems, therefore we should understand and know how to apply some of its properties.

An important property known as the **Theorem of Pythagoras** states:

'The square on the hypotenuse of a right-angled triangle is equal in area to the sum of the squares on the other two sides.'

Space is not available for a formal proof of this property, but Fig. 9.6 shows that it is true.

A right-angled triangle has sides of 3, 4 and 5 units in length. The square on the hypotenuse c, Fig. 9.6, contains 25 equal squares, the square on the side a contains 16 equal squares and the square on the side b contains 9 equal squares. Now all these small separate squares are equal to each other in area. Therefore, the sum of the squares on a and b is 16 plus 9 which is equal to 25 squares. These 25 squares are equal in area to the 25 squares contained in the square on the hypotenuse c.

We are now able to state the foregoing property of a right-angled triangle by means of the following formula:

$$c^2 = a^2 + b^2$$

This relationship between the sides can be applied to any right-angled triangle whatever the length of the sides may be.

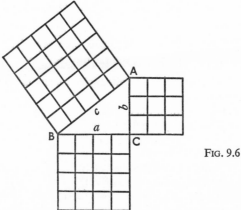

FIG. 9.6

Example. See Fig. 9.6. Let the length of the hypotenuse AB equal 5 m; the length of the side AC equal 3 m and the length of the side BC equal 4 m, then

$$AB^2 = AC^2 + BC^2 \quad \text{or} \quad c^2 = a^2 + b^2$$

according to the previous formula given,

$$\text{i.e. } 5^2 = 3^2 + 4^2$$
$$25 = 9 + 16$$
$$25 = 25$$

If the length of any two sides of a right-angled triangle are known, then we can always find the length of the remaining side.

Example. Given that in Fig. 9.6 $AC = 6$ m and $BC = 8$ m, what is the length of AB?

Now
$$AB^2 = 6^2 + 8^2$$
$$= 36 + 64 = 100$$
$$\therefore AB = \sqrt{100}$$
$$\therefore \text{Length of AB} = \underline{10 \text{ m}}$$

Example. Given that in Fig. 9.6, $AB = 13$ m and $AC = 12$ m, what is the length of BC?

Now
$$BC^2 + 12^2 = 13^2$$
$$BC^2 + 144 = 169$$
$$BC^2 \quad\quad = 169 - 144$$
$$\therefore BC \quad\quad = \sqrt{25}$$
$$\therefore \text{Length of BC} = \underline{5 \text{ m}}$$

In the foregoing examples the square root was evident by inspection; where the root is not obvious use the method shown in Chapter 3.

Example. The hypotenuse of a right-angled triangle is 7 m and the length of one side is 3·5 m.

Calculate the length of the third side.

Let $x =$ the length of the third side.

Then
$$x^2 + 3 \cdot 5^2 = 7^2$$
$$x^2 \quad\quad = 7^2 - 3 \cdot 5^2$$
$$x^2 \quad\quad = 49 - 12 \cdot 25$$
$$x \quad\quad = \sqrt{36 \cdot 75}$$
$$\therefore \text{Length of } x = \underline{6 \cdot 063 \text{ m}}$$

Example. A certain engine has a stroke of 100 mm and the connecting rod is 175 mm long between the centres of its bearings. Calculate the distance moved by the piston from the t.d.c. position when the connecting rod reaches its maximum angularity relative to the cylinder axis.

The connecting rod will be at its maximum angularity when the crankpin is at right angles to the cylinder axis. Fig. 9.7 shows the piston at t.d.c., and the position of the piston when the connecting rod reaches its maximum angularity. The stroke is 100 mm, therefore the length of

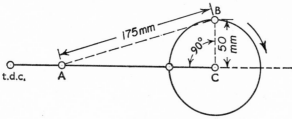

Fig. 9.7

the crank arm will be 50 mm. From Fig. 9.7 we are able to construct a right-angled triangle ABC, of which it is necessary to find the length of the side AC.

Then
$$AC^2 + 50^2 = 175^2$$
$$AC^2 = 175^2 - 50^2$$
$$AC = \sqrt{28\ 125}$$
$$\therefore \text{Length of AC} = \underline{167 \cdot 7 \text{ mm}}$$

In Fig. 9.7 the combined length of the connecting rod and crank arm is shown to be 175 + 50 = 225 mm.

∴ the amount of piston travel will be:

Combined length of connecting rod and crank arm minus the length of AC, i.e.

$$225 - 167 \cdot 7 = \underline{57 \cdot 3 \text{ mm}}$$

Note.—This example shows an important fact, i.e. the piston travels further and therefore faster in the first half than in the second half of the crank movement from t.d.c. to b.d.c.

Example. When a valve of an O.H.V. engine is open 10 mm, the distance from the centre of the rocker arm bearing to the centre of the valve stem is 82·55 mm. The rocker arm is horizontal when the valve is closed. Calculate the distance between the centre of the rocker arm bearing and the centre of the valve stem when the valve is closed.

Fig. 9.8 will be found useful in solving this problem.
Let x = the unknown distance in mm, then

$$x^2 + 10^2 = 82{\cdot}55^2$$
$$x^2 = 6817 - 100$$
$$= 6717$$
$$\therefore x \sqrt{6717}$$
$$\therefore \text{Distance } x = \underline{81{\cdot}95 \text{ mm}}$$

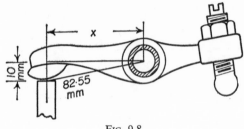

FIG. 9.8

Trigonometry

Trigonometry is that section of calculations concerning the measurement of triangles.

We have already seen that every triangle has three sides and three angles; these sides and angles are called the **parts** of the triangle. If the value of any three of these parts are known and one of them is a side, then the value of the remaining parts can be calculated. In the right-angled triangle, however, we need only know the value of two of the parts, one of which must be a side, because the right angle is always constant at 90 degrees.

Trigonometrical Ratios

Consider the right-angled triangle ABC, Fig. 9.9(a). The two sides forming the right angle C are represented by a and b and the hypotenuse by c. The angle B is represented by the symbol θ (theta), which is a Greek letter. Other Greek letters used as symbols for angles are ϕ (phi) and α (alpha). Now the side b is opposite the angle θ; the side a is adjacent the angle θ, and the side c is the hypotenuse.

The ratios between the various sides are called the **trigonometrical ratios** and these ratios are used to calculate the value of the angles in degrees and the length of the various sides. There are six ratios of which we shall first consider three:

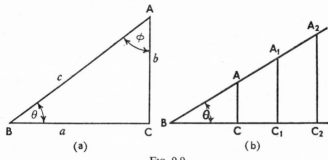

FIG. 9.9

(1) The **tangent** of an angle is the ratio which the side opposite the angle bears to the side adjacent the angle. Thus, in Fig. 9.9(a),

$$\text{tangent of the angle } \theta = \frac{\text{side opposite}}{\text{side adjacent}} = \frac{b}{a};$$

this is abbreviated to $\tan \theta = \frac{b}{a}$.

Consider the triangle, Fig. 9.9(b). The tangent of the angle θ at B is the ratio $\frac{AC}{BC}$ or $\frac{A_1C_1}{BC_1}$ or $\frac{A_2C_2}{BC_2}$, that is, the ratios $\frac{AC}{BC}$; $\frac{A_1C_1}{BC_1}$, and $\frac{A_2C_2}{BC_2}$ will always have the same value provided the angle remains the same. (This statement is equally true for the other ratios now to be considered.)

(2) The **sine** of an angle is the ratio which the side opposite the angle bears to the hypotenuse. Thus, in Fig. 9.9(a),

$$\text{sine of the angle } \theta = \frac{\text{side opposite}}{\text{hypotenuse}} = \frac{b}{c};$$

this is abbreviated to $\sin \theta = \frac{b}{c}$.

(3) The **cosine** of an angle is the ratio which the side adjacent the angle bears to the hypotenuse. Thus, in Fig. 9.9(a),

$$\text{cosine of the angle } \theta = \frac{\text{side adjacent}}{\text{hypotenuse}} = \frac{a}{c};$$

this is abbreviated to $\cos \theta = \frac{a}{c}$.

The foregoing ratios are the foundations of trigonometry.

Before making use of these ratios to find the value of an angle or the length of a side, the following should be noted (see Fig. 9.9(a)).

If the angle at A should be used as ϕm, then *a* would be the side opposite and *b* would be the side adjacent ϕ.

The foregoing ratios can be applied to a right-angled triangle of any size, provided the value of two of its parts are known.

Example. In Fig. 9.9(a), let $a = 4$ m, $b = 3$ m and θ the angle B, then:

$$\tan \theta = \frac{\text{side opposite}}{\text{side adjacent}} = \tfrac{3}{4} = 0\cdot75$$

$$\therefore \text{ the tangent of the angle B} = 0\cdot75$$

If $a = 36$ m and $b = 27$ m, then the ratio between them will be $\tfrac{27}{36}$ or $0\cdot75$ as before, i.e. the value of the angle at B remains unchanged.

The foregoing ratios for angles between 0 degrees and 90 degrees have been carefully calculated and compiled in tables sometimes headed **Functions of Angles;** in others the headings used are Natural Sines, Natural Cosines and Natural Tangents. These tables, usually called **trig** tables, are used to find the value of an angle; they will be found at the end of this book.

Use of Tables

The method of using the tables is shown in the worked examples for the three ratios which follow, we shall begin with the tangent.

Example. Calculate the value of the angle B to the nearest minute (Fig. 9.9(a)) when $a = 4$ m and $b = 3$ m.

When $a = 4$ m and $b = 3$ m, we have already found that

$$\tan \theta = 0\cdot75$$

$$\therefore \tan \text{B} = 0\cdot75$$

In order to find the value of the angle B in degrees we refer to the tables.

Look down the page headed Natural Tangents until the nearest decimal less than $0\cdot75$ is found. This decimal will be seen to be $0\cdot7481$, in line with the decimal in the degree column we find $36°$. To find the minutes we look at the top of the vertical column in line with $0\cdot7481$; here we find $48'$.

We now have 36° 48′. To find the remaining minutes we refer to the mean difference column and proceed:

$$\text{Given value} = 0{\cdot}75$$
$$\tan 36° 42′ = \underline{0{\cdot}7481}$$
$$\text{difference} = \qquad 19$$

From the difference column 19 (18 nearest) corresponds to an increase of 4′, therefore the angle is 36° 48′ + 4′ = 36° 52′.

∴ angle B = 36° 52′ (to nearest minute).

Example. In measuring a camber angle a vertical line XY was measured to be 540 mm. From Y, YZ measured at right angles to XY was found to be 32 mm. Find the magnitude of the angle YXZ to the nearest degree. (N.C.T.E.C.)

Fig. 9.10 shows a line diagram of the layout.

Now
$$\tan \theta = \frac{YZ}{XY}$$

$$= \frac{32}{540} = 0{\cdot}0592$$

∴ the angle YXZ = 3° (to nearest degree)

Example. In Fig. 9.10 the side XZ is known to be 540 mm. Find the magnitude of the angle YZX to the nearest minute using the cosine ratio.

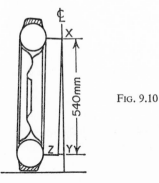

Fig. 9.10

Now

$$\cos \phi = \frac{YZ}{XZ} = \frac{32}{540} = 0.0592$$

From the tables

$$0.0592 = 86° \ 36'$$

∴ the angle YXZ = 86° 36′ (to nearest minute)

Example. The diameter of the taper end of a shaft is measured at two points 30 mm apart measured along the surface of the taper. The larger diameter is found to be 12 mm and the smaller 6·5 mm. Find, to the nearest degree, the angle between the surface of the taper and its axis; also the included or total angle.

Fig. 9.11(a) shows a line diagram of the taper end of the shaft. Fig. 9.11(b) shows another diagram which will assist in the solution of the problem.

Let x = the side opposite the angle θ in Fig. 9.11(b).

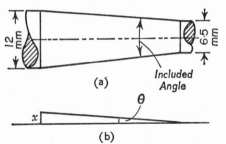

FIG. 9.11

Then, the length of $x = \dfrac{12}{2} - \dfrac{6\cdot5}{2} = 2\cdot75$ mm

Now, $\sin \theta = \dfrac{2\cdot75}{30} = 0\cdot0916$

∴ the angle $\theta = 5°$

The included angle is shown by Fig. 9.11(a) to be 10°, i.e. $5 \times 2 = 10°$.

Example. A certain vehicle has a wheel-base of 4 m and a wheel track of 1·6 m. When the vehicle is turning on a certain radius the steering angle of the inner wheel is 22 degrees,

Calculate (*a*) The angle of the outer wheel.

(*b*) The length of the radius (measured to the centre of the rear axle).

See Fig. 9.12.

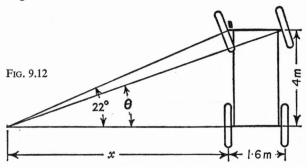

FIG. 9.12

(*a*) First find the distance *x*:

$$\tan 22° = \frac{4}{x}$$

and
$$\tan 22° = 0.4040$$

Then
$$x = \frac{4}{0.4040}$$

$$= \frac{4}{0.4040} \text{ m} = 9.9 \text{ m}$$

Angle of outer wheel is as follows:

$$\tan \theta = \frac{4}{9.9 + \text{wheel track}}$$

$$= \frac{4}{9.9 + 1.6}$$

$$= \frac{4}{11.5} = 0.3478$$

$$\therefore \theta = 19° 11'$$

∴ Angle of outer wheel = $\underline{19° 11'}$ (to nearest minute)

(*b*) Radius = length of *x* + half wheel track

$$= 9.902 + 0.8 \text{ m} = \underline{10.702 \text{ m}}$$

Angles of Elevation and Depression

Problems containing the terms **elevation** and **depression** are sometimes found in examination papers.

Fig. 9.13 shows that the **angle of elevation** refers to the angle made when we raise our eyes from the horizontal to an object higher than ourselves, e.g. the top of a hill. Fig. 9.13 shows that the angle of depression refers to the angle made when we lower our eyes from the horizontal to an object lower than ourselves, e.g. a valley from the top of a hill.

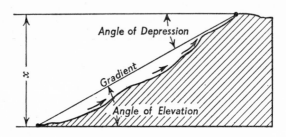

Fig. 9.13

Example. The angle of elevation from the starting point of a certain hill climb is 15 degrees and the direct length of the gradient is 1000 metres. Calculate the height of the hill to the nearest metre.

Let x = the height of the hill (see Fig. 9.13).

Then $\qquad \sin 15° = \dfrac{x}{1000}$ and $\sin 15° = 0.2588$

$$\therefore 0.2588 = \frac{x}{1000} \text{ m}$$

$$\therefore x = 258.8 \text{ m}$$

Height of hill = $\underline{259 \text{ m}}$ (to nearest metre)

Example. The starting-point of a hill-climb course has an angle of depression of 12 degrees when viewed from the finishing line which is 100 metres above the level of the starting point.

Find the distance of the course assuming that it is 12 per cent longer than the gradient.

Let y = length of gradient (see Fig. 9.13).
The angle of depression is 12°.

Then $\qquad \sin 12° = \dfrac{100}{y} \quad$ and $\quad \sin 12° = 0\cdot2079$

$$\therefore y = \frac{100}{0\cdot2079} \text{ m} = \underline{481 \text{ m}}$$

$\therefore$ Length of course $= 481 + 12\%$ of 481 m

$$= 481 + 58 \text{ m}$$

$$= \underline{539 \text{ m}} \text{ to the nearest metre}$$

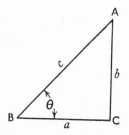

FIG. 9.14

Further Ratios

The three remaining ratios, which are not often used, can be defined:

(1) **Cotangent** (see Fig. 9.14). The cotangent (cot) of the angle ABC is the tangent of this angle inverted, thus

$$\cot \theta = \frac{\text{side adjacent}}{\text{side opposite}} = \frac{a}{b}$$

The cotangent is sometimes expressed as the **reciprocal** of the tangent, i.e. $\dfrac{1}{\tan}$.

Note, the reciprocal of a number is 1 divided by the number, e.g. the reciprocal of 5 is $\dfrac{1}{5}$.

(2) **Cosecant** (see Fig. 9.14). The cosecant (cosec) of the angle ABC is the sine of this angle inverted, thus

$$\text{cosec } \theta = \frac{\text{hypotenuse}}{\text{side opposite}} = \frac{c}{b}$$

The cosecant is also expressed as the reciprocal of the sine, i.e. $\dfrac{1}{\sin}$.

(3) **Secant** (see Fig. 9.14). The secant (sec) of the angle ABC is the cosine of this angle inverted, thus

$$\sec \theta = \frac{\text{hypotenuse}}{\text{side adjacent}} = \frac{c}{a}$$

The secant is the reciprocal of the cosine, i.e. $\dfrac{1}{\text{cosine}}$.

Piston Travel

During engine calculations it is often necessary to calculate the distance moved by the piston (**piston travel**) from t.d.c. for a given crank angle. Piston travel depends on:

(1) The angle through which the crank moves.
(2) The ratio of the length of the connecting rod to the crank radius.
(3) The angle which the connecting rod makes with the centre line of the cylinder, known as the **angle of obliquity**, when the piston is at any point between t.d.c. and b.d.c.

Piston travel can be calculated (see Fig. 9.15).

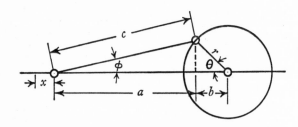

Fig. 9.15

Let x = piston travel from t.d.c. in millimetres

r = crank radius, in millimetres = $\frac{1}{2}$ stroke

c = length of connecting rod, in millimetres

ϕ = angle of obliquity of connecting rod, in degrees

θ = crank angle from t.d.c. in degrees

n = ratio of connecting rod to crank radius = $\dfrac{c}{r}$

$$\cos \phi = \frac{a}{c}$$

$$\therefore c \cos \phi = a$$

Also
$$\cos \theta = \frac{b}{r}$$

$$\therefore r \cos \theta = b$$

$$\therefore a + b = c \cos \phi + r \cos \theta$$

Also
$$c + r = \text{distance } x + a + b$$

$$\therefore c + r = x + a + b$$

$$= x + c \cos \phi + r \cos \theta$$

$$\therefore x = c + r - c \cos \phi - r \cos \theta$$

$$= c - c \cos \phi + r - r \cos \theta$$

$$= c(1 - \cos \phi) + r(1 - \cos \theta)$$

Also
$$\sin \phi = \frac{r}{c} \sin \theta = \frac{1}{n} \sin \theta$$

Example. An engine has a 75 mm bore and 88 mm stroke, and the connecting rod is 176 mm long. Calculate:

(*a*) Piston travel when the crank angle is 45° from t.d.c.

(*b*) The angle of obliquity of the connecting rod when the crank angle is 45° from t.d.c.

Find (*b*) first.

Then,
$$\sin \phi = \frac{r}{c} \sin \theta = \frac{1}{n} \sin \theta$$

Now
$$n = \frac{176}{44} = 4$$

$$\sin \phi = \frac{\sin 45°}{4} = \frac{0 \cdot 7071}{4} = 0 \cdot 1768$$

$$\therefore \text{Angle of obliquity} = \underline{10° \ 11'}$$

(*a*) $x = c(1 - \cos \phi) + r(1 - \cos \theta)$ mm

$$= 176(1 - 0 \cdot 9841) + 44(1 - 0 \cdot 7071) \text{ mm}$$

$$= 2 \cdot 799 + 12 \cdot 887 = \underline{15 \cdot 686 \text{ mm}}$$

Angles of any Size

In Chapter 8, we used OX and OY axes (see Fig. 8.7), for the graphical solution of simultaneous equations. We can apply this principle to angles.

The axes OX and OY divide the paper into four **quadrants**, Fig. 9.16. Let OP represent an arm rotated anti-clockwise. For angles between $0°$ and $90°$ the arm will be in the 1st quadrant, between $90°$ and $180°$ in the 2nd quadrant, between $180°$ and $270°$ in the 3rd quadrant and between $270°$ and $360°$ in the 4th quadrant. When the angles are greater than $360°$, the arm will move again into the 1st quadrant, and so on.

The size of a large angle is given by a spiral showing the number of revolutions involved, e.g. in the 4-stroke engine cycle the flywheel turns through two complete revolutions, i.e. $720°$ (see Fig. 9.17). For mathematical purposes the flywheel is viewed from the rear of the engine.

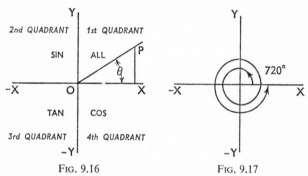

FIG. 9.16   FIG. 9.17

Trigonometrical Ratios of Angles greater than $90°$

Using Fig. 9.16, when the arm OP is in the 1st quadrant $\sin \theta$, $\cos \theta$ and $\tan \theta$ are all positive. In the 2nd quadrant $\sin \theta$ only is positive, in the 3rd quadrant $\tan \theta$ only is positive, and in the 4th quadrant $\cos \theta$ only is positive. Fig. 9.16 shows where the foregoing ratios of the angles are positive.

The Sine and Cosine Rules

In Fig. 9.18 the triangle is acute-angled with a perpendicular p drawn from C to AB.

Then
$$p = b \sin A \text{ and } p = a \sin B$$
$$\therefore b \sin A = a \sin B$$

Thus
$$\frac{a}{\sin A} = \frac{b}{\sin B}$$

In Fig. 9.19, the perpendicular p is drawn from A to BC.

Then $$p = c \sin B \text{ and } p = b \sin C$$

$$\therefore c \sin B = b \sin C$$

Thus $$\frac{b}{\sin B} = \frac{c}{\sin C}$$

$$\therefore \frac{a}{\sin A} = \frac{b}{\sin B} = \frac{c}{\sin C}$$

Fig. 9.20 shows the obtuse-angled triangle ABC which may also be proved by extending the line BC to D and drawing the perpendicular from D to A.

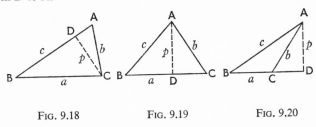

FIG. 9.18   FIG. 9.19   FIG. 9.20

The **sine rule** can now be expressed:
The sides of any triangle are proportional to the sines of the angles opposite those sides. Thus side a is proportional to sin A, side b to sin B and side c to sin C.

The Cosine Rule

The cosine rule states that in any triangle the square of a given side is the sum of the squares of the other two sides minus twice the product of the other two sides and the cosine of the angle opposite the given side.

Thus $$a^2 = b^2 + c^2 - 2bc \cos A$$
$$b^2 = a^2 + c^2 - 2ac \cos B$$
$$c^2 = a^2 + b^2 - 2ab \cos C$$

These formulae can be proved by using the foregoing figures in a similar manner as for the sine rule.

Triangles Not Having a Right-angle

To solve this type of triangle it is usually necessary to use angles greater than 90°, as follows:

Fig. 9.21 shows an obtuse angle XOP of 150°. Then the angle XOZ, which is known as the supplement of the angle XOP, will be (180° − 150°) = 30°.

To obtain the sine and cosine of the obtuse angle of 150° we use the tables to find the ratio of its supplement of 30° and then apply one or more of the following rules:

(1) The sine of an obtuse angle is the sine of its supplement, i.e. the sine is the same for both angles.

(2) The cosine of an obtuse angle is minus the cosine of its supplement. Using the foregoing values, the cosine of 150° will be the cosine of its supplement 30°; cos 30° = 0·8660, i.e. cos 150° = − 0·8660.

Using the angles in Fig. 9.21, we have:

(1) Sin (180° − 150°) = sin 30° = 0·5000

(2) Cos (180° − 150°) = − cos 30° = − 0·8660

Using the sine rule we can solve a triangle when given one side and two angles.

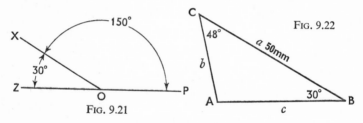

FIG. 9.21   FIG. 9.22

Example. Solve the triangle ABC. Fig. 9.22, in which B = 30°, C = 48° $a = 50$ mm

The angle A is found:

$$\text{Angle A} = 180° − (48° + 30°)$$
$$= \underline{102°}$$

Then,　　$\dfrac{b}{\sin B} = \dfrac{a}{\sin A}$　　　　　　$\dfrac{c}{\sin C} = \dfrac{a}{\sin A}$

∴　　　$b = \dfrac{a \sin B}{\sin A}$　　　∴　$c = \dfrac{a \sin C}{\sin A}$

$$= \dfrac{50 \times \sin 30°}{\sin (180° − 102°)} \qquad = \dfrac{50 \times \sin 48°}{\sin (180° − 102°)}$$

$$= \dfrac{50 \times 0·5}{0·9781} \qquad\qquad = \dfrac{50 \times 0·7431}{0·9781}$$

$$= \underline{25·57 \text{ mm}} \qquad\qquad = \underline{38 \text{ mm}}$$

Using the cosine rule we can solve a triangle when two sides and the included angle are given and also when the three sides are given.

Example. Solve the triangle ABC when $b = 6$ m; $c = 2$ m; $A = 25°$. Fig. 9.23 shows that ABC is an obtuse-angled triangle.

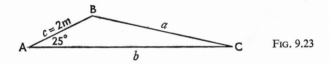

Fig. 9.23

Now
$$a^2 = b^2 + c^2 - 2 bc \cos A$$
$$a^2 = (6)^2 + (2)^2 - 2 \times 6 \times 2 \times 0.9063$$
$$= 40 - 21.751$$
$$a = \sqrt{18.249}$$
$$= \underline{4.272 \text{ m}}$$

Now
$$c^2 = a^2 + b^2 - 2 ab \cos C$$
$$\therefore \cos C = \frac{a^2 + b^2 - c^2}{2 ab}$$
$$= \frac{18.249 + (36 - 4)}{2 \times 6 \times 4.273}$$
$$= \frac{50.249}{51.264}$$
$$= 0.9802$$
$$\therefore C = 11° 25'$$
$$B = 180° - (25° + 11° 25')$$
$$= \underline{143° 35'}$$

Example. An engine has a 88 mm stroke and the connecting rod is 175 mm long between bearing centres. Assume that the piston has travelled 19 mm down the bore from t.d.c. Calculate:

(*a*) The angle between the crank and the connecting rod.

(*b*) The crank angle from t.d.c.

(*c*) The angle of obliquity of the connecting rod.

(*a*) Fig. 9.24 shows a line diagram of the crank and connecting rod. We require to know the distance BC. When the piston is at t.d.c. the combined length of the connecting rod and crank is 175 + 44 = 219 mm. The distance BC is therefore 219 − 19 = 200 mm.

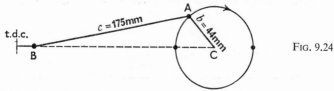

Fig. 9.24

Using the cosine rule,

$$a^2 = b^2 + c^2 - 2bc \cos A$$

$$\cos A = \frac{b^2 + c^2 - a^2}{2bc}$$

$$\cos A = \frac{(44)^2 + (175)^2 - (200)^2}{2 \times 44 \times 175}$$

$$= \frac{1936 + 30\,625 - 40\,000}{15\,400}$$

$$= -\frac{7439}{15\,400}$$

$$= -0 \cdot 4830$$

$$\therefore\ A = -61° 7'$$

Because cos A is a minus quantity, the angle A is an obtuse angle and is the supplement of 61° 7′. The true angle is therefore:

$$A = 180° - 61° 7'$$
$$= \underline{118° 53'}$$

(*b*) $c^2 = a^2 + b^2 - 2ab \cos C$ and $\cos C = \dfrac{a^2 + b^2 - c^2}{2ab}$

$$\cos C = \frac{(200)^2 + (44)^2 - (175)^2}{2 \times 200 \times 44}$$

$$= \frac{11\,311}{17\,600}$$

$$= 0 \cdot 6426$$

$$\therefore\ C = \underline{50° 1'}$$

(*c*) Angle B = 180° − (118° 53′ + 50° 1′)

$$\therefore\ B = \underline{11° 6'}$$

Steering Geometry

Camber, castor and king-pin inclination are usually measured, without calculation, by means of a special combined gauge.

The principles on which this type of gauge operates are:

The tangent of the camber angle is converted by the gauge to give a direct reading of this angle in degrees.

The calculation of the castor and king-pin inclination angles depends on the fact that the camber angle changes as the wheels are steered through a certain angle, usually 20 degrees either side of the straight ahead position. The camber angle is measured in both these positions and the difference between the readings is taken.

Let A = camber angle (straight ahead position)

B = camber angle (steered 20° left)

C = camber angle (steered 20° right)

Then $\quad$ Castor angle $= (B - C) \times \dfrac{1}{2 \sin 20°}$

and

King-pin inclination $= (B + C) - 2A \times \dfrac{1}{2(1 - \cos 20°)}$

Example. The following procedure was adopted in order to measure the castor angle of one front wheel of a motor car.

A straight edge was mounted vertically for the purpose of measuring the camber (angle with respect to the ground) of the wheel normal to its own plane. The road wheel was turned through 20° on the front lock and the camber was then measured. It was then turned backwards through 40° (i.e. 20° on the back lock) and a second camber reading was taken. The difference between the two readings was 2° 55′ (positive camber).

Calculate the corresponding castor angle. Note: You may accept the premise that variations in wheel offset, or initial wheel camber or swivel-pin inclination in the plane of the axle beam, do not affect the result of the calculation and may thus be neglected.

(C. and G.)

$$\text{Castor angle} = (B - C) \times \frac{1}{2 \sin 20°}$$
$$= 2° 55′ \times 1\cdot462 = \underline{\underline{4° 16′}}$$

Exercise 9

1. An overhead camshaft of a certain engine is driven by a pair of equal bevel wheels each having 40 teeth. If the camshaft bevel wheel is taken out of mesh and turned through one tooth and then re-engaged, through what angle is the camshaft turned? (9°)

2. A magneto drive is fitted with a vernier coupling which has 19 teeth on one side and 20 teeth on the other side. Calculate the smallest amount in degrees that the ignition timing can be varied. (0·9473°)

3. In a belt drive for a dynamo and water pump, the belt has contact with a 140 mm diameter pulley over an arc of length 170 mm. Find the angle of contact of the belt. (139·1°) (U.E.I.)

4. The diameter of the taper end of a shaft is measured at two points 35 mm apart measured along the surface of the taper. The larger diameter is found to be 12·44 mm and the smaller 7·56 mm. Find to the nearest degree, the angle between the surface of the taper and its axis. (4°) (C. and G.)

5. A steering drop arm is 175 mm long from the centre of the steering box shaft to the centre of the ball-joint in the free end. If the arm swings through 18 degrees fore and aft of the vertical position, calculate for the free end (*a*) length of arc swung through and (*b*) horizontal distance between the extreme fore and aft positions.

((*a*) 110 mm; (*b*) 108·16 mm) (N.C.T.E.C.)

6. A fine adjustment for ignition timing consists of a screw and nut operating on the end of a lever. If the screw has 1 thread per millimetre and the effective length of the lever is 40 mm, calculate the angle through which the lever turns when the screw is given $2\frac{1}{2}$ turns.

(3° 35′) (N.C.T.E.C.)

7. A taper of 2 degrees included angle is required on a shaft, the diameter of the small end being 13·75 mm. Calculate the length of the shaft necessary to give a large end diameter of 14·37 mm.

(17·7 mm) (N.C.T.E.C.)

8. A brake lining 35 mm wide subtends an angle of 125 degrees at the centre of a circle 280 mm diameter. Find the area of lining in contact and the pressure per mm² on the lining when a braking force of 1500 N is applied to the shoe.

(10 694 mm²; 0·1403 N/mm²) (N.C.T.E.C.)

9. A rectangular chassis frame is 3·808 m long and 1·016 m wide. What is the length to the nearest 0·001 m of the diagonal from the front offside corner to the rear near-side corner? Using the mathematical tables supplied, determine the angle between the diagonal and the side member. (3·941 m; 14° 56′) (C. and G.)

10. A vee groove is 32 mm wide at the top and it has an angle of 45°. A 25 mm diameter test bar is placed in the groove. Calculate the distance from the top of the groove to the centre of the bar.

(5·97 mm)

11. Calculate the smallest variation possible in the valve timing of a certain engine, using the following data:
Camshaft wheel—58 teeth.
Number of studs securing camshaft wheel—3.

(2·068°)

12. The base of an isosceles triangle is 4 m and the equal sides are 3 m. Use trigonometry to find all the angles of the triangle.

(48° 11′; 48° 11′; 83° 38′) (E.M.E.U.)

13. A certain vehicle has a wheel base of 3·05 m; the distance between the steering pivot pins is 1·42 m and the steering angle of the inner wheel is 38 degrees when the vehicle is turning on a given radius. Make use of the foregoing data and calculate the steering angle of the outer wheel to the nearest degree. (30°)

14. * An engine has a bore of 63·5 mm and a stroke of 88 mm with a connecting rod 176 mm long. When the crank is 30° past t.d.c. on the power stroke the pressure on the piston is 2067 kN/m². Set out a line diagram full size, showing the lines of action of the forces under these conditions. Calculate the total piston force and determine the force in the connecting rod and the twisting moment at the crankshaft.

(6546 N; 6598 N; 171·55 Nm) (C. and G.)

15. Using the data given in the last question, calculate:
   (*a*) The angle of obliquity of the connecting rod.
   (*b*) The distance moved by the piston from t.d.c.
   (*c*) The side thrust of the piston on the cylinder bore.

((*a*) 7° 11′; (*b*) 7·286 mm; (*c*) 808 N)

16. Find the value of $3 \tan^2 \theta \cos \phi$ when $\theta = 44°$ and $\phi = 30°$.

(2·422)

17. The radius of a road curve is 36·5 m. Find the angle turned through in 1 second in radians and degrees by a car travelling at 100 km/h. (0·761 rad; 43·6°)

* See Chapters 10 and 11.

18. The efficiency of a worm gear is given by the formula:
$$e = \frac{\tan \theta (1 - \mu \tan \theta)}{\mu + \tan \theta}$$
Find the efficiency e when $\theta = 16° 9'$ and $\mu = 0.02$.

(93 per cent)

19. An engine has a stroke of 100 mm and a connecting rod 200 mm long. Find the angle (to the nearest minute) between the connecting rod and the centre line of the engine (*a*) when the crank is at right angles to the connecting rod, (*b*) when the crank has moved 90° from t.d.c. What is the angular movement of the crank from t.d.c. in case (*a*)? ((*a*) 14° 2′; (*b*) 14° 29′; 75° 58′)

20. Two holes A and B are 44 mm in from centre to centre. A third hole C lies on a centre line drawn midway between A and B and at right angles to centre line AB. If the distances CA and CB are each 83 mm, calculate the perpendicular distance of C from AB.

(80·02 mm)   (U.E.I.)

21. The track and wheelbase of a motor vehicle are 1·8 m and 3·65 m.

When cornering, the inner front wheel is turned through an angle of 16°.

Calculate: (*a*) The angle turned through by the outer front wheel so that true rolling is obtained; (*b*) The rev/min of the outer front wheel when the rev/min of the inner front wheel is 320.

(14° 6′;   363 rev/min)

22. The inertia force of each of the reciprocating parts of an engine is given by the formula:

$$\frac{WN^2 r}{1\,031\,000}\left(\cos \theta + \frac{\cos 2\theta}{n}\right).$$

From the following data find the inertia force when the crankpin is 180° from top dead centre position. $N = 4000$; $n = 4$; $W = 3.5$ kg; $r = 45$ mm. (1833 N)

23. Two rollers, whose diameters are 10 mm and 30 mm, rest on a horizontal surface with their cylindrical surfaces in contact. How far apart horizontally are their centres X and Y? What angle does XY make with the horizontal? Use trigonometry to obtain your answers.

(17·32 mm;   30°   (E.M.E.U.)

24. A rectangular tank 900 mm wide contains water to a depth of 520 mm when the base is horizontal. What angle will the surface of the water make with the sides of the tank if the tank is tilted so that the base makes an angle of 20° with the horizontal? How far along one of the sides will the water now reach?

(70°; 683·9 mm; 356·1 mm) (E.M.E.U.)

25. A wheel 900 mm in diameter, whose axis is horizontal, rotates through an angle of 130°. What is then the height of a point on its rim above what was originally its lowest position? Use trigonometry.

(739·26 mm) (E.M.E.U.)

26. A parallelogram ABCD has AB = 40 mm; BC = 30 mm; angle ABC = 120°. Construct the figure and calculate:

(a) The length of the diagonal AC

(b) The angle CAB.

(60·83 mm; 25° 16′)

27. A small engine has a 50 mm stroke and the connecting rod is 100 mm long. Calculate:

(a) The distance the piston has moved from t.d.c. when the crank is at right-angles to the centre line of the cylinder.

(b) The angle of the crank when the piston is at half-stroke.

(c) The angle of the crank when the piston is at three-quarters stroke.

(28·17 mm; 82° 47′; 113° 16′)

28. Determine the end thrust T in N on a spiral bevel gear when

$$T(\text{N}) = F\left(\frac{\tan \alpha \sin \beta}{\cos \gamma} + \tan \gamma \cos \beta\right)$$

given that $F = 145$, $\alpha = 20·5°$, $\beta = 65°$, $\gamma = 23·4°$.

(51·46 N) (N.C.T.E.C.)

29. If an engine has a stroke of 75 mm and a con. rod length of 110 mm, calculate the distance between the gudgeon-pin centre and the crankshaft centre when the crankshaft has turned through 90° from t.d.c. (103·4 mm) (E.M.E.U.)

30. When measuring the camber angle of the steered wheels of a car, a vertical line measured 400 mm. From the lower end of the line and at right angles to it, a further measurement was found to be 10 mm. The road wheel made up the third side of the triangle.

What was the camber angle in degrees?

(1° 26′) (E.M.E.U.)

31. A motor vehicle having a wheelbase of 2·45 m is moving in a curve so that the outer front wheel has a turning circle of 10 m radius ᴊased on the Akerman principle. Through what angle has the outer front wheel been steered from the straight ahead position?

(13° 44′)   (E.M.E.U.)

32. Two cars leave a garage at the same time. One travels along a straight road to the north-west at 28 km per hour. The other travels along a straight road N.N.E. at 24 km per hour. Use the cosine rule to discover how long it will take before the cars are 60 km apart.

(1 h 49 min)   (I.M.I.)

10 Force

A force is that which produces or prevents motion or tends to produce or change the motion of a body. Note the word 'tends' in the definition; motion is not always produced or changed by a force. Force is measured in **newtons (N)** or kilonewtons (kN).

Tensile forces are forces acting on a body tending to make it longer in the direction in which the forces are acting.

Fig. 10.1 shows a body in a state of tension. This type of force exists in the brake rod when the brake is applied (see Fig. 10.2) or in the crane

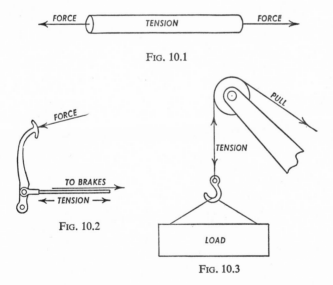

FIG. 10.1

FIG. 10.2

FIG. 10.3

rope as shown in Fig. 10.3; other examples are the bolt or stud when the nut has been tightened and the belt which drives the fan.

Compressive forces are forces acting on a body tending to make it

shorter in the direction in which the forces are acting. Fig. 10.4 shows
a body in a state of compression. An example is shown in Fig. 10.5,
the connecting rod during the first part of the power stroke; also the
push rod when the valve is opening and clutch lining when the clutch is
engaged.

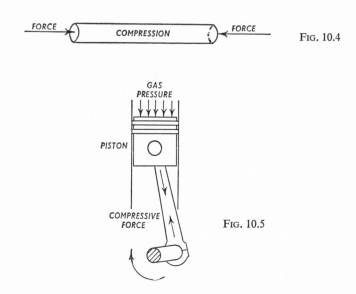

FIG. 10.4

FIG. 10.5

Shearing forces tend to produce sliding of one surface over another.
Fig. 10.6 shows two plates riveted together; these plates are subjected
to a tensile force, which produces a shearing force on the rivet at the
section XX and the rivet is subjected to 'single shear'. This type of force
occurs in the brake-shoe rivets, chassis rivets or bolts and the bolts
which hold the flywheel to the crankshaft.

Fig. 10.7 shows three plates riveted together. The shearing force
now occurs at two points, XX and X_1X_1; this is known as a 'double
shear'. This type of force occurs at many points on the motor car, such
as the clevis pin (Fig. 10.8); also the gudgeon pin, swivel axle pin and
road spring shackle bolt.

Fig. 10.9 shows another type of shearing force which is produced by
twisting; this occurs in the crankshaft, gear-box shaft, axle shaft and
speedometer driving cable.

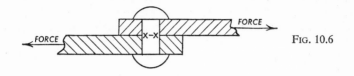

FIG. 10.6

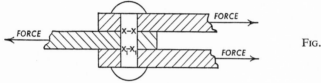

FIG. 10.7

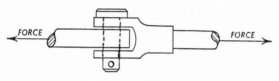

FIG. 10.8

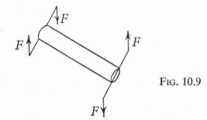

FIG. 10.9

Attractive forces. A magnet produces a force without coming in contact with another body; if the bodies are drawn together it is a 'force of attraction', but if the bodies are separated or pushed apart it is a 'force of repulsion'.

All bodies are said to have 'weight'; this is a force due to the pull of the earth and known as the 'force of gravity'.

Force and Pressure

These should not be confused. Force is the total amount of thrust or effort exerted on a body; it is assumed to be acting at a point.

The standard unit of force is the **newton (N)**; for very small forces the **millinewton (mN)** is used and for large forces the **kilonewton (kN)** is used. These units are 1000 times smaller and larger than the standard unit.

Pressure is the amount of force per unit of area. The standard unit of pressure is the newton per square metre (N/m^2).

For very high pressures the kilonewton per square metre (kN/m^2) may be used, also, for small areas the newton or kilonewton per millimetre squared (N/mm^2) or (kN/mm^2) may be used.

Triangle of Forces

When solving problems of forces it is often easier and quicker to use scale drawing or graphical methods. Each force is represented by a straight line.

Firstly, the **space diagram** is drawn to show the layout of the forces, and each line will show the direction in which the force is acting. Fig. 10.10 is a space diagram showing three forces P, Q and R acting at a point; the magnitude of P and Q are known and a force R is required to maintain a state of **equilibrium** or rest. The forces on the space diagram, each represented by one letter, are now given two new capital letters by using the method known as **Bow's notation.** One letter is placed on each side of the line: force P now becomes AB, Q becomes BC and R becomes CA.

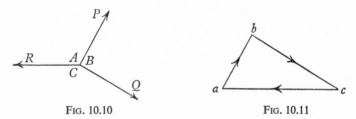

FIG. 10.10   FIG. 10.11

The **force diagram**, Fig. 10.11, is now constructed, each force being represented by a **vector**, that is, a straight line drawn to scale whose length represents the magnitude and direction of the force. A suitable scale is chosen and the vector ab is drawn parallel to AB; from point b the vector bc is drawn parallel to BC; then by connecting the two fixed

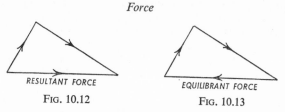

RESULTANT FORCE
FIG. 10.12

EQUILIBRANT FORCE
FIG. 10.13

points *ca* we have the vector of the unknown force *CA(R)*. This force is known as the 'equilibrant', since it prevents movement. If, however, the force acted in the opposite direction, it would be known as the 'resultant', since it would be a single force replacing the other two forces. These are shown in Figs. 10.12 and 10.13.

Parallelogram of Forces

When only three forces are concerned, the problem can be solved by the method of the parallelogram of forces. Consider the space diagram as shown in Fig. 10.14. To find the magnitude of the force *P* a suitable scale is selected. Measure a distance O*A* along the line O*R* to represent 8 N and a distance O*B* along O*Q* to represent 6 N. From *A* draw a

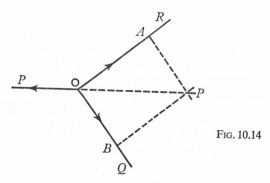

FIG. 10.14

line parallel to O*Q* and from *B* draw a line parallel to O*R*; the point where these two lines intersect will be *P*$_1$; the length O*P*$_1$ will be equal and opposite to the force O*P*. (Ans. 10 N.)

Resolution of a Force

In the previous problems two forces were compounded into one force; now one force is to be divided into two forces or components. When any single force is resolved into its component forces we must state their direction; this is usually done in the vertical and horizontal directions

and they become known as the vertical component and horizontal
component. To find the component forces, draw a vector to represent
the force R (Fig. 10.15). From O, the point of origin or starting, draw
a horizontal line ON and a vertical line OM. From a draw a vertical

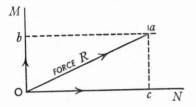

FIG. 10.15

line to cut ON at c and from a a horizontal line to cut OM at b. Then
Ob represents the vertical component and Oc represents the horizontal
component.

Worked Examples
The rear axle of a vehicle is lifted by a crane and it exerts a force of
2796 N in the lifting wire sling which is attached to the axle at points
1·6 m apart and to the crane hook. If each half sling is 1·2 m long, find
the tension in each wire.

In this problem the space diagram must be drawn to scale in order
to find the direction of the unknown forces. The arrow heads are inserted
from the point of origin, i.e. the crane hook, and the forces lettered by
Bow's notation, as shown in Fig. 10.16.

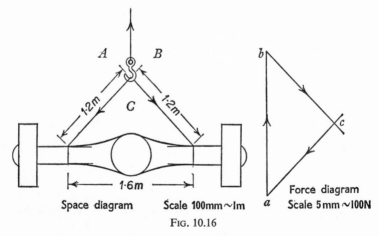

Space diagram   Scale 100mm ∼1m   Force diagram
                                            Scale 5mm ∼100N
FIG. 10.16

The force diagram is started by drawing the only known force, the vector *ab* vertical which represents the force on the hook in direction and magnitude.

From the point *b* the line for the vector *bc* is drawn for direction only, because the length is not yet known.

From point *a* draw the line for the vector *ca* parallel to *CA* to cut the line *bc*; the point of intersection is *c*.

It will be noted that when only one force is given the directions of the other forces are used to find the magnitudes of the unknown forces.

$$\text{Answer. Vector } bc = 1900 \text{ N}$$
$$\text{Vector } ca = 1900 \text{ N}$$
$$\text{Vector } ab = 2796 \text{ N}$$

Polygon of Forces

A development of the parallelogram of forces is the **polygon of forces** which we may use to determine either the equilibrant or the resultant force of any given number of forces acting at a point.

A polygon is a plane rectilineal figure usually having four or more sides which are used to represent the forces acting at one point.

Example. Fig. 10.17 shows the space diagram of four forces acting at one point; the forces are not in equilibrium. Construct a polygon of forces and draw in the vector representing the force required to maintain equilibrium (equilibrant force).

Fig. 10.18 shows the force diagram, the vector a_1a represents the equilibrant force.

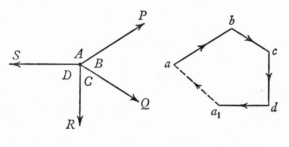

FIG. 10.17   FIG. 10.18

In all examples where the force diagram becomes a 'closed' polygon the forces are in equilibrium. If, however, the force represented by the vector a_1a acted in the opposite direction it would be the resultant force replacing all the other four forces.

The resultant of any number of forces acting at a point may be calculated as follows:

Example. Fig. 10.19 shows four forces N, O, P, Q acting at a point. Calculate the magnitude and direction of the resultant force R when $N = 4$ N, $O = 5$ N, $P = 3$ N and $Q = 2$ N.

Through the point of application draw the horizontal and vertical centre lines $-$ X, X and $-$ Y, Y.

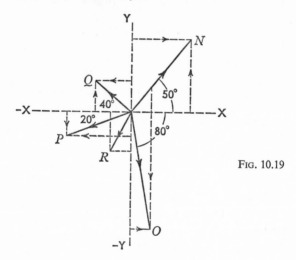

Fig. 10.19

If we consider the four forces as separate resultants, then each force can be resolved into horizontal and vertical components as follows:

(1) By means of dotted lines complete the parallelogram of forces for each of the four forces, as shown in Fig. 10.19.
(2) Calculate the magnitude and note the direction and signs of the horizontal and vertical components.

The forces acting towards the minus side of the centre lines are minus quantities and the forces acting towards the plus side of the centre lines are plus quantities. From Fig. 10.19 we obtain the following:

Force N, horizontal component $= \cos 50° \times 4 = 2\cdot5712$ (plus)
vertical component $= \sin 50° \times 4 = 3\cdot1040$ (plus)

Force *O*, horizontal component = cos 80° × 5 = 0·8680 (plus)
          vertical component   = sin 80° × 5 = 4·9240 (minus)
Force *P*, horizontal component = cos 20° × 3 = 2·8191 (minus)
          vertical component   = sin 20° × 3 = 1·0260 (minus)
Force *Q*, horizontal component = cos 40° × 2 = 1·5320 (minus)
          vertical component   = sin 40° × 2 = 1·2856 (plus)

Horizontal component =
  + 2·5712 + 0·8680 − 2·8191 − 1·5320 = − 0·9119 N
Vertical component =
  + 3·1040 − 4·9240 − 1·0260 + 1·2856 = −1·5604 N
Neglecting the minus signs, then:
Magnitude of resultant = 0·9119 + 1·5604
$$= \underline{2·4723 \text{ N}}$$

Because of the above minus signs, the resultant *R* will act in a minus direction, i.e. between − X and − Y. Because we know the value of the components and their resultant which form the sides of the final force parallelogram, we can calculate the angle below the − X,X axis at which the resultant is acting as follows:

Let θ represent the angle required, then:

$$\cos \theta = \frac{0·9119}{2·4723}$$
$$= 0·3668$$

Direction of *R* = $\underline{68° 29'}$ below the horizontal

centre line

Exercise 10

1. A load C exerts a force of 890 N and is suspended by two ropes, AC and BC, attached to a horizontal beam at A and B, 1·2 m apart. AC = 1·2 m, BC = 0·9 m. Determine the tension in each rope.
          (AC = 380 N; BC = 720 N) (E.M.E.U.)

2. A force of 3500 N acts horizontally on a car which exerts a downward force of 8000 N. Find the resultant of this force and the direction in which it acts.
          (8750 N; 66° to the horizontal) (E.M.E.U.)

3. A load of 890 N hangs vertically by a rope from an overhead support. It is pulled sideways by a horizontal force of 355 N. What angle will the supporting rope then make with the vertical, and what will be the force acting in it?   (21° 48′; 956 N) (E.M.E.U.)

4. The two connecting rods on a V8 engine are attached to the same crankpin. The downward thrust along rod A is 20 kN and the downward thrust along rod B is 7 kN, and the angle between them is 60°. Construct the space and force diagrams to determine the magnitude and direction of the resultant force relative to rod A.

(24·4 kN;   15°)

5. An oil engine exerts a downward force of 3600 N when it is lifted from the chassis by two wire slings, one 0·7 m long, the other 0·8 m. One end of each sling is attached to a crane hook, the other ends to lifting hooks fitted to the engine at points 0·65 m apart. If the lifting hooks remain horizontal, find by constructing force and space diagrams the tension in each wire sling.

(2535 N;   (1425 N)

6. A pressure of 965 kN/m² acts vertically downwards on a piston crown; the piston is 72·5 mm in diameter. The angle of the connecting rod causes a side thrust of 1555 N on the piston. Construct a space and force diagram to determine the thrust along the connecting rod, and its angle in relation to the cylinder bore axis.   (4225 N, 20° 14′)

7. An engine exerts a downward force of 1246 N when hanging on a chain whose upper end is attached to an overhead support. A horizontal force exerted on the engine causes the chain to take up a position inclined at 30 degrees to the vertical. What is then the horizontal force and the force in the chain?   (735 N;   1445 N)   (E.M.E.U.)

8. The jib and tie-rod of a simple crane meet at a point A. The jib is inclined at 60 degrees to the horizontal and the tie at 40 degrees to the horizontal. What force is produced in each by suspending a load of 19·94 kN from A?

(35·77 kN;   29·19 kN)   (E.M.E.U.)

9. A clutch pedal lever is cranked at the point where it is hinged to a fixed pivot. Below this pivot the arm is vertical and 100 mm long. Above the pivot it is inclined at an angle of 45° to the vertical and is 300 mm long.

Find the force required at the end of the upper arm, at right-angles to its length, to balance a horizontal force of 1200 N at the lower end, and the magnitude and direction of the force on the fixed pivot.

(400 N;   1512 N;   11°)   (C and G.)

10. The axial load on a piston is 7120 N when the connecting rod is inclined at 15° to the centre line of the cylinder.

(a) By means of a scale drawing, find the force acting along the connecting rod.
(b) Neglecting friction, determine the guiding force which has to be applied by the cylinder to the piston.
(c) Verify your results by calculation.

((a) 7370 N;   (b) 1843 N)

11. In a petrol engine, the connecting rod is 200 mm long and the piston has a stroke of 100 mm.

When the connecting rod lies at an angle of 10° to the line of the piston stroke, the force on the piston is 1335 N. Determine:

(a) the force in the connecting rod and
(b) the side force between the piston and the cylinder walls.

((a) 1356 N;   (b) 222 N)

12. Four forces in equilibrium are acting at a point. The magnitudes of three of the forces are 15 N acting in a North-East direction, 8 N acting due South and 18 N acting in a direction 30° East of South.

Determine the magnitude and direction of the fourth force.

(23·4 N;   33° 12′ North of East)

13. Find the resultant force exerted by two men pulling (a) with a force of 270 N at 30° to the axis of a car, (b) with a force of 222 N at 45° on the other side of the car axis. In what direction will the car tend to move?

(389 N;   5° towards the 222 N force)   (E.M.E.U.)

11 Moments

The **moment of a force** is a term used to describe the turning effect of that force. Consider the crankshaft of an engine and the force which passes along the connecting rod to the crankpin. Fig. 11.1 shows a layout where the centre lines or axes of the connecting rods and crank

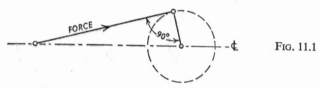

Fig. 11.1

are perpendicular or at right angles to each other. The turning moment of the force will be the product of the force along the connecting rod and its distance from the centre of the shaft about which the rotation takes place. If, however, the connecting rod and crank are not at right angles, the true perpendicular distance from the line of the force to the point of rotation or turn must be found. A simple method by scale drawing is shown in Fig. 11.2. The line AB is extended to point C, and the line DO is drawn at an angle of 90° to AC. The length of DO

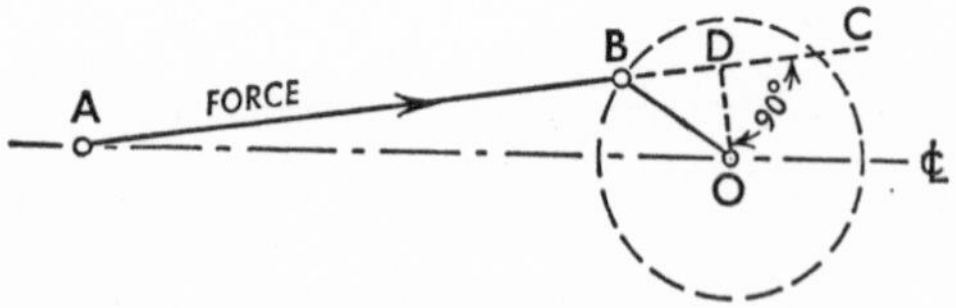

Fig. 11.2

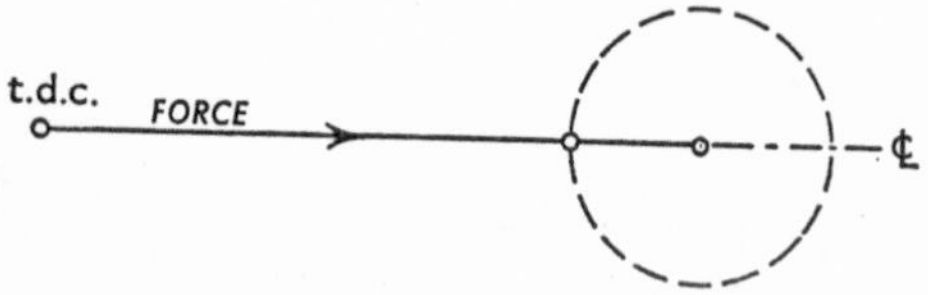

Fig. 11.3

represents the perpendicular distance from the point O, the axis of rotation, to the point D at which the force is acting.

A force can have no moment when the direction of the force passes through the point of rotation; this is shown in Fig. 11.3. This condition exists when the piston is in the t.d.c. position.

The 'moment of a force' may be defined as the product of that force and its perpendicular distance from the point of turn.

∴ Moment of a force = Force × perpendicular distance

When the force is measured in newtons (N) and the distance in metres (m), the unit of measurement will be Nm. Other units are the Nmm and kNm.

Fig. 11.4 shows a lever with two downward forces acting to produce a state of balance. Force A is tending to turn the lever in a direction opposite to the direction in which the hands of a clock rotate; the

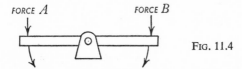

FIG. 11.4

moment produced is known as an 'anti-clockwise' or 'counter-clock-wise moment'. Force B is tending to turn the lever in the direction in which the hands of the clock rotate; the moment produced is known as a 'clockwise moment'. If these two forces produce a state of balance or equilibrium, no movement is produced, since the clockwise turning moments equal the anti-clockwise turning moments.

This turning moment is sometimes known as the **twisting moment** or **torque**.

The Lever

Three common types of lever are in everyday use; some examples are the clutch pedal, pliers, spanner, jack-handle and hand-brake lever. A lever may be defined as a rigid body, capable of transmitting a leverage in any direction except along its own axis. The common lever has three points of interest:

(1) The fulcrum or pivot.
(2) The point where the force or effort is applied, usually indicated by the capital letter F.
(3) The point where the lever exerts the force or acts against the resistance (load); this is indicated by the capital letter W.

Class I lever. This is shown in Fig. 11.5. It will be seen that the fulcrum is between the points where the effort is applied and the load is in contact.

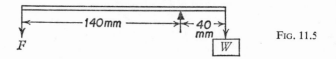

Fig. 11.5

Example. Find the effort required to overcome a resistance (load) of 49 N at the end of the lever shown in Fig. 11.5.

Let F (N) be the effort required to produce equilibrium in the lever, then:

$$\text{Anti-clockwise moments} = \text{Clockwise moments}$$
$$\text{Effort} \times \text{distance} = \text{Load} \times \text{distance}$$
$$F \text{ (N)} \times 140 \text{ (mm)} = 49 \text{ (N)} \times 40 \text{ (mm)}$$

The units are the same on each side of the equation.

$$\therefore 140F = 49 \times 40$$
$$F = \frac{49 \times 40}{140}$$
$$= 14$$
$$\therefore \underline{\text{The effort } F = 14 \text{ N}}$$

Class II lever. Fig. 11.6 shows this type of lever. The fulcrum is at one end, the applied effort acts at the opposite end of the lever and the load is between these two points.

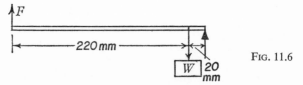

Fig. 11.6

Example. Find the effort required to overcome resistance (load) of 480 (N) by the lever shown in Fig. 11.6.

Let F (N) be the effort required to produce equilibrium in the lever, then:

$$\text{Clockwise moments} = \text{Anti-clockwise moments}$$
$$F \text{ (N)} \times 240 \text{ (mm)} = 480 \text{ (N)} \times 20 \text{ (mm)}$$

The units are the same on each side of the equation.

$$\therefore 240F = 480 \times 20$$

$$F = \frac{480 \times 20}{240}$$

$$= 40$$

$$\therefore \underline{\text{The effort } F = 40 \text{ N}}$$

Class III lever. Fig. 11.7 shows this type of lever. The fulcrum is at one end and the load at the opposite end; the effort is applied between these two points.

Example. Find the effort required to support a load (force) of 12 N by the lever shown in Fig. 11.7.

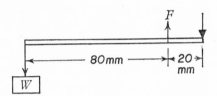

Fig. 11.7

Let F (N) be the effort required to produce equilibrium in the lever, then:

Clockwise moments = Anti-clockwise moments

$$F \text{ (N)} \times 20 \text{ (mm)} = 12 \text{ (N)} \times 100 \text{ (mm)}$$

The units are the same on each side of the equation.

$$\therefore 20F = 12 \times 100$$

$$F = \frac{12 \times 100}{20}$$

$$= 60$$

$$\therefore \underline{\text{The effort } F = 60 \text{ N}}$$

The **principle of moments** has been used to solve the unknown force in each of these three types of lever. This principle may be defined as: If a body remains at rest when acted on by several forces in one plane, then the total anti-clockwise moments will equal the total clockwise moments.

The following examples each have several known forces acting in one plane.

Example. Find the value of F (as shown in Fig. 11.8) which will keep the beam horizontal.

Let F (N) be the effort required, then:

Clockwise moments = Anti-clockwise moments

$(F \times 100) + (10 \times 40)$ Nmm $= (14 \times 50) + (8 \times 80)$ Nmm

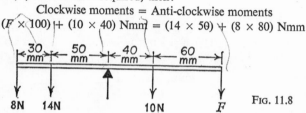

FIG. 11.8

The units are the same on each side of the equation.

$$\therefore 100F + 400 = 700 + 640$$
$$100F = 700 + 640 - 400$$
$$= 940$$
$$F = \frac{940}{100} = 9 \cdot 4$$
$$\therefore \text{ The effort } F = 9 \cdot 4 \text{ N}$$

Example. Find the value of F (as shown in Fig. 11.9) which will keep the beam horizontal.

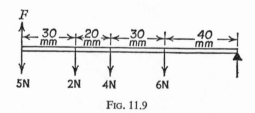

FIG. 11.9

Let F (N) be the effort required, then:

Clockwise moments = Anti-clockwise moments

$F \times 120$ Nmm $= (6 \times 40) + (4 \times 70) + (2 \times 90)$
$$+ (5 \times 120) \text{ Nmm}$$

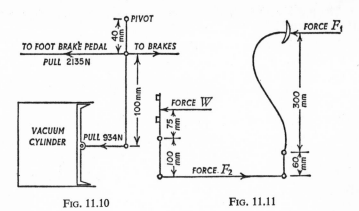

FIG. 11.10   FIG. 11.11

The units are the same on each side of the equation.

$$\therefore 120F = 240 + 280 + 180 + 600$$

$$F = \frac{1300}{120} = 10\cdot83$$

$$\therefore \text{The effort } F = 10\cdot83 \text{ N}$$

Example. Fig. 11.10 shows the layout of a vacuum servo brake unit.

Find the pull in the brake rod when the foot-brake pedal exerts a pull of 2135 N and the vacuum piston a pull of 934 N.

Let W (N) be the pull in the brake rod, then:

Anti-clockwise moments = Clockwise moments

$$(W \times 40) \text{ Nmm} = (2135 \times 40) + (934 \times 140) \text{ Nmm}$$

The units are the same on each side of the equation.

$$\therefore 40W = 85\,400 + 130\,760$$

$$W = \frac{216\,160}{40}$$

$$= 5404$$

$$\therefore \text{ Pull in brake rod } W = 5404 \text{ N}$$

Example. Fig. 11.11 shows the layout of the clutch-operating mechanism. What force is exerted by the thrust on the clutch fingers when the force on the pedal is 267 N?

This problem is worked in two stages: first find the pull F_2 in the rod, then the value of W.

Let F_2 (N) be the pull in the clutch rod, then:

Clockwise moments = Anti-clockwise moments

$$F_2 \times 60 \text{ Nmm} = F_1 \times 300 \text{ Nmm}$$

$$F_2 \times 60 \text{ Nmm} = 267 \times 300 \text{ Nmm}$$

The units are the same on each side of the equation.

$$\therefore 60 F_2 = 267 \times 300$$

$$\therefore F_2 = \frac{267 \times 300}{60}$$

$$= 1335$$

$$\therefore \underline{\text{The effort } F_2 = 1335 \text{ N}}$$

Let W (N) be the force on the clutch fingers, then:

Clockwise moments = Anti-clockwise moments

$$W \times 75 \text{ Nmm} = F_2 \times 100 \text{ Nmm}$$

$$W \times 75 \text{ Nmm} = 1335 \times 100 \text{ Nmm}$$

The units are the same on each side of the equation.

$$\therefore 75W = 1335 \times 100$$

$$W = \frac{1335 \times 100}{75}$$

$$\therefore \underline{\text{The force on the clutch fingers } W = 1780 \text{ N}}$$

Reaction

This may be defined as that which opposes or resists another action. To every action, load or force there is an equal and opposite reaction.

In the horizontal beam, reaction is the upward force which is opposing or supporting the downward load of the beam.

When the force and reaction are equal in magnitude, no movement will take place. If, however, the force is greater than the resistance, movement will occur.

Reactions of a Horizontal Beam

This type of beam is supported at two points, which need not be at the ends of the beam. Consider the beam as shown in Fig. 11.12. It could represent the front or rear axle of a car and the unequal loads are shown at the points where the road springs are attached to the axle. The difference in loads would suggest that the vehicle is either cornering, subjected to a side wind or on a cambered road. The arrowhead and letters R_A are always put at the left-hand support to indicate the reaction (R) at the point (A), likewise R_B is the right-hand support or point of reaction. The downward force of any uniform beam is always

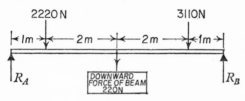

Fig. 11.12

considered to be concentrated at the centre of the beam, not the centre between the points of reaction unless they are both at the extreme ends.

The calculation to find the load supported by each reaction is carried out in two parts.

To find the value of R_A, the point R_B is assumed to be a fulcrum or pivot and all moments are taken about this point.

(1) Taking moments about B.

Let R_A (N) be the reaction at the point A, then:

Clockwise moments = Anti-clockwise moments

$$R_A \times 6 \text{ Nm} = (3110 \times 1) + (220 \times 3) + (2220 \times 5) \text{ Nm}$$

The units are the same on each side of the equation.

$$\therefore 6R_A = 3110 + 660 + 11\,100$$

$$= 14\,870$$

$$R_A = \frac{14\,870}{6}$$

$$= 2478$$

The reaction $R_A = 2478$ N

(2) Taking moments about A to find the downward load on R_B.
Let R_B (N) be the reaction at the point B, then:

Anti-clockwise moments = Clockwise moments

$$R_B \times 6 \text{ Nm} = (2220 \times 1) + (220 \times 3) + (3110 \times 5) \text{ Nm}$$

The units are the same on each side of the equation.

$$\therefore \ 6R_B = 2220 + 660 + 15\,550$$
$$= 18\,430$$
$$R_B = \frac{18\,430}{6}$$
$$= 3072$$

The reaction $R_B = 3072$ N

To check the answers obtained, all the downward loads must equal the two reactions R_A and R_B.

$$\therefore \ \text{Downward loads} = R_A + R_B$$
$$2220 + 220 + 3110 = 2478 + 3072$$
$$5550 = 5550$$

Problems of this type sometimes result in one of the loads acting in an upward direction and the other in a downward direction. An example of this is shown in Fig. 11.13, where points A and B represent the bearings supporting a shaft and the downward loads are the forces acting on the gear wheels or pulleys.

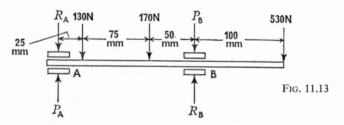

Fig. 11.13

Assuming that the shaft is pivoted at B and the bearing A is removed, by taking moments about B,

Anti-clockwise moment $= (130 \times 125) + (170 \times 50) = 24\,750$ Nmm

Clockwise moment $= 530 \times 100 = 53\,000$ Nmm

From this it will be seen that, as the clockwise moment is greater than the anti-clockwise moment, there will be an upward thrust load at A. This load is resisted by bearing A, hence the reaction at A is downwards, see Fig. 11.13.

Let P_A represent the upward load at A and R_A the reaction of the load P_A at A. Then P_A will be equal in value to R_A, Fig. 11.13.

Taking moments about B,

Anti-clockwise moments $=$ Clockwise moments

$$(R_A \times 150) + (170 \times 50) + (130 \times 125) \ \text{Nmm} = 530 \times 100 \ \text{Nmm}$$

The units are the same on each side of the equation.

$$\therefore 150R_A + 24\,750 = 53\,000$$
$$150R_A = 53\,000 - 24\,750$$
$$R_A = \frac{28\,250}{150}$$
$$= 188 \cdot 3 \text{ N}$$

Because R_A is the reaction to P_A it has the same value as P_A. Therefore $P_A = 188 \cdot 3$ N, and

Load on the bearing A = <u>188·3 N</u>

Let P_B represent the downward load at B and R_B the reaction of the load P_B at B. Then P_B will be equal in value to R_B.

Taking moments about A,

Anti-clockwise moments = Clockwise moments

$$R_B \times 150 \text{ Nmm} = (130 \times 25) + (170 \times 100) + (530 \times 250) \text{ Nmm}$$
$$R_B = 3250 + 17\,000 + 132\,500$$
$$= 150$$
$$R_B = \frac{152\,750}{150}$$
$$= 1018 \cdot 3 \text{ N}$$

Because $P_B = R_B$,

Load on the bearing B = <u>1018·3 N</u>

This load acts in a downward direction and is the sum of the total loads acting downwards on the shaft **plus** the reaction at A, thus:

$$1018 \cdot 3 = 530 + 170 + 130 + 188 \cdot 3$$
$$1018 \cdot 3 = 1018 \cdot 3$$

Centre of Gravity

The lever shown in Fig. 11.4 is in a state of balance, since the position of the fulcrum or pivot produces balances in the lever and its loads. The load acting on the pivot is equal to the downward force of the lever and its loads, therefore the total force is concentrated at one point; this is known as its **centre of gravity**. If the lever were suspended from a hook by a cord, the cord would have to be attached to exactly the same point to produce balance.

The centre of gravity, abbreviated c.g., can be defined as a single point through which the system of forces is considered to act.

To find the c.g. of objects having a regular shape, their centre only has to be found. In a square sheet of thin metal having sides, say, 50 mm long or a disc having a diameter of 75 mm, the c.g. is in the centre of both.

To find the c.g. of irregular shapes of thin flat material the method of suspension is used. The point of intersection of the various vertical lines drawn from different points of suspension is the position of the c.g.

A lever or bar of uniform cross-section will have its c.g. at a point in the middle of its length. If the cross-section is not uniform, such as a connecting rod, the c.g. can be found experimentally by placing it on a knife edge at various points until balance is obtained.

The c.g. can also be found by calculation, using the principle of moments.

The connecting rod would be placed in a horizontal position and supported by spring balances at the centre line of each bearing. Knowing the magnitude of the downward load on each spring balance and the distance between them, the position of the c.g. can be found.

Spring balances and similar equipment are calibrated in newtons (N) for recording force and kilogrammes (kg) for recording mass, so a conversion may be needed, i.e. kilogrammes $\times$ 9·8 = newtons (N)

newtons $\div$ 9·8 = kilogrammes (kg)

Example. A connecting rod 300 mm long between its bearing centres is suspended at these centres from two spring balances. The balances are adjusted so that the connecting rod is horizontal.

If the balance reading at the big end is 12 N and at the small end

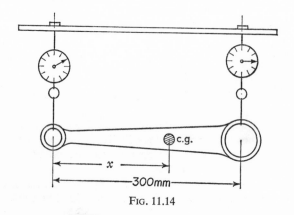

Fig. 11.14

bearing is 10 N, calculate the position of the centre of gravity of the connecting rod.

Fig. 11.14 shows the connecting rod and spring balances.

Let $x =$ distance of c.g. from the small end bearing.

Now, the total mass of the rod will act at the point of c.g. of the rod, as shown in Fig. 11.14.

Therefore, taking moments about the small end bearing,

$$\text{Clockwise moments} = \text{Anti-clockwise moments}$$

$$x \times 22 \text{ Nmm} = 300 \times 12 \text{ Nmm}$$

$$x = \frac{300 \times 12 \text{ Nmm}}{22 \qquad \text{N}}$$

$$= 163 \cdot 6 \text{ mm}$$

$$\therefore \text{ Position of c.g. } (x) = \underline{163 \cdot 6 \text{ mm}}$$

The position of the c.g. of a motor vehicle will be found on the centre line of the vehicle between the axles, i.e. the wheelbase, at a point usually nearer the front axle for cars but nearer the rear axle for commercial vehicles, see Fig. 11.15.

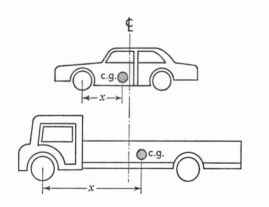

FIG. 11.15

To determine the position of the c.g. of a vehicle, the downward load on each axle and the length of the wheelbase must be known. At this stage the height of the c.g. above ground level is not taken into account.

Example. A vehicle has a wheelbase of 2·5 m and the distribution of load, when the vehicle is at rest, is: front axle 3980 N, rear axle 5970 N.

Determine the distance of the c.g. behind the front axle.　(C. and G.)

Let x = distance of c.g. from the front axle, see Fig. 11.15.

Then, taking moments about the front axle,

$$\text{Clockwise moments} = \text{Anti-clockwise moments}$$
$$x \times 9950 \text{ Nm} = 5970 \times 2 \cdot 5 \text{ Nm}$$
$$x = \frac{5970 \times 2 \cdot 5 \text{ Nm}}{9950 \quad \text{N}}$$
$$= 1 \cdot 5 \text{ m}$$
$$\therefore \text{ Distance of c.g.} \quad = \underline{1 \cdot 5 \text{ m}}$$

A more difficult problem is the lever supporting several loads instead of one load at each end.

Fig. 11.16 shows a lever which has a downward force of 40 N and supporting loads of 130, 80 and 170 N at the points shown. The following should be noted.

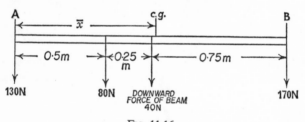

FIG. 11.16

(1) The left-hand end of the lever is point A, and the right-hand end point B.

(2) The resultant downward force is the sum of the downward loads including that of the lever.

(3) $\bar{x}$ is the distance of the c.g. from point A.

(4) The moment of the resultant is equal to the product of the resultant × distance $\bar{x}$.

(5) The moment of each load is the product of its load and its distances from point A.

Now the moment of the resultant acting at an unknown distance from point A will equal the sum of moments of all the loads acting at their own distances from A.

$$\text{Resultant} = \text{Sum of loads}$$
$$= 130 + 80 + 40 + 170$$
$$= 420 \text{ N}$$
$$\therefore \text{ Moment of resultant} = 420 \times \bar{x}$$

Moment of loads
$$= (130 \times 0) + (80 \times 0 \cdot 5) + (40 \times 0 \cdot 75) + (170 \times 1 \cdot 5) \text{ Nm}$$
$$= 0 + 40 + 30 + 255 \text{ Nm}$$
$$= 325 \text{ Nm}$$

Note that $(130 \times 0) = 0$, not 130.

Let $\bar{x}$ (m) be the distance of the c.g. from point A, then:

$$\text{Moment of resultant} = \text{Moment of loads}$$
$$420 \times \bar{x} \text{ Nm} = 325 \text{ Nm}$$

The units are the same on each side of the equation.

$$\therefore 420 \bar{x} = 325$$
$$\bar{x} = \frac{325}{420}$$
$$= 0 \cdot 7738$$
$$\therefore \text{ Position of c.g. } \bar{x} = \underline{0 \cdot 7738 \text{ m}}$$

This can now be checked by taking moments about the c.g.

$$\text{Anti-clockwise moments} = \text{Clockwise moments}$$
$$(130 \times 0 \cdot 7738) + (80 \times 0 \cdot 2738) + (40 \times 0 \cdot 0238) = 170 \times 0 \cdot 7262$$
$$123 \cdot 45 = 123 \cdot 45$$

The above procedure could have been carried out by working from point B instead of point A and producing the same answer.

Torque
This has already been defined as the **turning moment** or twisting

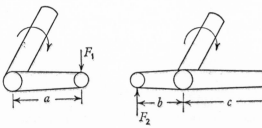

Fig. 11.17   Fig. 11.18

moment. Consider the diagram Fig. 11.17; a lever is attached at right angles to the end of a shaft, a force F_1 acting perpendicular to the lever produces an effect tending to rotate the shaft, so the torque, turning or twisting moment will be the product of the force F_1 and its perpendicular distance from the axis of the shaft.

$$\therefore \text{ Torque or Moment of force} = \text{Force} \times \text{distance}$$
$$= F_1 \times a$$

The units will be (Nm)

Fig. 11.18 shows a double-ended lever; the forces F_2 and F_3 both tend to rotate the shaft in a clockwise direction. Since the levers are of different lengths the torque produced $= (F_2 \times b) + (F_3 \times c)$.

Torque is a term used in the workshop and service station when overhauling various vehicle components. The torque wrench is a standard piece of equipment and it can be adjusted to show the torque produced by the mechanic or fitter when tightening a nut. Manufacturers usually state the torque required for tightening the nuts on the cylinder head, main and big-end bearing studs. This prevents damage to the bearing, stud and thread. Torque is also used to measure the preload given to some of the ball and roller bearings. The maximum torque produced by an engine is the factor which governs the size and type of clutch to be fitted. It is important that the principle is properly understood.

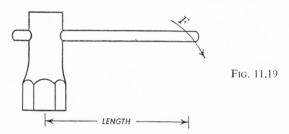

FIG. 11.19

Fig. 11.19 shows a box spanner which will produce a torque equal to the force applied perpendicularly to the end of the bar multiplied by the length of the bar from the axis to the point where the force is applied. It is interesting to note that as the length of the bar is increased the torque will also increase, the applied force remaining constant. That is why a tight or rusted-up nut can be freed by connecting an extension to the bar.

Example. A force of 220 N is applied at right angles to the end of a spanner whose effective length is 230 mm. What is the applied torque?

$$\text{Torque} = \text{Force} \times \text{perpendicular distance}$$
$$= 220 \times 230 \text{ Nmm}$$
$$= 50\ 600 \text{ Nmm}$$
$$= 50 \cdot 6 \text{ Nm}$$
$$\therefore \text{Torque} = \underline{50 \cdot 6 \text{ Nm}}$$

Example. The bearings of a bevel pinion shaft require a preload of 1250 Nmm. What load must be attached to the cord to produce slow uniform motion which indicates the correct preload? Fig. 11.20 shows the layout of the test rig.

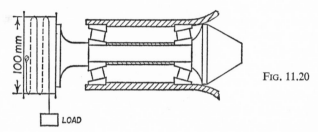

100 mm

LOAD

Fig. 11.20

$$\text{Torque} = \text{Force} \times \text{perpendicular distance}$$
$$\therefore \text{Force} = \frac{\text{Torque}}{\text{Distance}}$$
$$= \frac{1250}{50} \text{ N}$$
$$= \underline{25 \text{ N}}$$

The diameter of the drum is 100 mm, so the perpendicular distance or radius is 50 mm.

Example. A torque of 484 Nm exists in the axle shafts of the driving wheels of a motor vehicle. The road wheels are 680 mm in diameter. What is the tractive effort?

Fig. 11.21 shows the layout of forces at the road wheels; the perpendicular distance or radius = 680 ÷ 2 = 340 mm

The radius is converted from mm to m as the units must be the same as those for the torque which is measured in Nm, i.e. 340 ÷ 1000 = 0·340 m.

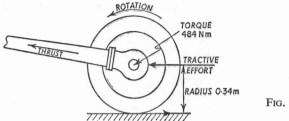

Fig. 11.21

The tractive effort is the horizontal force parallel to the road and opposite in direction to the reaction at the road.

Now   Torque = Force × perpendicular distance

$$\therefore \text{Force} = \frac{\text{Torque}}{\text{Distance}}$$

$$= \frac{484}{0.34}. \text{ N}$$

$$= \underline{1420 \text{ N}}$$

Example. The propeller shaft of a motor vehicle transmits a torque of 104 Nm. If the bolts attaching the universal joint to the driving flange are a p.c.d. (pitch circle diameter) of 75 mm, what shearing force are the bolts subject to (see Fig. 11.22)?

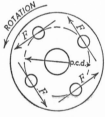

Fig. 11.22

Torque = 104 Nm

Torque = Force × perpendicular distance

$$\therefore \text{Force} = \frac{\text{Torque}}{\text{Distance}}$$

$$= \frac{104}{0.0375} \text{ N}$$

Shearing force = $\underline{2773 \text{ N}}$

Exercise 11

1. A trailer with a single axle is hitched to the vehicle hauling it at a point 2 m in front of the trailer axle. The trailer exerts a downward force of 2990 N at a point 0·7 m in front of the axle, while the load in the trailer is 6770 N, and this acts at a point 1·2 m in front of the axle. Calculate the load on the axle and the forces acting on the trailer hitch.

(4651·5 N;   5108·5 N)   (N.C.T.E.C.)

2. A bellcrank lever forming part of a braking system has its arms at right angles and the pull at each end is at right angles to the arm. One arm is 104 mm long and the pull in the rod connected to it is 665 N. If the other arm is 56 mm long, calculate (*a*) the pull in the other rod; (*b*) the magnitude and direction of the force acting on the fulcrum pin of the lever.

((*a*) 1235 N;   (*b*) 1403 N;   direction relative to (*a*) 28° 18′)
(N.C.T.E.C.)

3. The distance between the front and rear axles of a four-wheeled vehicle is 4 m. The load on the front axle is 6540 N, the load on the rear axle is 7780 N. Find how far behind the front axle of the vehicle lies its centre of gravity.   (2·18 m)   (E.M.E.U.)

4. The distance between the front and rear axles of a four-wheeled vehicle is 4·34 mm. The load on the front axle is 10 000 N, and the load on the rear axle is 12 460 N. Calculate how far the centre of gravity of the vehicles lies in front of the rear axle.

(1·933 m)   (U.E.I.)

5. The lifting gear on a tipping lorry is 2·8 m in front of the pivot point. The body contains two loads, one of 17 440 N, which is 0·75 m in front of the pivot point, and one of 4980 N, which is 1·6 m in front of the pivot. Calculate the force to be exerted by the lifting gear to just commence tipping the body. (Neglect the mass of the body.)

(7517 N)   (U.E.I.)

6. A ratchet lifting-jack handle is 1m long from the fulcrum and lifts 1745 N at a point 0·032 m from the fulcrum. Calculate the force required on the handle.   (55·84 N)   (U.E.I.)

7. A motor vehicle front axle is 1·27 m long between swivel pins centres, and the spring seat centres are 0·75 m apart. Under certain conditions the load on one spring seat is 3550 N and on the other 2220 N. Find the forces at the two swivel pins.

(3278 N;   2492 N)   (C. and G.)

8. A hand-brake lever is pivoted at a point 360 mm from the handle and the brake pull rod is coupled to the lever 88 mm beyond this point. If a force of 90 N is applied to the handle of the lever, what will be the pull in the brake rod, assuming that the forces are parallel and perpendicular to the lever?　　　　　　　　　(368 N)　(C. and G.)

9. A pinion shaft is supported by two bearings 100 mm apart with the pinion outside the bearings. A load of 11 120 N acts on the pinion at a point 45 mm from the centre of the nearest bearing and at right angles to the shaft. Calculate the load on each of the bearings.

(16 124 N;　5004 N)　(C. and G.)

10. A lorry exerts a total downward force of 58 620 N and has a wheelbase of 3·75 m. The centre of gravity is 1·75 m behind the front wheels. What upward force must a jack exert on the front axle beam to lift the front wheels just clear of the ground?　　　　(31 264 N)

11. To hold the valve in its closed position the valve spring exerts a force of 245 N. The valve rocker arm of this o.h.v. engine measures 105 mm between the centre lines of the point of contact of the valve stem and push rod; the centre line of the rocker shaft is 9 mm nearer the push-rod end. Find the force required along the push-rod just to lift the valve off its seat, assuming the forces are parallel and perpendicular to the rocker arm.　　　　　　　　(290·9 N)

12. A duralumin connecting rod has a length of 190 mm between the centres of the gudgeon pin and crankpin bearings, and exerts a downward force of 6·18 N with the gudgeon pin in place. The gudgeon pin is now supported in a pair of vee-blocks and a spring balance is attached to the big end exactly in line with the centre of the crankpin bearing. With the rod horizontal the reading on the spring balance is 4·12 N.

    (*a*) Find the position of the centre of gravity of the rod and gudgeon-pin combination.

    (*b*) If the gudgeon pin load is 1·03 N, find the position of the rod alone with the pin removed.

    ((*a*) 63·4 mm or 126·6 mm;　(*b*) 38 mm or 152 mm)　(C. and G.)

13. A gear lever has an overall length of 700 mm and is pivoted at a point 100 mm from its lower end. If a force of 108 N is required at the lower end to engage gears, what effort would be required at the other end of the lever?

If the overall length of the lever was increased by 150 mm, retaining the position of the pivot at 100 mm from its lower end, determine the amount by which the effort would be decreased.

(18 N;　3·6 N)　(C. and G.)

14. (*a*) State the principle of moments.

(*b*) A vehicle exerts a downward force of 8000 N and has a wheelbase of 3 m; the total concentrated load may be assumed to act 1·75 m in front of the rear axle. Find the static axle reactions.

(*c*) When a caravan towing hitch equal to a downward load of 600 N is coupled at a point 0·5 m behind the rear axle, determine the new axle reactions.

((*b*) 3333·3 N and 4666·6 N;   (*c*) 4033·3N;   4566·6N)

15. In an overhead valve engine with push rod type of operation, the push rod exerts a force of 420 N on the rocker. The horizontal distance measured between the centre of the valve and the fulcrum is 75 mm, the horizontal distance between the fulcrum and the push rod is 60 mm. Calculate (*a*) the force exerted on the valve stem; (*b*) the approximate movement of the push rod when the lift of the valve is 9·5 mm.

((*a*) 336 N;   (*b*) 7·6 mm)

16. A valve rocker shaft is supported by a bearing at each end, the bearing centres are 200 mm apart. At a given instant the shaft is subjected to two vertical loads, one of 1200 N at 50 mm from the front bearing centre and one of 1000 N at 150 mm from the front bearing centre. Calculate the load carried by each bearing.

(1050 N;   1150 N)

17. The layshaft in a gearbox is supported by two bearings which are 350 mm apart. The constant mesh gear is 50 mm from the front end of the gearbox and the first speed gear is 38 mm from the rear end of the gearbox. If the load on the constant-mesh gear is 7000 N and the load on the first gear is 6000 N, what is the load on each bearing?

(6348·5 N;   6651·5 N)

Work and Power

Work

Work is done when a force acting on a body causes it to move. If the force acting on the body does not produce movement, no work is done. When movement is in the direction of the force, the work done will be the product of that force and the distance moved.

Work is done when a car is lifted by a jack. The amount of work done will be the product of the upward force exerted by the jack and the distance the car is raised above the ground level.

Work is a form of energy and the unit for this is the **joule (J)**, it is the product of the force of 1 **newton (N)** moving a distance of 1 **metre (m)**.

$$\text{So 1 joule} = 1 \text{ newton metre}$$
$$\text{J} = \text{Nm}$$

If the work is done in one second, then 1 J/s = 1 Nm/s.

This is known as **Power (P)** since the unit of time has been introduced. Now power is measured in **watts (W)**. Therefore 1 J/s = 1 Nm/s = 1 W. The watt is a small unit, so the **kilowatt (kW)** may be used in its place, when high powers are calculated. The force which propels or moves the motor vehicle along the road is known as the **tractive force** or **tractive effort,** while the forces which oppose the forward motion of the vehicle are called the **tractive resistance.** In problems dealing with liquid force, this often has to be converted from the volume measurement of litres into newtons.

Work done, then, is the product of the applied force (F) and the distance (S) through which it moves.

Example. Find the work done when a force of 5970 N is required to lift an engine through a vertical distance of 1·35 m.

$$\text{Work done} = \text{Force} \times \text{distance}$$
$$= 5970 \times 1\cdot35 \text{ J}$$
$$\underline{8060 \text{ J of work}}$$

Example. A tractive effort of 1335 N propels a car at 50 km/h on a level road. How much work is done in one minute?

$$\text{Force} = 1335 \text{ N}$$

The distance must be expressed in m/min

$$50 \text{ km/h} = \frac{50\,000}{60} \text{ m/min}$$

$$\therefore \text{ Work done per min } = \text{Force} \times \text{distance}$$

$$= 1335 \times \frac{50\,000}{60} \text{ J}$$

$$\therefore \text{ Work done } = \underline{1\,112\,500 \text{ J/min}}$$

Suppose the vehicle considered in the previous question was ascending a hill with a gradient of 1 in 20; additional work would be done against the force of gravity To find this, the downward force of the vehicle and the vertical distance moved through in one minute must be found.

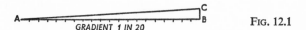

A ———————————— C
GRADIENT 1 IN 20 B   FIG. 12.1

Since the gradient is not very large, the vertical distance moved through in one minute can be found by dividing the distance covered in one minute by the gradient. This can be easily checked by drawing a right-angled triangle (Fig. 12.1) making AC the distance covered and the vertical axis CB the height climbed in one minute.

Let the downward force of vehicle be 12 460 N

$$\therefore \text{ Force } = 12\,460 \text{ N}$$

$$\text{Vertical distance} = \frac{\text{Distance covered}}{\text{Gradient}}$$

$$= \frac{50\,000}{60 \times 20}$$

$$= 41 \cdot 6 \text{ m}$$

Work done per minute against force of gravity

$$= \text{Force} \times \text{vertical distance}$$

$$= 12\,460 \times 41 \cdot 6 \text{ J}$$

$$= 518\,336 \text{ J}$$

Then work done per minute to propel vehicle up hill = Work done in propelling + work done against force of gravity

$$\therefore \text{ Total work done} = 1\ 112\ 500 + 518\ 336 \text{ J/min}$$
$$= \underline{1\ 630\ 836 \text{ J/min}}$$

Work done in Rotation

Force, however, does not always move in a straight line or path as previously considered; it often moves in a circular path such as the crankshaft of an engine, the propeller shaft, the axle shaft or the starting handle of a car.

Consider the starting handle of a car. Work done per revolution is the product of the applied force and the distance moved; this distance will be the circumference of a circle made by the point at which the force is applied.

$$\therefore \text{ Work done per rev} = \text{Force} \times \text{distance}$$
$$= \text{Force} \times 2\pi r$$

when r is the crank radius.

$$\text{Work done per min} = \text{Force} \times \text{distance moved per min}$$
$$= \text{Force} \times 2\pi r \times \text{rev/min}$$

when rev/min is the revolutions per minute.

$$\therefore \text{ W.D./min} = F \times 2\pi r \text{ rev/min (W.D. is work done)}$$

It will be seen that this equation contains two terms, force (F) and radius (r), whose product represents torque (T); so by rearranging the equation

$$\text{W.D./min} = Fr \times 2\pi \text{ rev/min}$$
$$= T \times 2\pi \text{ rev/min}$$

or
$$\text{W.D./min} = 2\pi\ T \text{ rev/min}$$

Example. To rotate a car engine at 40 rev/min an average force of 130 N is applied perpendicular to the crank arm of the starting handle The distance from the axis of the starting nut to the point of the applied force is 0·152 m

Find (*a*) Resisting torque (torque opposing rotation).

(*b*) Work done per minute.

(*a*) Resisting torque = Force × perpendicular distance

$$130 \times 0\text{·}152 \text{ Nm}$$
$$= \underline{19\text{·}76 \text{ Nm}}$$

(*b*) Work done per minute $= 2\pi\,T$ rev/min

$$= 2 \times 3\cdot1416 \times 40 \times 19\cdot76 \text{ J}$$
$$= \underline{4966 \text{ J}}$$

Part (*b*) of the problem was solved by using the torque value (*Fr*).

Efficiency of a Machine

The mechanical efficiency of a machine is the ratio of useful work done by a machine to the amount of work given to the machine.

Engineers always try to increase the efficiency of a machine by reducing to a minimum the frictional losses caused by the bearings, gear wheels, moving parts and lubricant.

In motor vehicles most of the power lost is in the engine, gear box and rear axle. The mechanical efficiency of the engine is between 80 and 90 per cent, while the gear-box efficiency in top gear exceeds 90 per cent, but is reduced when the indirect gears are used. The rear axle efficiency is between 90 and 95 per cent when bevel gears are used, but a lower figure when the worm type of drive is used.

Mechanical efficiency when expressed as a fraction will be

$$= \frac{\text{Work done by the machine}}{\text{Work given to the machine}}$$

or expressed as a percentage

$$= \frac{\text{Work done by the machine}}{\text{Work given to the machine}} \times 100$$

or

$$\frac{\text{Power output}}{\text{Power input}} \times 100$$

Example. The power developed in the cylinders of an engine is 56 kW and the power at the flywheel is 49 kW. What is the efficiency of the engine?

$$\text{Efficiency} = \frac{\text{Work done by the engine}}{\text{Work given to the engine}} \times 100$$

$$= \frac{49}{56} \times 100$$

$$= \underline{87\cdot5 \text{ per cent}}$$

Example. The rear axle of a car has an efficiency of 95 per cent when the power input is 45 kW. What is the power output?

$$\text{Efficiency} = \frac{\text{Power output}}{\text{Power input}} \times 100$$

$$\therefore \text{Power output} = \frac{\text{Efficiency} \times \text{power input}}{100}$$

$$= \frac{95 \times 45}{100}$$

$$= \underline{42\cdot75 \text{ kW}}$$

Example. A man does 2710 J of work operating a crane to lift an engine which requires a vertical force of 1270 N; the distance lifted is 1·22 m. What is the efficiency of the crane?

$$\text{Efficiency} = \frac{\text{Work done in lifting engine}}{\text{Work done by man}} \times 100$$

$$= \frac{1270 \times 1\cdot22}{2710} \times 100$$

$$= \underline{57\cdot18 \text{ per cent}}$$

Example. The power required to drive a car dynamo is 373 W and the electrical output is equivalent to 261 W. What is the efficiency of the dynamo?

$$\text{Efficiency} = \frac{\text{Power output}}{\text{Power input}} \times 100$$

$$= \frac{261}{373} \times 100$$

$$= \underline{70 \text{ per cent}}$$

Power

This is the rate of doing work; it is a measurement of the work done in one second.

$$\therefore \text{Power (W)} = \frac{\text{Work done}}{\text{Time in seconds}}$$

$$= \frac{\text{Force (N)} \times \text{distance moved (m)}}{\text{Time in seconds}} \text{ (Nm/s)}$$

i.e. $$\frac{(1 \text{ N} \times 1 \text{ m})}{1\text{s}}$$

When N, m and s each have **one** as a figure, then the power is one **watt (W)**

If a certain amount of work has to be done it could be completed in a short interval of time by a powerful machine or by a lower powered machine in a longer time; the power required to do work depends entirely on the length of time during which the work is done.

The rate of doing work $= \dfrac{\text{Total work done}}{\text{Time taken}}$

Example. A vertical force of 58 720 N lifts a vehicle through a distance of 1·5 m on a hydraulic ramp or hoist. Find the power required to lift it in (*a*) $\frac{1}{4}$ min, (*b*) $\frac{1}{2}$ min, (*c*) 1 min.

$$\text{Total work done} = \text{Force} \times \text{distance}$$
$$= 58\ 720 \times 1\cdot5 \text{ Nm}$$
$$= 88\ 080 \text{ Nm}$$

(*a*) Power required to lift vehicle in 15 sec

$$= \frac{88\ 080}{15}\left(\frac{\text{Nm}}{s}\right)$$
$$= 5872 \text{ W or } 5\cdot872 \text{ kW}$$

(*b*) Power required to lift vehicle in 30 sec

$$= \frac{88\ 080}{30}\left(\frac{\text{Nm}}{s}\right)$$
$$= 2936 \text{ W or } 2\cdot936 \text{ kW}$$

(*c*) Power required to lift vehicle in 60 sec

$$= \frac{88\ 080}{60}\left(\frac{\text{Nm}}{s}\right)$$
$$= 1468 \text{ W or } 1\cdot468 \text{ kW}$$

Example. The tractive resistance to forward motion of a motor vehicle is 1460 N when the vehicle is travelling at 54 km/h. What power does this represent?

Now 54 km/h = 15 m/s

$$\text{Power} = \frac{\text{Force} \times \text{distance}}{\text{Time}} \left(\frac{N \times m}{s} \right)$$

$$= \frac{1460 \times 15}{1} = 21\,900 \text{ W}$$

$$= \underline{21 \cdot 9 \text{ kW}}$$

Example. The torque of a propeller shaft is 120 Nm when it is rotating at 3000 rev/min. Find the power transmitted.

Work done per min = Torque × 2π × revolutions per minute

Torque (T) = 120 Nm

Rev/min = 50 rev/s

$$\text{Power} = \frac{\text{Force} \times \text{distance}}{\text{Time}} \left(\frac{N \times m}{s} \right)$$

$$= \frac{120 \times 2\pi \times 50}{1} = 37\,700 \text{ W}$$

$$= \underline{37 \cdot 7 \text{ kW}}$$

Example. A force of 200 N is exerted on the cutting tool of a lathe, the steel shaft being machined is 100 mm in diameter and rotating at 300 rev/min, what power does this represent?

Force F = 200 N

Circumference of shaft = $2\pi r$

rev/min = 300

$$= 2\pi \times 50 \text{ mm}$$

$$= \frac{2\pi \times 50 \text{ m}}{1000}$$

Distance moved/s $\qquad = \dfrac{100\pi}{1000} \times \dfrac{300}{60} \text{ m/s}$

Power $\qquad = \dfrac{200 \times 100\pi}{1000} \times \dfrac{300}{60} \text{ W}$

$$= \frac{200 \times 100 \times 3 \cdot 1416}{1000} \times \frac{300}{60} \text{ W}$$

$$= \underline{314 \cdot 16 \text{ W}}$$

Work done against Rotation

This is one method used for testing the power output of an engine or machine. The mechanical energy of the engine is changed by friction into heat energy, which in turn is dissipated to air or water.

Absorption dynamometers, as they are generally known, vary in design; the hydraulic type is normally used for testing motor vehicle engines.

The Hydraulic Dynamometer

This type of dynamometer is suitable for testing all types of automobile engines because it can operate over a wide range of speed and absorb high power outputs. Fig. 12.2 shows the general layout of the dynamometer.

The rotor which is coupled to the engine rotates in the casing through which water flows steadily, and the casing together with the torque arm is mounted on ball bearings fitted to the trunnion brackets. As the rotor rotates, water is flung from its cups into the cups of the casing; this force tends to turn the casing and the torque arm in the direction of rotation, thus lifting the 'load' carrier which is attached to the end of the arm. Adjustment for load is carried out by means of a handwheel which slides thin metal plates, known as 'sluice gates', between the rotor and the casing cups; this controls the exposed cup area and the larger the area, the greater the turning effort.

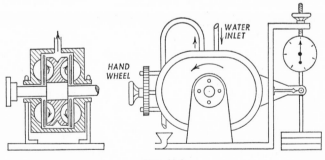

FIG. 12.2

To adjust the torque arm to a horizontal position the handwheel above the spring balance is rotated; when the torque arm is horizontal, the balance will record the downward force acting at its end. If this force is found to be greater than the balance scale range, a 'weight' (load) must be placed on the hanger and its force value added to that of the spring balance.

Large powers can be absorbed with this type of dynamometer since the heat energy is carried away by the water circulating through the casing.

In the following paragraph it is assumed that existing dynamometers using British units of force (lbf) and length (ft) will be in general use for several years. These dynamometers, however, can be used without modification for determining torque and power in SI units as shown on the following page.

Let $\qquad F$ = Downward load at the end of the torque arm (lbf)

$\qquad$ rev/min = Speed in revolutions per minute

$\qquad r$ = Length of torque arm (ft)

Then $\qquad$ Torque = Downward load × length of arm

$$= Fr$$

Work done per revolution = $F \times 2\pi r$ ft lbf

Work done per minute = $F \times 2\pi r \times$ rev/min ft lbf

$$\text{power} = \frac{\text{Work done per minute}}{33\ 000}$$

$$= \frac{F \times 2\pi r \times \text{rev/min}}{33\ 000}$$

The power formula for the Heenan-Froude dynamometer is reduced to the simple form of $\dfrac{F \text{ rev/min}}{K_\text{C}}$

The terms $\dfrac{2\pi r}{33\ 000} = \dfrac{1}{K_\text{C}}$.

To make the term K_C an easy figure for calculation the torque arm is made a definite length, and its length is therefore not given since it is included in the value of K_C.

The value of K_C varies with the size or capacity of the dynamometer and some of the values used are 2400, 2800, 3500, 4500 and 5500.

The formulae used to determine torque and power in SI units are:

$$\text{torque} = \frac{F \times 7121}{Kc} \text{ Nm}$$

and

$$\text{power} = \frac{F \times \text{rev/min} \times 0.7457}{Kc} \text{ kW}$$

Example. An engine undergoing power tests is coupled to a Heenan-Froude dynamometer. At 3500 rev/min the downward load is 65 lbf. If the constant Kc is 2800, what power is being developed in kW?

$$\text{Power P} = \frac{F \times \text{rev/min} \times 0.7457}{2800} = \frac{F \times \text{rev/min}}{3750}$$

$$= \frac{65 \times 3500}{3750} = \underline{60.66 \text{ kW}}$$

Later types of dynamometers will be provided with meters enabling the torque in Nm to be read directly, but it will not be possible for the dynamometer constant K to be a round figure number.

Determination of torque and power will require calculation using the following formulae.

Torque	*Power*
Nm = dial reading	$\text{kW} = \dfrac{\text{Nm} \times \text{rev/min}}{9549}$

Example. An engine on test running at 3000 rev/min has a torque meter reading of 175 Nm. Calculate the power of the engine.

$$\text{Power} = \frac{\text{Nm} \times \text{rev/min}}{9549}$$

$$= \frac{175 \times 3000}{9549}$$

$$= \underline{54.99 \text{ kW}}$$

Exercise 12

1. Determine the additional power which has to be expended by the engine if a car exerting a downward force of 8970 N has to climb an incline which raises it vertically at the rate of 33·5 m/min.

(5·008 kW)   (E.M.E.U.)

2. A pump raises 22 500 litres of water per hour through a height of 14 m. If the efficiency of the pump is 85%, what is the power expended?

(1008·8 W)   (E.M.E.U.)

3. The engine of a bus develops 60 kW at a speed of 72 km/h. If the efficiency of the transmission gear is 85%, what is the effective force propelling it on a horizontal road?

(2450 N)   (E.M.E.U.)

4. The force acting tangential to the pitch circle circumference of a gear wheel is 710 N. If the pitch circle diameter is 135 mm and the gear makes 1350 rev/min, calculate (a) the turning moment acting on the shaft carrying the gear, (b) the work done in joules (J) per minute as the gear rotates.   ((a) 47·94 Nm;   (b) 406·4 kJ)   (E.M.E.U.)

5. A turning moment of 45 Nm acts on a shaft to which is keyed a gear wheel having a pitch circle diameter of 100 mm. If the shaft makes 1200 rev/min, calculate (a) the force acting tangential to the pitch circle circumference of the wheel, (b) the work done in joules per minute by this force.   ((a) 900 N;   (b) 339 290 J)   (U.E.I.)

6. A loaded vehicle exerting a downward force of 52·31 kN climbed a gradient of slope 1 in 200, the gradient being 1463 m long. Calculate (a) the work done, (b) the power used for climbing if the speed of the vehicle was 9·5 km/h.   ((a) 382·6 kJ;   (b) 0·68 kW)   (U.E.I.)

7. If an engine drives a car against a total resistance of 1112 N over a distance of 402·5 m in half a minute, what power is being delivered by the crankshaft?   (15 918 W)   (C. and G.)

8. A motor vehicle exerting a downward force of 12·46 kN is raised 1·6 m above ground level on a lift in 40 seconds. How much work is done in lifting the vehicle?

What power does this represent?   (19·936 kJ;   (0·4984 kW)

9. An oil engine is connected to a Froude dynamometer for testing. When the engine speed is 1650 rev/min, the torque meter reading is 350 Nm. Find the power of the engine.   (138·8 kW)

10. The torque in the axle shaft of a vehicle travelling at 45 km/h is 615 Nm. If the rolling diameter of the road wheels is 797·5 mm, find (a) the tractive effort, (b) the power at the road wheels.

((a) 1544 N;   (b) 19·3 kW)

11. A vehicle exerting a downward force of 19 930 N descends an incline of 1 in 15 at a uniform speed with the engine switched off.

(a) What is the total resistance to its motion in newtons?

(*b*) What power would be required to drive the vehicle at 63 km/h against this resistance on a horizontal road?

((*a*) 1329 N;   (*b*) 23·26 kW)   (E.M.E.U.)

12. A motor vehicle with a load exerts a downward force of 19·93 kN and it is driven up an incline at a constant speed of 36 km/h. If at this speed the engine develops 14·92 kW and the efficiency of transmission is 80%, calculate the maximum gradient which can be climbed when the total resistances amount to 107 N.   (1 in 16·12)   (I.M.I.)

13. An engine drives a vehicle against a total resistance of 1068 N when travelling at 54 km/h.

Calculate the power developed by the engine.

(16·02 kW)   (E.M.E.U.)

14. A petrol engine connecting rod is 140 mm long and drives a crank of 38 mm radius. When the angle between the connecting rod and the crank is 90 degrees, calculate:

- (*a*) the angle between the centre lines of the connecting rod and cylinder;
- (*b*) (i) the torque on the crankshaft
- (*b*) (ii) the power developed when the thrust along the connecting rod is 2135 N and the crankshaft rotates at 3000 rev/min.

((*a*) 15° 17′;   (*b*) (i) 81·03 Nm;   (ii) 25·29 kW)   (U.E.I.)

15. An engine on test running at 3500 rev/min has a torque meter reading of 200 Nm.

Calculate the power of the engine   (73·31 kW)

13 Stress and Strain

The terms **stress** and **strain** tend to be loosely used in everyday life; in engineering, however, these terms have a precise meaning and they are normally applied to metals.

Every part of a vehicle has some form of load placed on it. These loads come from various sources, such as power impulses from the engine, road conditions, the vehicle's own mass and the load carried. Because of these loads a certain amount of strength is essential in the material used for the construction of the vehicle. The **strength** of a material means its resistance to stress; now what do we mean by **stress**? Stress is the internal reaction of a material to an outside load placed on it; this stress produces a corresponding deformation (change of shape) called **strain,** which is however usually slight. Several forms of stress will now be described.

(1) **Tensile stress** (Tension). See Fig. 10.2, Chapter 10.

When a material is subjected to a tensile stress, the material is stretched or an attempt is made to stretch it. Fig. 13.1 shows a bar loaded to produce tension and the extension (stretch).

(2) **Compressive stress** (Compression). See Fig. 10.5, Chapter 10.

When a material is subjected to a compressive stress, the material is under a pushing or crushing force. Fig. 13.2 shows a bar loaded to produce compression and reduction in length.

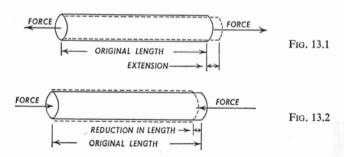

FIG. 13.1

FIG. 13.2

(3) **Shearing stress** (Shear). See Figs. 10.6 and 10.7, Chapter 10.

When a material is subjected to a shearing stress, the material is cut through or an attempt is made to cut it through at right angles—or nearly so—to its length. Fig. 13.3 shows a loaded clevis pin and fork end which produces a shearing action on the pin.

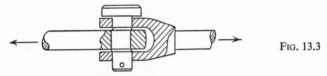

FIG. 13.3

(4) **Torsional stress** (Torsion). See Fig. 10.9, Chapter 10.

When a material is subjected to torsional stress the material is twisted or an attempt is made to twist it. This stress is in the nature of a shear. Fig. 13.4 shows a loaded rear axle half-shaft with the wheel hub at the left-hand end and the splines at the right-hand end. The splined end of the shaft is entered into the side-bevel gear where the splines are subjected to twist owing to the torque or load.

TWISTED SPLINES

FIG. 13.4

The foregoing stresses often combine to give compound stresses; for example, bending, which is partly a compressive stress and partly a tensile stress. Fig. 13.5 shows a loaded spring leaf which is subjected to tension in the upper half and compression in the lower half of the leaf.

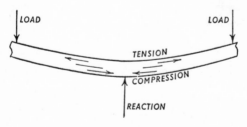

FIG. 13.5

We are able to calculate stress by using the following formula:

$$\text{Stress} = \frac{\text{Load (N)}}{\text{Area resisting load (m}^2)} \; \text{N/m}^2$$

The N/m^2 is the standard unit for stress, but, since m^2 is a large area it is often more convenient to use N/mm^2 or kN/mm^2.

Example. The tensile load or pull in a steel brake rod of 6·4 mm diameter is $12 \cdot 2 \times 10^3$ N. Find the maximum stress in the rod.

$$\text{Stress} = \frac{\text{Load}}{\text{Area resisting load}}$$

In this example, the area resisting the load is the cross-sectional area of the rod, and as the rod is 6·4 mm diameter, then this area will be:

$$\text{Area} = \pi \times 3 \cdot 2^2 = 32 \cdot 15 \text{ mm}^2$$

$$\therefore \text{Stress} = \frac{12200}{32 \cdot 15} = \underline{37 \cdot 93 \text{ N/mm}^2}$$

Strain. When a load is applied to any part of a vehicle, the material from which the part is made changes its shape. The change in the shape of the material, caused by the load, is called **strain,** and it is defined:

Strain is the deformation or change of shape, normally very small, caused by the stress.

It should be realized, however, that although all parts of a vehicle are under stress the efficiency of the vehicle would be lowered if the parts were unduly strained. The various stresses, already outlined, each have their particular form of strain, i.e. stretching, compression, twisting, and so on.

Strain is calculated by using the following formula:

$$\text{Strain} = \frac{\text{Change in length, in millimetres}}{\text{Original length, in millimetres}}$$

Example. A mild steel bar 250 mm long and 12·5 mm diameter is subjected to a direct pull of 20 000 N. Calculate the stress in the material and the strain produced when the bar is stretched to 250·05 mm.

$$\text{Stress} = \frac{\text{Load}}{\text{Area}} = \frac{20\,000}{\pi \times 6 \cdot 25^2} = \underline{163 \text{ N/mm}^2}$$

Note, when calculating stress, we do not take into account the length of the rod.

$$\text{Strain} = \frac{\text{Change in length}}{\text{Original length}} = \frac{250 \cdot 05 - 250}{250} = \underline{0 \cdot 0002}$$

Note that strain is a **ratio** of lengths and thus has no units.

Elasticity

When a loaded and therefore stressed material returns to its original shape after removing the load, we call such a material **elastic**. This property of elasticity holds good up to a point called the **elastic limit** of the material. Should a part however be loaded so that the stress in the material exceeds the elastic limit, then the part will remain deformed when the load is removed. For example, when sheet metal for vehicle bodies is formed into various shapes, the metal will remain in its new shape and is said to have a **permanent set**.

An important law called **Hooke's Law** deals with the stress and strain set up in an elastic material when the material is loaded. This law applies to every form of strain, including stretching (tension), compression, shearing, and so on.

Hooke's law states: 'The strain produced in a material is directly proportional to the stress producing it.'

By this we mean that if a certain stress causes a material to stretch, say, 0·01 mm, then, if the stress is doubled, the stretch will be doubled also, i.e. 0·02 mm, and when the stress is trebled, the stretch will be trebled also, i.e. 0·03 mm.

Hooke's Law is expressed by a formula:

$$\frac{\text{Stress}}{\text{Strain}} = \text{a ratio}$$

which is a constant, but depends on the material and the type of the stress.

The ratio for tension is called **Young's Modulus of Elasticity**, which is represented by the symbol E. The meaning of the term modulus is 'a number which measures'; thus E can be considered as a number which measures the elasticity of a material per unit of area.

The following list gives the approximate values of E for various metals:

Material	*Modulus of Elasticity* (N/mm^2)
Steel	207 000
Cast iron	117 000
Phosphor-bronze	96 000
Copper	83 000
Brass	69 000

Now, $$\text{Stress} = \frac{\text{Load}}{\text{Area}}$$

and
$$\text{Strain} = \frac{\text{Extension}}{\text{Original length}}$$

also
$$E = \frac{\text{Stress}}{\text{Strain}} \text{ or } E = \frac{\text{Load}}{\text{Area}} \div \frac{\text{Extension}}{\text{Original length}}$$

$$\therefore E = \frac{\text{Load}}{\text{Area}} \times \frac{\text{Original length}}{\text{Extension}}$$

It will be seen that this last formula is a combination of the stress and strain formulae and we can use it to calculate the value of any one unknown quantity if all the other values are known. The following worked example shows this formula in use.

Example. A mild steel rod 200 mm long and 25 mm diameter is subjected to a tensile load of 99 630 N. Calculate the stretch caused by this load. ($E = 207\,000$ N/mm^2)

$$E = \frac{\text{Load} \times \text{length}}{\text{Area} \times \text{extension}}$$

$$207\,000 = \frac{99\,630 \times 200}{\pi \times 12 \cdot 5^2 \times \text{stretch}}$$

Transposing,
$$\text{Stretch} = \frac{99\,630 \times 200}{\pi \times 12 \cdot 5^2 \times 207\,000} = \underline{0 \cdot 196 \text{ mm}}$$

Hooke's Law, however, holds good only up to the elastic limit of a material. Beyond this point the metal is no longer elastic and strain is no longer proportional to stress.

The following worked examples show the method of solving simple problems concerning two forms of shear stress, namely, the punching of holes in metal and the double shear as found in clevis pins, rivets, and so on, see Fig. 13.3.

Example. Calculate the force required to punch a hole 6·3 mm diameter in a plate 6·3 mm thick if the shear strength of the metal is 207 N/mm^2.

In this example the area resisting shear is equal to the circumference of the hole multiplied by the thickness of the plate, then:

$$\text{Area resisting} = 6 \cdot 3\,\pi \times 6 \cdot 3$$
$$= 124 \cdot 7 \text{ mm}^2$$

Now
$$\text{Stress} = \frac{\text{Load or force}}{\text{Area}}$$

$$207 = \frac{\text{Force}}{124 \cdot 7}$$

Transposing,

$$\text{Force} = 207 \times 124 \cdot 7$$
$$= \underline{25\ 810\ \text{N}}$$

Example. A brake rod is connected to the hand brake by a forked end and clevis pin of 12·5 mm diameter. If the pull in the rod is 4894 N, what is the shear stress in the clevis pin?

In this example the pin is in double shear and the total area resisting shear is *twice* the area of the clevis pin.

$$\text{Stress} = \frac{\text{Load}}{\text{Area} \times 2}$$

$$= \frac{4894}{\pi \times 6 \cdot 25^2 \times 2} \ \text{N/mm}^2$$

$$= 19 \cdot 9 \ \text{N/mm}^2$$

Exercise 13

1. A steel brake rod is subjected to a maximum tensile load of 1120 N. If the diameter of the rod is 6 mm, calculate the tensile stress in the rod in N/mm². $(39 \cdot 5 \ \text{N/mm}^2)$

2. Calculate the average value of the shear stress in a solid gudgeon pin of 25 mm diameter when the load on the pin is 37 800 N.

$(38 \cdot 5 \ \text{N/mm}^2)$ (E.M.E.U.)

3. To what kinds of stress are the following parts of a motor vehicle subjected?

(*a*) Connecting rod. (*b*) Rear axle shafts. (*c*) Cylinder head studs. (*d*) Propeller shaft. (*e*) King-pins.

Explain how the stress is caused in each part.

4. A hand-brake lever has the effort applied at 375 mm from the fulcrum. The brake-actuating rod, which has a diameter of 6·3 mm, is attached at 75 mm from the fulcrum. Both forces act at right angles to the lever which is straight throughout its length. If the applied effort is 355 N, find the tensile stress in the rod.

$(56 \cdot 94 \ \text{N/mm}^2)$ (C. and G.)

5. A metal bar of length 250 mm and cross-sectional area 145 mm² is gradually loaded in tension up to the elastic limit. It is found that a load of 24·91 kN produces an extension of 0·22 mm. Find Young's Modulus for the metal.

(197 200 N/mm²) (N.C.T.E.C.)

6. A steel rod 19 mm diameter carries a pull of 59·78 kN. Calculate the extension in mm on a length of 305 mm.

(E = 207 000 N/mm²)   (0·311 mm) (N.C.T.E.C.)

7. A piece of 25 mm square mild steel bar is placed between the jaws of a parallel bench vice and the vice is tightened. Explain the kind of stress that will be caused in (*a*) the bar; (*b*) the screw of the vice; (*c*) the vice handle, as the jaws are tightened on the bar. (U.E.I.)

8. A 25 mm diameter hole is punched out of a plate 1·5 mm thick. The shear strength of the material is 241 N/mm². Calculate the load on the punch and the work done.

(28 403 N; 42·604 J) (U.L.C.I.)

9. The bearing cap of a crankshaft main bearing is secured by two 16 mm bolts which have a core diameter of 13·2 mm. Find the average stress in the bolts if the maximum force against the bearing cap is 17·79 kN.   (65·03 N/mm²) (U.L.C.I.)

10. With the aid of sketches distinguish between tensile stress and shearing stress.

Calculate the force required to punch a hole 19 mm diameter in a plate 12·5 mm thick if the shear strength of the material is 510 N/mm².

(380·6 kN) (N.C.T.E.C.)

11. A vertical steel wire 4·572 m long and 2·03 mm diameter carries a load of 445 N. Calculate the extension of the wire if E = 193 100 N/mm².   (3·25 mm) (N.C.T.E.C.)

12. (*a*) Explain clearly what is meant by the terms 'stress', 'strain', 'modulus of elasticity'.

(*b*) A mild steel rod has to carry an axial pull of 47·82 kN. The maximum permissible stress is 123·5 N/mm². Calculate a suitable diameter for the rod.   (22·2 mm) (U.E.I.)

13. A brake rod of 16 mm diameter is subjected to a tensile force of 2446 N. Calculate the tensile stress in N/mm².

(12·2 N/mm²) (E.M.E.U.)

14   Heat

Heat and Temperature

The terms **heat** and **temperature** are often confused. **Heat** is a form of energy; motor-vehicle engines are known as 'heat' engines, making use of the heat energy released when petrol or oil vapour is ignited and 'burnt'. **Temperature** is the degree of hotness or coldness of a body. Heat is the energy required to increase the temperature of a body and the amount of heat required for any temperature rise depends on the mass of the body being heated. A large kettle full of water will take longer to boil than a small kettle when heat is applied at a constant rate.

Other examples are thermostats fitted in engine cooling systems to ensure rapid 'warming-up' of the engine. In this instance, only a small part of the water in the system is heated; the thermostat valve prevents complete water circulation until a certain temperature is reached. More heat is required for welding cylinder blocks than for welding wings.

To decrease the temperature of a body, heat must be removed; e.g. water in the cooling system of an engine removes heat from the engine and finally dissipates (gets rid of) this heat mainly through the radiator into the air.

When heat is applied to most materials, certain effects may be noticed:

(1) Change of shape or size. When heat is added to or subtracted from metals, liquids or gases they expand or contract, e.g. a starter ring gear is expanded by heating it in order to assist fitting.

(2) Change of condition. Water will boil and be converted into steam when sufficient heat is applied to it or will turn into ice when sufficient heat is extracted from it.

(3) Change of composition. When petrol and oil are heated in air they burn to form carbon and a mixture of gases.

(4) Change of colour. When bright steel is heated it shows several different colours, e.g. blue, purple, dark straw, light straw, and so on.

(5) Electrical effect. If heat is applied to the junction of two metals of different composition, a small electric current is produced which can be measured by a **galvanometer** (a sensitive electrical measuring device). The junction of the two metals is called a **thermocouple**, and its use for measuring high temperature will be described later in this chapter.

Measurement of Temperature

The usual method of measuring temperature is by means of a **thermometer**. This device consists of a glass tube of uniform bore, sealed at its upper end, with a small bulb containing mercury at its lower end. A change in temperature causes the mercury to expand or contract more than the glass which contains it. The level of mercury will rise or fall in the tube as the temperature rises or falls and the change in the level of the mercury is used as an indicator of temperature.

A thermometer is sometimes fitted in the water cooling system of an engine in order to indicate the working temperature of the engine.

The temperature scale is the degree Celsius (°C) and will be known as the customary temperature of heat.

The fixed points on the scale are 0° and 100°, with 100 equal divisions between. When the atmosphere pressure is 101·4 kN/m^2, then water freezes or ice melts at 0°C. At 100°C water boils.

High Temperature Measurement

In the measurement of high temperatures, e.g. as required in the heat treatment of metals, the mercury thermometer is unsuitable and other methods must be used. One such instrument, called the **pyrometer**, indicates temperature readings by the small current of electricity produced when heat is applied to a thermocouple.

Measurement of Heat

To find the quantity of heat required to change the temperature of a given substance, the following must be considered:

(1) The mass of the substance.

(2) The nature of the substance.

(3) The number of degrees of temperature change.

For example: (1) A large soldering- 'iron' takes longer to heat than a small iron on the same gas heater.

(2) A piece of copper of mass 1 kg requires only one tenth the quantity of heat required by 1 kg of water in order to change its temperature by the same amount.

(3) When the cooling water of an engine boils we say the engine is 'overheated'. By this we mean that the temperature of the water has risen to boiling point because more than the normal quantity of heat has passed to the cooling water.

The unit for the measurement of heat is the joule (J) or the kilojoule (kJ) for large quantities.

Specific Heat Capacity

As stated earlier in this chapter, the nature of a substance affects the quantity of heat required to change its temperature. So far we have only compared copper and water, but many other substances also require less heat than water to change their temperature when equal masses of the substances are considered. Water is therefore taken as a standard for comparison and a figure of 4·187 kJ/kg °C has been assigned as the specific heat capacity of water. This figure of 4·187 kJ/kg °C serves as a comparison with the quantity of heat required to give 1 degree rise in temperature to 1 kg of a substance and a figure of specific heat capacity is given to each substance. A list of the specific heat capacities of the common materials used in motor vehicles is given:

Water	4·187	Steel	0·485
Alcohol	2·512	Copper	0·4187
Petrol	1·817	Brass	0·397
Aluminium	0·879	Lead	0·129
Cast iron	0·502		

The values given are only accurate at one given temperature, but for practical purposes they may be considered as correct at all normal temperatures.

The following example will show the method employed to calculate the number of heat units required to raise a certain mass of water by a given number of degrees. The general expression for calculating quantities of heat is:

Heat required or given out = The mass of the substance × temperature interval × the specific heat capacity.

Example. In the cooling system of a certain engine the mass of water is 11·5 kg. How much heat is given by the engine to the water if its temperature increases from 15°C to 95°C?

Mass of water $= 11\cdot5$ kg

Temperature interval $= 95 - 15 = 80°C$

Heat to cooling water $=$ Mass of water $\times$ temperature interval $\times$ specific heat capacity

$$= 11\cdot5 \times 80 \times 4\cdot187 \text{ kJ}$$
$$= \underline{3825 \text{ kJ}}$$

Specific heat capacity is often used in carburation problems, e.g. in the design of an efficient 'hot-spot'.

Example. In order to give efficient carburation, the temperature of a certain carburettor 'hot-spot' has to be raised from 15°C to 150°C. What quantity of heat must be passed by the exhaust system to the cast-iron induction pipe weighing 0·27 kg? (Specific heat capacity of cast-iron 0·502).

Heat required $=$ Mass $\times$ specific heat capacity $\times$ temperature interval

$$= 0\cdot27 \times 0\cdot502 \times (150 - 15)$$
$$= \underline{18\cdot3 \text{ kJ}}$$

Example. A certain engine is fitted with a pump which circulates the cooling water at a rate of 90 litres per minute. The temperature at the top of the radiator is 84°C and the temperature at the bottom of the radiator is 75°C. Calculate the quantity of heat passed to the cooling water (1 litre of water has a mass of 1 kg).

Heat passed to cooling water

$$= \text{Mass} \times \text{specific heat capacity} \times \text{temperature interval}$$
$$= 90 \times 4\cdot187 \times (84 - 75) \text{ kJ}$$
$$= \underline{3391\cdot47 \text{ kJ}}$$

Heat Transfer

Heat always flows from the hotter to the colder body or substance (from one at a high temperature to one at a low temperature). For example, two substances at different temperatures when mixed together will reach the same temperature, i.e. the heat lost by one substance (hot) equals the heat gained by the other substance (cold); neglecting any loss of heat during the transfer.

The following examples deal with heat transfer and show the methods used.

Example. A piece of iron of mass 1·8 kg is heated in a furnace to a temperature of 500°C and then placed in a tank containing 45 litres of water at a temperature of 15°C. If the final temperature of the water and iron in the tank is found to be 17·3°C, what is the specific heat capacity of the iron? (Neglect any other loss of heat.)

$$\text{Initial temperature of iron} = 500°C$$
$$\text{Final temperature of iron } 17·3°C$$
$$\therefore \text{ Temperature change of iron} = 500 - 17·3 = 482·7 \text{ degrees C}$$
$$\text{Mass of iron} = 1·8 \text{ kg}$$
$$\text{Let the specific heat capacity of iron} = s$$
$$\text{Then heat lost by iron} = 1·8 \times s \times 482·7$$
$$\text{Initial temperature of water} = 15°C$$
$$\text{Final temperature of water} = 17·3°C$$
$$\therefore \text{ Temperature change} = 2·3 \text{ degrees C}$$
$$\text{Mass of water} = 45 \text{ kg}$$
$$\therefore \text{ Heat gained by water} = 45 \times 2·3 \times 4·187 \text{ kJ}$$

Now, neglecting other losses, the heat lost by the iron must pass to the water.

$$\text{Thus, heat lost by iron} = \text{heat gained by water}$$
$$\therefore 1·8 \times s \times 482·7 = 45 \times 2.3 \times 4·187$$
$$\therefore s = \frac{45 \times 2·3 \times 4·187}{1·8 \times 482·7}$$
$$= \underline{0·498}$$

Example. A piece of copper of mass 1·5 kg is heated to 140°C and then quickly placed in a copper vessel called a calorimeter, of mass 0·75 kg and containing 0·75 kg of water both at a temperature of 10°C. The temperature of the calorimeter and its contents is thus increased to 30°C. What is the specific heat of the copper?

Let s = Specific heat capacity of copper, then:

Heat lost by copper = Heat gained by water + heat gained by calorimeter

Now,

$$\text{Heat lost by copper} = \text{Mass of copper} \times s \times \text{temp. change}$$
$$= 1·5 \times s \times (140 - 30)$$
$$= 165s \text{ kJ}$$

$$\left. \begin{array}{l} \text{Heat gained by water} \\ + \text{ heat gained by} \\ \text{calorimeter} \end{array} \right\} = \left\{ \begin{array}{l} \text{Mass of water} \times \text{temp. change} \\ + \text{ Mass of copper} \times s \times \text{temp.} \\ \text{change} \end{array} \right.$$
$$= 0·75 \times 4·187 \times (30 - 10) + 0·75 \times s \times (30 - 10)$$
$$= 15 \times 4·187 + 15s$$

$$\text{Heat lost } = \text{ Heat gained}$$
$$165s = 15 \times 4 \cdot 187 + 15s$$
$$165s - 15s = 15 \times 4 \cdot 187$$
$$150s = 15 \times 4 \cdot 187$$
$$s = \frac{15 \times 4 \cdot 187}{150} = \underline{0 \cdot 4187}$$

The calorimeter containing the water will absorb some heat because its temperature will always be the same as that of the water, and in this example an allowance is made for the heat absorbed in this way.

Sensible heat. Heat which results in a change of temperature of a substance is called **sensible heat.** For example, in order to raise the temperature of 1 kg of water from 0°C to 100°C, the quantity of heat required (all of which is sensible heat) will be 100 × 4·187 kJ.

Latent heat. When additional heat is applied to boiling water the condition of the water will change, i.e. steam will form, but there will be no further rise in temperature. The quantity of heat required to bring about this change is called **latent heat** and it is the quantity of heat producing a change of condition without a change of temperature or pressure. The term latent heat means 'hidden' heat and there are two forms of this heat:

(1) When a substance changes from a solid to a liquid, the heat required to bring about this change is called the **latent heat of fusion**; there is no change of temperature. For example, sodium-filled valves are used in certain engines and in service the salts change into a liquid at high temperatures. In this way heat is transferred from the head of the valve to the stem, where it can easily pass through the guide into the cooling water and thus prevents the valve temperature rising too high.

(2) When a substance changes from a liquid to a vapour or a gas, the heat required to bring about this change is called the **latent heat of vaporization** and again there is no change of temperature. For example, in the vaporization of petrol, as it passes from the carburettor to the induction pipe and cylinders, heat is required. This heat is drawn from the induction pipe and surrounding metal. In order to assist vaporization it is usual to apply heat to the petrol–air mixture by means of a 'hot-spot'.

The amount of heat required for the complete vaporization of 1 kg of ordinary petrol is from 315 to 325 kJ; the alcohol type of fuel takes considerably more heat.

The following list gives the latent heat of vaporization of various common substances.

						J/kg	kJ/kg
Water	.	.	.	.	.	2 256 000	2256
Ethyl alcohol	.	.	.	.	.	1 191 000	1191
Alcohol	.	.	.	.	.	998 600	998·6
Methyl alcohol	.	.	.	.	.	923 400	923·4
Paraffin	.	.	.	.	.	607 000	607
Benzol	.	.	.	.	.	395 400	395·4
Petrol	.	.	.	.	.	313 900	313·9

Example. A radiator holds 10 litres of water. When cold, the temperature of the water is 10°C. How many kilo-joules would it take to evaporate all this water at the ordinary boiling temperature?

1 litre of water has a mass of 1 kg

Latent heat of steam = 2256 kJ/kg

Heat to raise temp of 10 kg of water

from 10°C to 100°C = Quantity × sp. ht. capacity × temp. rise

= 10 × 4·187 kJ (100 − 10)

= 3768 kJ

Heat to convert 10 kg of water at 100°C

into 10 kg of steam at 100°C = Quantity × latent heat

= 10 × 2256 kJ

= 22 560 kJ

Total heat required = 22 560 + 3768 kJ

= 26 328 kJ

Transfer of Heat

There are three ways in which heat can be transferred:

(1) **Radiation** (heat travels across open space).

For example, from a fire, radiator or hot-water pipe.

(2) **Conduction** (heat travels through the material from the hotter to the colder part of a body).

For example, heat is conducted through the cooling 'fins' of an air-cooled engine into the air.

(3) **Convection** (heat travels from one point to another point by the movement of gases or liquids).

For example, exhaust gases and the cooling water in an engine. The cooling system of a vehicle employs all three methods:

(*a*) Heat is radiated from the radiator to the air.

(*b*) Heat is conducted from the cylinder walls and pistons to the cooling water or the air or both.

(*c*) Heat is convected to the air by means of the cooling water and the exhaust gases.

Thermal (Heat) Conductivity

Materials have different degrees of heat **conductivity,** i.e. the ability to conduct or dissipate heat. The following list gives the conductivity of various metals; for the purpose of comparison, silver, the best conductor, is given the value 100.

Silver	100·0	Iron	11·9
Copper	74·0	Steel	11·6
Aluminium	32·0	Lead	8·5
Tin	15·2		

When compared with cast iron, the fitting of aluminium-alloy pistons and cylinder heads is preferred owing to the superior heat dissipation of the aluminium alloy. Copper tubes and sheets are used in the manufacture of radiator 'cores' because they are excellent conductors of heat.

Calorific Value of Fuels

The **calorific** (heat) value of a fuel is the number of heat units, in J or kJ, released when 1 kg of the fuel is burnt completely. For example, the calorific value of petrol is about 47 500 kJ/kg, i.e. 47 500 kJ are released when 1 kg of petrol is burnt completely.

The following list gives the calorific value of the fuels normally used in motor vehicles.

Fuel	*Calorific Value* (kJ)
Petrol	47 500 per kg
Benzol	42 600 ,, ,,
Alcohol	28 000 ,, ,,
Diesel fuel-oil	40 500 ,, ,,

These figures give what is called the **lower calorific value** of the fuel. A higher figure, called the **higher calorific value** of the fuel, is sometimes given, but this takes into account the latent heat of the steam produced during the burning of the fuel. This latent heat however does not appear as sensible heat in the combustion chamber of an engine and it cannot be used by the engine for useful work. It is usual, therefore, to subtract the value of the latent heat of the steam in order to give the lower calorific value of the fuel.

EXPANSION AND CONTRACTION OF MATERIALS

When most materials are heated they **expand** and thus increase their volume. One example of expansion is the fitting of the starter ring gear to the flywheel. The gear is heated until it expands sufficiently to pass over the rim of the flywheel, and when it is cool the gear tries to return to its original size, thus gripping the flywheel with considerable force.

All metals do not expand equally when heated through the same range of temperature, e.g. aluminium alloy expands more than cast iron; copper and brass expand more than mild steel. Gudgeon pins (hardened steel) are removed and replaced by dipping aluminium-alloy pistons in boiling or very hot water; the difference in expansion—the piston expands more than the gudgeon pin—makes the pin an easy push fit.

Coefficient of Expansion

A number which denotes the degree of expansion of a substance is called the **coefficient of expansion** of the material. There are three types of expansion namely, **linear, superficial** and **cubical,** and each has its own coefficient of expansion:

(1) The **coefficient of linear expansion** is the increase in unit length of a material when its temperature is raised by 1 degree C. The co-efficients of linear expansion for various metals have been found by experiment and they are given in the list below.

(2) The **coefficient of superficial expansion** is the increase in unit area of a material when its temperature is raised by 1 degree C. Its value is double that of the coefficient of linear expansion for the same material.

(3) The **coefficient of cubical expansion** is the increase in unit volume of a material when its temperature is raised by 1 degree C. Its value is three times that of the coefficient of linear expansion for the same material.

Heat

Coefficient of Linear Expansion

Material							Per 1 deg C
Mercury .	.	.	.	.	.	.	0·000 059 9
Aluminium	.	.	.	.	.	.	0·000 022 1
Brass .	.	.	.	.	.	.	0·000 018 9
Copper .	.	.	.	.	.	.	0·000 017 1
Iron .	.	.	.	.	.	.	0·000 011 7
Cast Iron	.	.	.	.	.	.	0·000 011 2
Steel .	.	.	.	.	.	.	0·000 011 9
Invar .	.	.	.	.	.	.	0·000 001 0

Taking aluminium as an example: one mm of aluminium expands 0·000 022 1 mm for 1 deg C rise in temperature. One metre of aluminium expands 0·000 022 1 metre for 1 deg C rise in temperature. If the temperature rise is doubled the expansion (increase in length) will be doubled also, e.g. one mm of aluminium will expand 0·000 022 1 multiplied by 2, equals 0·000 044 2 mm for a 2 deg C rise in temperature, and a two mm length of aluminium will also expand 0·000 022 1 multiplied by 2 for 1 deg C rise in temperature.

We are now able to calculate the increase in length (linear expansion) of a material and the following examples show the methods used. One example of cubical expansion is also given.

Example. An exhaust pipe 3 m long has its temperature raised from 15°C to 125°C; if the coefficient of expansion of the steel used is 0·000 011 9 per degree C, calculate the increase in length of the pipe.

Expansion = Original length × coefficient of expansion × temp. rise
= 3 × 1000 × 0·000 011 9 × (125 − 15)mm
= 3·927 mm

Example. An aluminium-alloy piston is machined to a diameter of 100 mm; the temperature is 20°C during this operation.

When in the cylinder the working temperature of the piston is 205°C. Calculate the increase in diameter of the piston at its working temperature. (Coefficient of expansion of the aluminium alloy 0·000 022 1 per degree C.)

Noting that any increase in diameter is a linear increase, then:

Increase in diameter = Original diameter × coefficient of expansion × temp. rise
= 100 × 0·000 022 1 × (205 − 20) mm
= 0·4089 mm

Example. Calculate the gap required in a piston ring to allow for expansion, under working conditions, given the following data:

Cylinder bore diameter, 60 mm

Normal temperature, 18°C

Working temperature, 162°C

Coefficient of expansion, cast iron, 0·000 011 2 per degree C

Ring circumference = 60 × π mm (linear measurement)

Ring expansion = Circumference × coefficient of expansion × temperature rise

$$= 60 \times \pi \times 0.000\ 011\ 2 \times (162 - 18)\ \text{mm}$$
$$= \underline{0.3041\ \text{mm}}$$

Therefore the gap necessary to allow for expansion should be at least 0·3 mm. In practice, however, the cylinder expands also and the ring gap would be rather less than this figure.

Liquids and gases have no definite form, and when heated cubical expansion only takes place. The cubical coefficients of expansion (each given as per degree C) of three common fluids are:

Water, 0·000 45

Petrol, 0·002 17

Air,   0·003 65

Further useful applications of expansion in motor vehicle operation are:

(1) Thermostats, which depend on the expansion and evaporation of a liquid for their operation.

(2) Automatic carburettor air-stranglers ('chokes') which use bi-metallic strips for their operation.

(3) Temperature correction of compensated voltage control units, also by means of bimetallic strips. The term 'bimetallic' refers to two strips of metal, one steel and the other brass or bronze, riveted together. Any temperature rise will cause the brass or bronze strip to expand more than the steel strip thus making the strip bend; this is sometimes called the 'differential expansion' of two metals.

Example. The cooling system of an engine contains exactly 9 litres of water. Before starting the engine, the temperature of the water is 15°C; after a run the temperature of the water is found to be 85°C. Calculate the volume of water lost by expansion through the overflow pipe (cubical expansion of water is 0·000 45 per 1 degree C).

Expansion of water = Volume of water × coefficient of expansion ×
(water lost)   temperature rise

$$= 9 \times 0.000\ 45 \times (85 - 15) \text{ litres}$$
$$= \underline{\underline{0.2834 \text{ litres}}}$$

Contraction

Contraction is the reverse of expansion, and reducing the temperature of a material results in a decrease of its dimensions, i.e. the material contracts. Most metals contract when subjected to low temperatures. The following are some examples of contraction:

(1) Cylinder liners and valve seat inserts are cooled and contracted by contact with liquid air which has a temperature of about minus − 80°C; after fitting, the liners and inserts return to normal temperature and they expand back to normal size and grip the cylinder block with great force. Owing to the varying temperatures to which valve inserts are subjected the fitting allowance for inserts is usually greater than that allowed for liners, Thus, a valve insert of 28·5 mm nominal diameter will have a fitting allowance of about 0·155 mm, but a liner of 75 mm nominal outside diameter will have a fitting allowance of 0·06 mm. heat.

(2) Chassis frame cross-members are sometimes riveted with red-hot rivets which cool and contract, thus drawing the side and cross-members tightly together at the joint.

MECHANICAL EQUIVALENT OF HEAT

Heat is a form of energy which can be used to do useful work, and work, useful or otherwise, can be changed into heat. The following examples illustrate this principle.

(1) In petrol and c.i. engines the heat produced by combustion of the air–fuel mixture results in an expansion of the gases thus formed. This expansion forces the piston along the cylinder and thus does useful work.

(2) When a vehicle is brought to rest by means of the brakes there is a rise of temperature of the brakes, i.e. the energy of the moving vehicle is changed into heat.

(3) During most machining operations the job and the tool become hot, and in order to keep the temperature fairly normal, a cooling

liquid (a 'coolant') is arranged to pass over the tool; the machining is thus carried out more efficiently.

From these examples we see there is a connection between work and heat.

Dr. **Joule** conducted numerous experiments and succeeded in finding the value of one heat unit in work units. This value is called **Joule's Mechanical Equivalent of Heat** denoted by the symbol J.

Mechanical and Heat Units of Power

We have already seen the relationship between work and power and also the relationship between work and heat. It follows therefore that a relationship between heat and power must also exist.

Now $\quad\quad (1 \text{ J/s} = \text{W}) = (1 \text{ Js} = 1 \text{ Nm/s})$

The foregoing units of heat and power are often used in testing engines in order to determine the distribution of the heat energy contained in the fuel.

Examples of this distribution will be given in the second part of this book.

Example. A heavy goods vehicle completes a journey in 5·5 hours; only 25 kg of the fuel consumed is converted into useful work. One kg of oil when burned gives out 40 500 kJ. Find how many joules of energy are available per minute and the power this represents.

Total heat supplied = Mass of fuel $\times$ calorific value of fuel
$$= 25 \times 40\ 500 \text{ kJ}$$

$\therefore$ Heat supplied in 5·5 h $= 25 \times 40\ 500 \text{ kJ}$

$$\therefore \quad ,, \quad\quad ,, \quad\quad ,, \quad 1 \text{ h} = \frac{25 \times 40\ 500}{5\cdot5} \text{ kJ}$$

$$\therefore \text{ Heat supplied in 1 min} = \frac{25 \times 40\ 500}{5\cdot5 \times 60} \text{ kJ}$$

$$\text{Work done per min} = \frac{25 \times 40\ 500}{5\cdot5 \times 60} \text{ kJ}$$

$$= \underline{3068 \text{ kJ/min}}$$

$$\text{Now 1 W} = 1 \text{ J/s}$$

$$\therefore 60 \text{ W} = 3\ 068\ 000 \text{ J}$$

$$\text{Power (W)} = \frac{3\ 068\ 000}{60}$$

$$= \underline{51\ 133 \text{ W or } 51\cdot133 \text{ kW}}$$

Example. A stationary petrol engine uses 0·3 kg of petrol for every 1000 watts. What proportion of the available energy in the petrol is converted into mechanical power? (Calorific value of petrol 47 500 kJ/kg.)

$$\text{Total heat supplied} = \text{Mass of fuel} \times \text{calorific value}$$
$$= 0\cdot3 \times 47\ 500\ \text{kJ}$$
$$\text{Heat to power} = 1\ \text{W} = 1\ \text{J/s}$$
$$\therefore\ 1000\ \text{W} = 1000\ \text{J/s}$$
$$= 1000 \times 3600\ \text{J/h}\ (3600\ s = 1\ \text{h})$$

Proportion of petrol converted into useful power

$$= \frac{\text{Power in heat units}}{\text{Heat units supplied in the fuel}}$$
$$= \frac{1000 \times 3600\ (\text{J/h})}{0\cdot3 \times 47\ 500\ 000\ (\text{J/h})}$$
$$\text{Expressed as a percentage} = 0\cdot25 \times 100$$
$$= \underline{25\ \text{per cent}}$$

Example. Express the heat required to raise the temperature of 5 kg of water from 60°C to 80°C, in the equivalent number of joules

$$\text{Heat supplied} = \text{Mass of water} \times \text{temp. rise} \times 4\cdot187$$
$$= 5 \times (80 - 60) \times 4\cdot187$$
$$= \underline{418\cdot7\ \text{kJ}}$$

Exercise 14*

1. When 58 kJ are given to a piece of metal of mass 7 kg the temperature rises from 12°C to 18·3°C. Find the specific heat capacity of the metal. (1·3147)

2. What are the freezing and boiling temperatures of water as expressed in Centigrade degrees? (0° and 100°C)

3. Express the heat required to raise the temperature of 5 kg of water from 4°C to 80°C in kJ. (1592 kJ) (E.M.E.U.)

4. An oil cooler fitted to an engine cools oil at the rate of 2·1 kg/min. If the inlet temperature is 64°C and the outlet temperature is 40°C,

* The coefficients of expansion given in Exercise 14 may be found to vary slightly from those given in the list. The coefficients in the list, however, are more accurate.

how many kJ are extracted from the oil per hour? (Specific heat capacity of oil is 2·223.)   (6720 kJ)

5. An engine is cooled by a radiator to which water is pumped from the engine. Using the factors given below, calculate the flow of water in litres per minute.

(*a*) Heat to cooling water, expressed as kJ = 1790 per min.

(*b*) Water temperatures of radiator:

$$Top = 90°C$$

$$Bottom = 85°C$$

(85·5 litres)

6. Calculate the quantity of heat required to raise the temperature of 11·25 litres of water from 15°C to 80°C. Express your answer in kJ.
(3062 kJ)

7. State three methods by which heat is transferred from hot to cold bodies. Give an example of each method as it occurs in motor engineering practice.   (E.M.E.U.)

8. Explain the difference between 'heat' and 'temperature'. How many heat units are required to raise the temperature of a steel tank containing 273 kg of water from 16°C to 95°C if the tank weighs 36 kg and the specific heat capacity of steel is 0·502?

(91 739 kJ)   (U.E.I.)

9. What is meant by the 'coefficient of linear expansion' of a metal? A steel crankarm is to be shrunk on to the crankshaft. The hole in the crankarm is 250 mm diameter at 15°C and is required to be 251·3 mm diameter when heated. To what temperature must the arm be heated for this diameter to be obtained? The coefficient of linear expansion of steel is 0·000 012 per degree C.   (448°C)   (N.C.T.E.C.)

10. By how much is the diameter of an aluminium piston increased when its temperature is raised from 4°C to 204°C? The diameter at 4°C is 75 mm. Coefficient of expansion for aluminum is 0·000 022 1 per degree C.   (0·3315 mm)   (E.M.E.U.)

11. By how much is the length of a steel rod, 3048 mm, increased when its temperature is raised from 4°C to 38°C? The coefficient of linear expansion is 0·000 011 9.   (1·233 mm)   (E.M.E.U.)

12. (*a*) A steel rod 2500 mm long lengthens 1·75 mm when its temperature is raised by 55°C. What is the coefficient of expansion of steel?

(*b*) By how much will a steel rod shorten when its temperature falls from 120°C to 10°C? Its original length is 3048 mm.

((*a*) 0·000 012 7;   (*b*) 4·258 mm)   (E.M.E.U.)

13. The coefficient of linear expansion of iron is 0·000 012 and that of aluminium 0·000 023. A rod of iron and a rod of aluminium are both 305 mm long at 100°C. What will be the difference in their length at 20°C?   (0·2684 mm)   (U.L.C.I.)

14. A brass rod measures 900 mm at 0°C and increases in length by 1·65 mm when heated to 100°C. What is the coefficient of linear expansion of brass per degree C?   (0·000 018 3)

15. A copper pipe in a heating system is 9145 mm long at the normal temperature of 15°C; find its length when water at a temperature of 85°C flows through it. Coefficient of expansion of copper per degree C = 0·000 017.   (9155·88 mm)   (U.L.C.I.)

16. The bearing friction in a machine absorbs 1865 watts. If all of this power is converted into heat, calculate the joules per hour.

(6714000 J)   (N.C.T.E.C.)

17. Express the heat required to raise the temperature of 4·5 kg of water from 4°C to 82°C in the equivalent number of work units.

(2 640 000 J)   (E.M.E.U.)

18. The combustion of 1 kg of fuel generates 40 500 kJ. If 70% of the heat is wasted, find how long a 186·5 kW oil engine, working at full load, would take to consume 200 kg of the fuel.

(217·1 min)   (N.C.T.E.C.)

19. In a test of a petrol engine, cooling water was circulated through the jacket at the rate of 7 kg per minute. The inlet temperature of the water was 63°C and the outlet temperature 90°C. Calculate the amount of heat carried away by the engine and express this amount as power.

(13·186 kW)

20. A vehicle travelling at 50 km/h overcomes a total resistance to motion of 245 N. How much work is being done per minute? Express this in heat units.   (204 200 J;   204 200 J)

21. An exhaust valve 150 mm in length has a tappet clearance of 0·38 mm at 20°C. Calculate the tappet clearance at 100°C to the nearest thousandth of a millimetre. The coefficient of linear expansion of the metal is 0·000 012 per degree Centigrade.

(0·235 mm)   (E.M.E.U.)

15

Velocity, Acceleration and Braking Efficiency

When a body, which is a quantity of matter, moves or changes its position relative to surrounding bodies, it is in 'a state of motion'; if, however, the body does not change its position, it is 'at rest'.

Speed is the rate at which a body changes its position. Speed is a scalar quantity of magnitude only.

Velocity is the rate at which a body changes its position in a given direction. Velocity is a vector quantity of both magnitude and direction.

Uniform or constant velocity is when the body moves or travels over equal distances in equal intervals of time, no matter how small the interval of time.

Variable velocity is when a body moves or travels over unequal distances in equal intervals of time.

The units used when dealing with these problems are m/s, km/s and km/h.

To find how far a body has travelled, when its speed and the time taken are known, an equation is used.

Distance travelled = Velocity in m/s × time taken in seconds.

Instead of writing distance travelled the letter s is used; for velocity in metres u and v are used, and for time in seconds t is used.

Then, our equation becomes

$$s = ut$$

This will be known as **equation 1**.

Example. If a car travels at a speed of 50 km/h (13·88 m/s) how far does it travel in 10 seconds?

$$\text{Now } u = 13\cdot88 \text{ m/s}$$
$$t = 10 \text{ seconds}$$
$$\text{From equation 1 } s = ut$$
$$= 13\cdot88 \times 10 \text{ m}$$
$$\therefore \text{ Distance} = \underline{\underline{138\cdot8 \text{ m}}}$$

The problem can also be solved by graphical methods, since the distance covered is equal to the product of time and speed. Fig. 15.1 shows the graph.

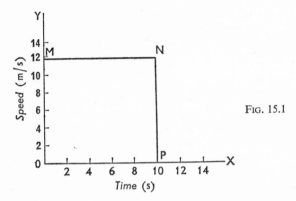

FIG. 15.1

Speed is represented on the 0Y axis. Time is represented on the 0X axis. The line MN will be parallel to the 0Y axis since the speed was uniform throughout.

$$0M = \text{speed } (u)$$
$$0P = \text{time } (t)$$

Therefore, the area 0MNP represents the distance covered.

$$\therefore \text{Distance covered} = \text{area 0MNP}$$
$$= 0M \times 0P$$

or
$$s = u \times t$$
$$= 12 \times 10 \text{ m}$$
$$\therefore \text{Distance} = \underline{120 \text{ m}}$$

Variable Velocity

Consider a body whose velocity increases uniformly from 4 m/s to 8 m/s during a period of 12 seconds. The starting or initial velocity will be u. Let the final velocity be v in equation 2, which will now be developed from a graph (Fig. 15.2). When the time is 0 second the velocity u is represented by 0M, 4 m/s. When the time is 12 seconds, the velocity v is represented by NP, 8 m/s. The area under the line represents the distance covered.

$$\therefore \text{Area 0MNP} = \left(\frac{0M + NP}{2}\right) \times 0P$$

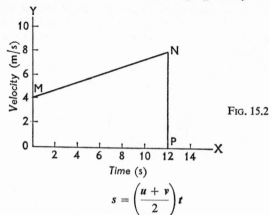

Fig. 15.2

or

$$s = \left(\frac{u + v}{2}\right) t$$

This is **equation 2.**

Substituting the values:

$$s = \frac{u + v}{2} t$$

$$= \frac{4 + 8}{2} \times 12 \text{ m}$$

$$= 6 \times 12 \text{ m}$$

Total distance covered = 72 m

Note: $\dfrac{u + v}{2}$ is the average velocity.

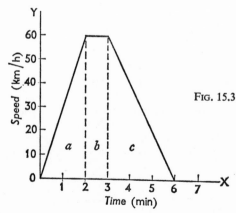

Fig. 15.3

Example. A car starts from rest and its speed increases uniformly to 90 km/h (25 m/s) in 2 minutes; the speed remains constant for 1 minute and then decreases uniformly, the car coming to rest in 3 minutes. How far has the car travelled?

To solve this problem the graph will be divided into sections, see Fig. 15.3. Total distance covered will be areas *a*, *b*, *c*.

Using equation 2 for area *a*:

$$\text{Initial velocity } u = 0$$
$$\text{Final velocity } v = 25 \text{ m/s}$$
$$\text{Time } t = 120 \text{ seconds}$$
$$\therefore \text{ Distance } s = \frac{u + v}{2} t$$
$$= \frac{0 + 25}{2} \times 120 \text{ m}$$
$$= 12 \cdot 5 \times 120 \text{ m}$$
$$= \underline{1500 \text{ m}}$$

Using equation 1 for area *b*:

$$\text{Velocity } u = 25 \text{ m/s}$$
$$\text{Time } t = 60 \text{ seconds}$$
$$\therefore \text{ Distance } s = ut$$
$$= 25 \times 60 \text{ m}$$
$$= \underline{1500 \text{ m}}$$

Using equation 2 for area *c*:

$$\text{Initial velocity } u = 25 \text{ m/s}$$
$$\text{Final velocity } v = 0 \text{ m/s}$$
$$\text{Time } t = 180 \text{ seconds}$$
$$\therefore \text{ Distance } s = \frac{u + v}{2} t$$
$$= \frac{25 + 0}{2} \times 180 \text{ m}$$
$$= 12 \cdot 5 \times 180 \text{ m}$$
$$= \underline{2250 \text{ m}}$$

$$\therefore \text{ Total distance covered } = \text{Areas } a + b + c$$
$$= 1500 + 1500 + 2250 \text{ m}$$
$$= 5250 \text{ m}$$
$$= \underline{5 \cdot 25 \text{ km}}$$

Acceleration

This is the rate at which the velocity of a body is increased. If the velocity of a body is 12 m/s and after 1 second it becomes 14 m/s, then the change of velocity or acceleration is 2 metres per second per second or 2 m/s². The first 's' represents the rate of the velocity and the second 's' represents the increase or change in velocity.

A change in velocity which gives a decrease is known as a retardation, a negative acceleration or deceleration.

The symbol a is used in equations for acceleration.

Equation 3 will now be developed, using the symbols as before.

$$\text{Initial velocity} = u$$
$$\text{Final velocity} = v$$
$$\text{Acceleration} = a$$
$$\text{Time} = t$$

Let the velocity of a car be 15 m/s; it then accelerates uniformly at 2 m/s² for 4 seconds.

$$\text{At 0 second velocity} = 15 \text{ m/s}$$

After 1st second velocity = Original velocity + acceleration
$$= 15 + (2 \times 1) = 17 \text{ m/s}$$

After 2nd second velocity $= 15 + (2 \times 2) = 19$ m/s

After 3rd second velocity $= 15 + (2 \times 3) = 21$ m/s

After 4th second velocity $= 15 + (2 \times 4) = 23$ m/s

It will be noticed that acceleration × time = the increase in velocity. Substituting the symbols:

After t seconds velocity $= u + at$

$$\therefore v = u + at$$

This is **equation 3**.

The graph, Fig. 15.4 will help to explain the development of this equation.

Since equation 3 deals only with velocity, time and acceleration, another equation must be developed to introduce the factor of distance. This is done by the method of substitution.

Now equation 3 states that $v = u + at$, and from equation 2 it was found that the average velocity $= \dfrac{u + v}{2}$.

If we take the value of v, i.e. $u + at$, from equation 3 and substitute this value in the place of v in equation 2, we shall get $\dfrac{u + (u + at)}{2}$.

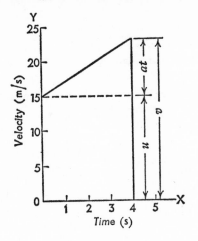

Fig. 15.4

Now
$$\frac{2u + at}{2} = \text{Average velocity}$$

$$\therefore \frac{2u}{2} + \frac{at}{2} = \text{Average velocity}$$

$$\therefore u + \tfrac{1}{2}at = \text{Average velocity}$$

Now the distance passed over by a uniformly accelerated body is its average velocity × time.

$$\therefore \text{Distance } s = (u + \tfrac{1}{2}at) \times t$$

$$s = ut + \tfrac{1}{2}at^2$$

This is **equation 4**.

An equation is also needed for distance and acceleration in terms of velocities.

From equation 2
$$s = \frac{u + v}{2}t$$

$$\therefore 2s = (u + v)t$$

$$\therefore \frac{2s}{t} = u + v \qquad (a)$$

From equation 3
$$v = u + at$$

$$\therefore v - u = at \qquad (b)$$

Multiplying (*a*) and (*b*)

$$(u + v) \times (v - u) = \frac{2s}{t} \times at$$

$$v^2 - u^2 = 2as$$

This is **equation 5**.

When the body starts from rest these equations can be simplified since the value of the initial velocity becomes 0.

Therefore the equations become

Eq. 1, $\qquad s = ut$

Eq. 2, $\qquad s = \left(\dfrac{u + v}{2}\right) t$ becomes Eq. 2a, $s = \dfrac{v}{2} t$

Eq. 3, $\qquad v = u + at \qquad$ becomes Eq. 3a, $v = at$

Eq. 4, $\qquad s = ut + \frac{1}{2}at^2 \qquad$ becomes Eq. 4a, $s = \frac{1}{2}at^2$

Eq. 5, $\qquad v^2 - u^2 = 2as \qquad$ becomes Eq. 5a, $v^2 = 2as$

Example. A car travelling at a speed of 50 km/h is braked with a deceleration of 7 m/s². How far does it travel before coming to rest?

Since both time and stopping distance are not known, equation 5 is used.

Then
$$v = 0$$
$$u = 13{\cdot}88 \text{ m/s}$$
$$a = 7 \text{ m/s}^2$$
$$s \text{ is to be found.}$$

Eq. 5,
$$v^2 - u^2 = 2as$$
$$\frac{v^2 - u^2}{2a} = s$$
$$\frac{0 - 13{\cdot}88^2}{2 \times 7} = s$$
$$\frac{13{\cdot}88 \times 13{\cdot}88}{2 \times 7} = s$$

$$\therefore s = \underline{13{\cdot}77 \text{ m}}, \text{ the stopping distance}$$

What would be the stopping distance if the car had been travelling at 100 km/h?

$$u = 27{\cdot}77 \text{ m/s}$$
$$a = 7 \text{ m/s}^2$$

$$\therefore s = \frac{27 \cdot 77 \times 27 \cdot 77}{2 \times 7}$$

$\therefore s = \underline{55 \cdot 08 \text{ m}}$, the stopping distance

These two solutions are interesting since they show that the stopping distance of a car is not proportional to its speed but to the square of its speed, i.e. speed × speed.

In the foregoing example the stopping distance at 100 km/h is four times the stopping distance at 50 km/h.

Braking Efficiency

To calculate braking efficiency we introduce the acceleration resulting from gravity, which is written as $9 \cdot 8$ m/s². This means that a falling object increases its speed by $9 \cdot 8$ m/s² for every second of the duration of its fall. How does this figure of $9 \cdot 8$ m/s² apply to the braking of a motor vehicle? The answer is, that contact between the tyres of a vehicle and the ground is dependent on the direct result of gravity. Since gravity is used to maintain contact between tyres and road during braking, then the force exerted can not exceed that of gravity. Thus, in theory, the maximum deceleration can only equal the acceleration due to gravity. In practice, however, the figure of $9 \cdot 8$ m/s² has been exceeded under special conditions.

Braking efficiency is the effectiveness of the brakes in both retarding and bringing a motor vehicle to rest. It is usual to express this efficiency as a percentage. When we say that the efficiency of the brakes is 100 per cent, the brakes are retarding the vehicle at a rate of $9 \cdot 8$ m/s² under which condition the horizontal braking force is equal to the downward force of the vehicle.

Example. The driver of a motor vehicle travelling at 50 km/h applies the brakes and stops in 15 m. What is the efficiency of the brakes?

We must find first the deceleration of the vehicle by using equation 5:

$$v^2 - u^2 = 2as$$
$$\frac{v^2 - u^2}{2s} = a$$
$$\frac{0 - 13 \cdot 88^2}{2 \times 15} = a$$
$$\frac{13 \cdot 88 \times 13 \cdot 88}{30} = a$$
$$a = 6 \cdot 422 \text{ m/s}^2$$

$$\text{Now } 9 \cdot 8 \text{ m/s}^2 = 100\% \text{ efficiency}$$
$$\therefore \ 6 \cdot 422 \text{ m/s}^2 = \frac{6 \cdot 422 \times 100}{9 \cdot 8}$$
$$= \underline{65 \cdot 53\%}$$

Exercise 15

1. A car moves at a uniform speed of 72 km/h. How many metres will it travel in 1 second, and how long will it take to travel 1 kilometre?

(20 m/s;   50 s)

2. A car laps a racing circuit, 4·62 km in length, in the time of 2·1 minutes. What is the speed in km/h and m/s?

(132 km/h;   36·66 m/s)

3. The acceleration tests of a car were: (1) From rest to 54 km/h in 6 seconds. (2) From rest to 72 km/h in 15 seconds. Find in each case (*a*) average acceleration, (*b*) distance covered.

((*a*) 2·5 m/s²;   1·33 m/s²;   (*b*) 45 m;   149·625 m)

4. A motor vehicle travelling at a speed of 72 km/h is accelerated at a uniform rate of 1·25 m/s². How long will it take before the speed is 108 km/h and what distance is covered during the period of acceleration?

(8s;   200 m)

5. Braking tests were carried out on a sports car and the average rate of deceleration was 8 m/s². Find the stopping distances and time taken when the car's speed was (*a*) 36 km/h, (*b*) 54 km/h, (*c*) 72 km/h, (*d*) 90 km/h, (*e*) 108 km/h, (*f*) 144 km/h.

((*a*) 6·25 m;   1·25 s;   (*b*) 14·0625 m;   1·875 *s*;
(*c*) 25 m;   2·25 s;   (*d*) 39·062 m;   3·125 s;
(*e*) 56·25 m;   3·75 s;   (*f*) 76·5625 m;   4·375 s;

6. A car moving at a speed of 54 km/h is stopped in a distance of 12 m. Find (*a*) time taken, (*b*) average rate of retardation, (*c*) brake efficiency (assume 9·8 m/s² as 100 per cent.)

((*a*) 1·6 s;   (*b*) 9·375 m/s²;   (*c*) 95·6 per cent)

7. A lorry starts climbing a hill 950 metres long at a speed of 54 km/h. If it takes 1 minute 35 seconds to reach the top, what will its speed then be? (Assume uniform retardation.)   (18 km/h)

8. A car is travelling at a uniform speed of 50 km/h. It maintains this speed for 2 minutes. It is then uniformly accelerated to 100 km/h in one minute and then immediately retarded and brought to rest after a total of 6 minutes' travelling time. The braking effort is uniform. Draw a velocity time graph and use it to find (*a*) the distance covered whilst accelerating, (*b*) the distance covered whilst braking, (*c*) the total distance covered.

((*a*) 1250 m or 1·25 km;   (*b*) 2500 m or 2·5 km;
(*c*) 5416·6 m or 5·4166 km)   (I.M.I.)

9. A car starting from rest and moving with uniform acceleration covers 50 metres from the start in 5 seconds. What is the velocity at this instant? If the car now continues moving with uniform speed for two minutes and then the brakes are applied so that it comes to rest with uniform retardation in 3 seconds, find the total distance travelled.

(20 m/s;   2480 m or 2·48 km)   (I.M.I.)

10. A body moves with uniform acceleration. (*a*) If the velocity increases from 4 m/s to 25 m/s in 3·2 seconds, calculate the acceleration and the distance covered in that time. (*b*) If with an initial velocity of 4 m/s it moves 32 m in 4·5 seconds, determine the new acceleration and the final velocity.

((*a*) 6·562 m/s²;   46·4 m; (*b*) 2·27 m/s²;   12·22 m/s)   (I.M.I.)

11. Determine the efficiency of the braking system of a car which is brought to a stop from a speed of 54 km/h with uniform deceleration in a distance of 20 m.

Calculate the additional distance which would be required if the driver's reaction time of 0·7 second is taken into account.

(57·3%;   11·9 m)   (C. and G.)

12. A car is brought to rest from a speed of 72 km/h in a distance of 20 m. Calculate the average deceleration and the efficiency of the brakes.   (10 m/s²;   98%)

13. Give four factors which affect the stopping distance of a car.

The distance, *S*m, in which a car, travelling at *V*m/s may be brought to rest is given by:

$$S = \frac{V^2}{2g\mu}$$

Rearrange the equation to give *V* in terms of the other quantities and calculate the initial velocity when the stopping distance is 13·75 m. *u* = 0·62 and *g* = 9·8.   (12·93 m/s)   (E.M.E.U.)

16

Electricity

The **electron** is responsible for a 'flow' of electricity called a current, and for all practical purposes the current is assumed to flow from the positive terminal of a battery or dynamo to the negative terminal when the electrons are acted on by a force. The current produced in this way is measured in **amperes** and the force acting on the electrons is measured in **volts**; these terms, amperes and volts, together with the **ohm**, which is the unit of resistance to a current, will be defined later in this chapter.

Conductors

Conductors are materials which offer a comparatively low resistance to the flow of an electric current; they are usually metals which conduct electricity with ease. Although most metals are good conductors, silver is the best because it offers the least resistance. Copper, however, is nearly as good, but as it is much cheaper than silver it is used a great deal in electrical equipment. In order to be effective a conductor should have a large cross-sectional area (thick) and it should be as short in length as practicable.

Several conductors, in order of excellence, are given in the following list:

(1) Silver
(2) Copper
(3) Other metals
(4) Carbon
(5) Damp earth
(6) Acidulated water (acid added to water)
(7) Tap water

Insulators

Insulators are materials which offer a high resistance to the flow of an electric current. Rubber, silk, mica, ebonite, p.v.c. and dry air are examples of excellent insulators.

Signs and Symbols

Fig. 16.1 shows the signs and symbols used in electrical work.

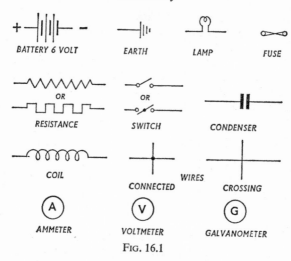

FIG. 16.1

Circuits

Any unbroken path of conductors along which an electric current flows is called a **circuit**, e.g. a battery, wiring, lamp and switch, as shown in Fig. 16.2, is a complete circuit, and with the switch in the closed or 'on' position the lamp will light.

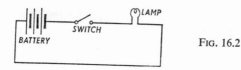

FIG. 16.2

'Open' Circuit

When we get an unintentional 'break' in a circuit we call this an 'open', e.g. a broken wire or a battery lead disconnected, and in these examples current cannot flow even with the switch 'on'.

'Short' Circuit ('Dead' Short)

When the insulation of a 'live' wire, i.e. a wire carrying current, is chafed through and the bare wire touches any metal part of the vehicle, we call this a 'dead' short. This fault, however, cannot occur when an insulated return system is used—it would only take place between the two wires.

Partial Open and Partial Short Circuits

Many of the faults in electrical systems are caused by what we call partial 'opens' and 'shorts'. A partial 'open' consists of a high resistance which has the effect of reducing the current, e.g. a loose or sulphated battery lug or a 'bad earth' connection at a lamp. By a 'bad earth' we mean that the connection between (in this case) the lamp body and its attachment to the wing is not complete; it may be loose, dirty, rusty or partially insulated by paint. The term 'earth' indicates any metal part of the vehicle.

A partial 'short' consists of an alternative path of low resistance which allows some of the current to by-pass or leak from the normal circuit, e.g. a wet insulator, such as a sparking-plug insulator, will cause a leakage of current.

Definitions

We will now define the three units of electricity which were given at the beginning of this chapter, namely, the ampere, the volt and the ohm.

The **volt** is the pressure required to force a current of one ampere through a conductor whose resistance is one ohm.

The **ampere** is the quantity of current forced through a resistance of one ohm by a pressure of one volt.

The **ohm** is the resistance offered by a circuit which allows a current of one ampere to be forced through the circuit when the pressure is one volt.

We are able to use instruments in order to determine the value of these units, e.g. the voltmeter, the ammeter and the ohmmeter.

The foregoing units can be illustrated simply by means of a water-mains system:

The driving pressure required to move water in a mains system is usually provided by means of a pump, and we can represent voltage by this driving pressure.

The volume of water represents the current in amperes and the diameter of the pipes will represent the resistance in ohms, i.e. the smaller the diameter of a pipe the greater its resistance.

Fig. 16.3 shows two pipes connected to a water-main containing water which is maintained at a constant pressure. Taps connect each pipe to the main supply. When the tap of the small diameter pipe is opened the volume of water flowing out the end of the pipe will be small and the pressure in the mains will only drop slightly owing to the high resistance of the small pipe. When the tap of the large diameter pipe is opened, however, the volume of water will be much greater and the pressure in the mains will drop considerably owing to the low resistance of the large pipe.

We can say therefore that a high resistance will allow only a small current to pass and the voltage will drop only slightly. A low resistance, however, will allow a large current to pass with a corresponding drop in voltage.

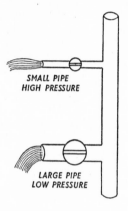

SMALL PIPE
HIGH PRESSURE

LARGE PIPE
LOW PRESSURE

FIG. 16.3

Ohm's Law

Ohm's Law gives the relationship existing between the three units voltage, current and resistance.

Ohm's Law states:

⌐ The quantity of current, in amperes, flowing in a circuit is proportional to the pressure in volts divided by the resistance in ohms.

This law is usually expressed by means of symbols:

$$I = \frac{E}{R}; \quad R = \frac{E}{I}; \quad E = IR$$

where
I = amperes (current)
E = volts (pressure)
R = ohms (resistance)

Ohm's Law should be carefully memorized because most of the problems which include the foregoing units are solved by applying this law. The following examples show that if the values of any two of the units are known, then the value of the other unit can be calculated.

Example. Calculate the amount of current flowing when a voltage of 12 is applied to a circuit of 6 ohms resistance.

$$I = \frac{E}{R}$$

$$\therefore I = \frac{12}{6} = \underline{2 \text{ amps}}$$

Example. In a certain circuit, a current of 10 amps flows when the pressure is 13 volts. What is the resistance of the circuit?

$$R = \frac{E}{I}$$

$$\therefore R = \frac{13}{10} = \underline{1 \cdot 3 \text{ ohms}}$$

Example. Calculate the voltage required to force a current of 3 amps through a resistance of 5 ohms.

$$E = I \times R$$

$$\therefore E = 3 \times 5 = \underline{15 \text{ volts}}$$

Electromotive Force. Potential Difference and Voltage Drop

Electromotive force (e.m.f.) is the voltage measured across the terminals of a battery or dynamo when they are not supplying current to an outside circuit; it is sometimes called the 'open circuit' voltage.

Potential difference (p.d.) is the voltage measured across the terminals of a battery or dynamo when it is supplying current to an outside circuit, i.e. p.d. equals e.m.f., minus the internal resistance of the battery, or dynamo, multiplied by the amount of current flowing. The p.d. will therefore always be less than the e.m.f. because a certain amount of voltage is required in order to force current through the battery or dynamo itself, or, as it is usually called, the internal resistance of the battery or dynamo.

Voltage drop (v.d.) is the loss of voltage occurring when current flows in a circuit. For example, when the starter motor is used with the lights switched on, the lights will dim; this shows that the voltage normally passing to the lamps is reduced. Every conductor, however good, possesses some resistance; thus in forcing current through a circuit some of the voltage is used for this purpose and it is therefore not available for useful work.

The following examples illustrate the application of these terms.

Example. When a resistance of 10 ohms is connected to a battery, a current of 0·6 amp flows through the resistance. If the internal resistance of the battery is 2 ohms, what is the e.m.f. of the battery?

$$\text{p.d.} = \text{Current flowing} \times \text{resistance}$$
$$= 0{\cdot}6 \text{ amps} \times 10 \text{ ohms}$$
$$= 6 \text{ volts}$$
$$\text{v.d.} = \text{Current flowing} \times \text{internal resistance of battery}$$
$$= 0{\cdot}6 \text{ amp} \times 2 \text{ ohms}$$
$$= 1{\cdot}2 \text{ volts}$$
$$\text{Now e.m.f.} = \text{p.d.} + \text{v.d.}$$
$$= 6 + 1{\cdot}2 \text{ volts}$$
$$= 7{\cdot}2 \text{ volts}$$

Example. The internal resistance of a dynamo (whose e.m.f. is 12 volts) is 0·01 ohm. What is the terminal voltage (p.d.) of the dynamo when supplying a current of 20 amps?

$$\text{v.d.} = \text{Current} \times \text{internal resistance of dynamo}$$
$$= 20 \text{ amps} \times 0{\cdot}01 \text{ ohm}$$
$$= 0{\cdot}2 \text{ volts}$$
$$\text{p.d.} = \text{e.m.f.} - \text{v.d.}$$
$$= 12 - 0{\cdot}2 \text{ volts}$$
$$= 11{\cdot}8 \text{ volts}$$

Units of Electrical Power

The practical unit of electrical power is called the **watt (W)** and it is defined:

A watt is the product of the current in amperes and the e.m.f. in volts.

Hence,
$$\text{Watts} = \text{amperes} \times \text{volts}$$
$$= I \times E$$

The unit of mechanical power is also the watt (W) or kilowatt (kW).

The following examples illustrate the application of these terms:

Example. Calculate the amount of current used by a 12-volt 50-watt cigar lighter.

$$\text{Watts} = I \times E$$
$$50 = I \times 12$$
$$\therefore \frac{50}{12} = I, \text{ and } I = 4{\cdot}16 \text{ amps}$$

Example. A starter motor draws a current of 185 amps when turning an engine. If the voltage at the starter terminals is 10, calculate the power (W) of the starter; neglect efficiency.

Power (W) $= I \times E$

$= 185 \times 10 = \underline{1850 \text{ W or } 1\cdot85 \text{ kW}}$

Series and Parallel Connections

Students are often confused by the **series** and **parallel** methods of circuit connection, and the following explanation and diagrams will show these methods. When we use the term 'resistance' in the following examples we mean any device that uses current, e.g. a lamp bulb, a windscreen wiper, a direction indicator, and so on.

Series

Fig. 16.4 shows three resistances connected in 'series' and the following points should be noted.

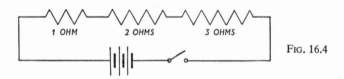

FIG. 16.4

(1) The value of the current flowing through each resistance is the same.

(2) The voltage is divided between the resistances in proportion to their values, i.e. the higher the resistance in ohms the greater the voltage across this resistance.

(3) Any resistance placed in a series circuit will increase resistance and reduce current.

Example. Three resistances, 1, 2 and 3 ohms respectively, are connected in series with a 12-volt battery. Calculate:

(*a*) The current flowing.

(*b*) The voltage across each resistance. (see Fig. 16.5).

Total resistance $= 1 + 2 + 3 = 6$ ohms

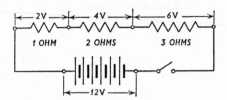

Fig. 16.5

(*a*) Current flowing $I = \dfrac{E}{R}$

$$= \dfrac{12}{6} = \underline{2 \text{ amps}}$$

(*b*) Voltage across each resistance

$$= \dfrac{\text{Battery voltage}}{\text{Total resistance}} \times \text{each resistance}$$

Voltage across 1-ohm resistance $= \dfrac{12}{6} \times 1 = \underline{2 \text{ volts}}$

,, ,, 2-ohm ,, $= \dfrac{12}{6} \times 2 = \underline{4 \text{ volts}}$

,, ,, 3-ohm ,, $= \dfrac{12}{6} \times 3 = \underline{6 \text{ volts}}$

The sum of 2, 4 and 6 equals 12 volts, i.e. the battery voltage.

Example. Calculate the resistance required to be fitted to the bulb holder of an ignition warning light connected in a 12-volt system. The bulb specification is 2·5 volts and 0·2 amp.

Fig. 16.6 shows the lamp bulb and resistance in series with the battery.

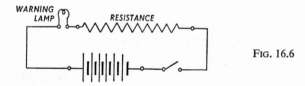

Fig. 16.6

Let R_1 = resistance of bulb

$$= \frac{2 \cdot 5}{0 \cdot 2} = 12 \cdot 5 \text{ ohms}$$

Now the total value of all the resistance in circuit should allow a current 0·2 amp to flow at a voltage of 12.

$$\therefore \text{ Total resistance of circuit} = \frac{12}{0 \cdot 2} = 60 \text{ ohms}$$

Let R_2 = value of resistance to be fitted to bulb holder, then:

R_2 = Total resistance − bulb resistance
   = 60 − 12·5
   = 47·5 ohms

Parallel

Fig. 16.7 shows three resistances connected in parallel and the following points should be noted.

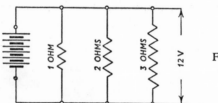

FIG. 16.7

(1) The value of the voltage across each of the resistances is equal.

(2) The total current flowing is divided between the resistances inversely proportional to their value, i.e. the higher the value of the resistance the less the current in amperes flowing through this resistance.

(3) Adding resistances in parallel reduces the total resistance of the circuit.

Example. Three resistances, 1, 2 and 3 ohms respectively, are connected in parallel with a 12-volt battery. Calculate:

(*a*) The current flowing through each resistance.

(*b*) The total resistance of the circuit.

(*b*) The total resistance of the circuit must first be calculated by using the following formula:

$$R = 1 \div \left(\frac{1}{R_1} + \frac{1}{R_2} + \frac{1}{R_3} \right)$$

where R = the total resistance, in ohms, and

R_1, R_2, R_3 = the value of the separate resistances, in ohms

$$\therefore R = 1 \div \left(\frac{1}{1} + \frac{1}{2} + \frac{1}{3} \right)$$

$$= 1 \div \frac{6 + 3 + 2}{6} = 1 \div \frac{11}{6} = \underline{0 \cdot 55 \text{ ohms}}$$

(*a*) Now the total current flowing is:

$$\text{Total current flowing} = \frac{\text{Battery voltage}}{\text{Total resistance}} = \frac{12}{0 \cdot 55} = 22 \text{ amps}$$

Using Ohm's Law, we can find the current flowing in each resistance:

$I = \dfrac{E}{R}$, thus current flowing in 1-ohm resistance $= \dfrac{12}{1} = \underline{12 \text{ amps}}$

$\qquad$,, $\qquad$,, $\quad$,, 2-ohm $\quad$,, $\quad = \dfrac{12}{2} = \underline{6 \text{ amps}}$

$\qquad$,, $\qquad$,, $\quad$,, 3-ohm $\quad$,, $\quad = \dfrac{12}{3} = \underline{4 \text{ amps}}$

The sum of 12, 6 and 4 amps equals 22 amps, which is the total current flowing.

The Effects of an Electric Current

Now let us see some of the effects of an electric current:

Heating. When current is applied to the filament of a lamp bulb, the fine wire, from which the filament is made, becomes white hot and thus produces a light.

Chemical. When current is applied to a battery from a battery charger, various chemical reactions are produced which enable electrical energy to be stored in a chemical form. When a current is required this can be produced by means of further chemical reactions.

Magnetic. At this stage it is sufficient to say that an electric current can be produced by magnetic means and magnetism can be produced by electrical means.

Lamp Bulbs

In recent years considerable development has taken place in the manufacture of vehicle lamp bulbs in order to improve their brightness and life.

Voltage and Wattage Rating

Vehicle lamp bulbs are rated by voltage and wattage, and the bulbs are stamped accordingly. For example, a headlamp bulb may be marked 12-volt 36-watt (12-V 36-W), a side lamp bulb 12-V 6-W, a pass-light bulb 12-V 60-W, and so on.

The amount of current used by a lamp bulb can be calculated.

Example. Calculate the amount of current used by a 12-volt 36-watt headlamp bulb.

$$\text{Watts} = I \times E$$
$$36 = I \times 12$$
$$\frac{36}{12} = I \text{ and } I = \underline{3 \text{ amps}}$$

Example. Calculate the amount of current used by a 12-volt 6-watt sidelamp bulb.

$$\text{Watts} = I \times E$$
$$6 = I \times 12$$
$$\frac{6}{12} = I \text{ and } I = \underline{0\cdot5 \text{ amps}}$$

Candela, Lumens and Bulb Efficiency

The foregoing terms are often used when the technical aspect of vehicle lamp bulbs is discussed.

The **candela** is the illuminating power of a source of light. The average vehicle lamp bulb produces up to one candela for each watt consumed. Headlamp bulbs, however, require only 0·7 watt per candela.

The **lumen** is the unit of luminous flux with the intensity of one candela.

Combining candela and lumens, when a lumen of light is uniformly distributed over an area of one square metre, the unit of illumination is called the **lux.**

Bulb efficiency is measured in lumens per watt. An average 12-volt 36-watt headlamp bulb will have an efficiency of 16–19 lumens per watt, but the newer iodine headlamp bulbs have an efficiency of about 25 lumens per watt. This increased efficiency produces a whiter and thus a brighter light.

The Battery

The purpose of the battery is to store electrical energy which can be used when the engine is not running or the dynamo output is too low to meet the load on the electrical system.

Two types of battery are used on motor vehicles:

(1) Lead–acid.
(2) Alkaline.

The Lead–Acid Battery

A container or case, usually moulded, is divided into compartments called cells. Each cell contains a group of **positive** and **negative** plates, these plates are insulated from each other by means of **separators** made of wood or a special material which has been developed during recent years. The plates are immersed in a solution of sulphuric acid and water, called the **electrolyte**, which has a specific gravity of about 1·300 when the battery is charged and about 1·180 when the battery is discharged.

The positive plates contain lead oxide when charged and lead sulphate when discharged. Negative plates contain spongy lead when charged and lead sulphate when discharged.

Each cell has a **nominal** voltage of 2 volts, although the voltage varies between 2·1 volts (charged) and 1·8 volts (discharged). The cells are assembled either in banks of three connected in series which gives 6 volts (nominal voltage) or six cells connected in series which gives 12 volts (nominal voltage).

We shall now see how the battery produces this electrical energy. During the charging and discharging process, which stores and releases the electrical energy, chemical changes take place in both the plates and the electrolyte. Assuming the battery to be in a discharged condition, then:

Charging (current passed into the cells). The positive plates change from lead sulphate into lead peroxide and the negative plates change from lead sulphate into spongy lead. The electrolyte is strengthened by the formation of sulphuric acid from lead sulphate released from the plates. The specific gravity of the electrolyte will rise during charging due to the strengthening. When fully charged, the colour of the positive plates becomes chocolate-brown and the negative plates become grey.

Discharging. When current is taken from the cells, both positive and negative plates tend to change to lead sulphate; this process reduces the sulphuric acid and water is formed, thus lowering the specific gravity of the electrolyte.

The changes can be represented by chemical symbols:

	During charge		*During discharge*
Positive Plate	PbO_2	$\longleftrightarrow$	$PbSO_4$
Electrolyte	$2H_2SO_4$	$\longleftrightarrow$	$2H_2O$
Negative Plate	Pb	$\longleftrightarrow$	$PbSO_4$

Battery Capacity

Battery **capacity** equals the product of the number of hours taken to discharge a battery and its rate of discharge; it is expressed in **ampere-hours** (Ah). The actual capacity of a battery, however, varies with the rate of discharge and the following example shows the importance of this fact.

A lead-acid battery, fully charged, rated at 75 Ah can supply 7·5 amps for about 10 hours, but will discharge in about 6·5 hours when supplying 10 amps. The battery will discharge in about 3·75 hours when supplying 15 amps. Thus the ampere-hour outputs are about 72, 65 and 56·5 ampere-hours before the voltage drops to 1·8 volts per cell. At this voltage the discharge should be discontinued and the battery recharged, otherwise excessive sulphation may occur.

Capacity Test

To make this test the battery must first be fully charged; this is best done off the vehicle. The battery should be charged at one-tenth of its ampere-hour capacity until the sp. gr. of the electrolyte in each cell remains constant between 1·270 and 1·290. The voltage of each cell should be 2·6 to 2·7 measured with an accurate voltmeter while the battery is on charge. These values indicate a fully charged battery.

When the charge is completed the battery should be allowed to stand idle for at least two hours until the open circuit reading of each cell has dropped to about 2·1 volts.

The battery is then discharged for ten hours through a variable resistance with an ammeter in circuit (see Fig. 16.8). The rate of discharge is one-tenth of its ampere-hour capacity, e.g. a battery of 60 Ah capacity will be discharged at 6 amps. If the capacity is about 100 per cent of the ampere-hour capacity, then the rate of discharge will be maintained for ten hours before the voltage of each cell falls to 1·8 with the discharge current still flowing. If the foregoing readings are obtained before the expiry of ten hours, then the battery capacity will be less than 100 per cent. The actual capacity can be determined by multiplying together the amps and the hours of discharge.

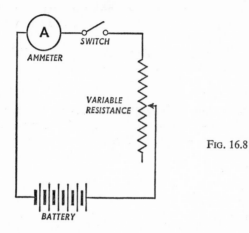

Fig. 16.8

Battery Resistance

The internal resistance of the lead-acid battery is low; it is about 0·001 to 0·01 ohm. This low resistance makes the lead–acid battery suitable for engine starting. The resistance depends on battery size (plates), state of charge and temperature.

Example. A battery has a p.d. of 6·25 volts when supplying a current of 25 amps. The e.m.f. of the battery rises to 6·5 volts when the load is switched off. Calculate the internal resistance of the battery.

$$\text{Voltage drop (v.d.)} = \text{e.m.f.} - \text{p.d.}$$
$$= 6·5 - 6·25 = 0·25 \text{ volts}$$
$$\text{Internal resistance} = \frac{\text{v.d.}}{\text{current flowing}} = \frac{0·25}{25} = \underline{0·01 \text{ ohm}}$$

Effect of Temperature on Capacity and Voltage

The density and resistance of battery electrolyte (lead–acid) both increase as the temperature falls, thus slowing down diffusion between the electrolyte and the plates. In general, the capacity of a battery is lower in winter than in summer.

The capacity of a fully charged battery at 20°C may fall to about 80 per cent at 0°C and to 60 per cent at −10°C. When a battery is only partly charged the capacity is even further reduced.

The following table shows the effect of temperature and discharge rate on the voltage drop in a lead–acid battery when the starter switch is first closed.

Battery condition	Temp. °C	Voltage drop %
Fully charged	20	25
Fully charged	0	33
Half charged	0	50

The electrolyte in a discharged ('flat') lead–acid battery may freeze at 0°C with possible bursting of the case. A fully charged battery will only freeze at about − 60°C, see Fig. 16.9.

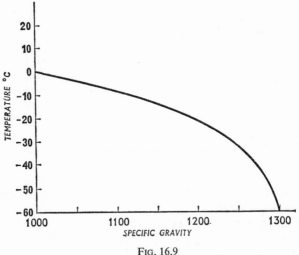

Fig. 16.9

Battery Charging

For the charging of batteries a D.C. supply is essential so that if only A.C. mains current is available a **rectifier** (battery charger) is necessary.

Batteries may be charged from a D.C. supply by inserting a variable series resistance between the positive side of the supply and the pos. (+) pole of the batteries, and the negative side of the supply is connected to the neg. (−) pole of the batteries (see Fig. 16.10).

The value of a suitable initial series resistance for a stated current can be calculated by using a modification of Ohm's Law:

$$R + r = \frac{E - e}{I}$$

where R = value of initial resistance, in ohms;
r = total internal resistance of cells, in ohms;
E = supply voltage;
e = total voltage of cells;
I = charging current, in amps.

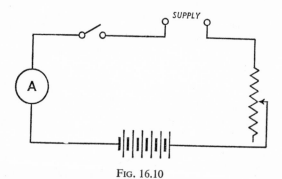

Fig. 16.10

Example. Six 12-volt lead–acid batteries, connected in series, are to be charged from a 200-volt d.c. supply. Assuming each cell to be discharged at 1·8 volts and the internal resistance of each cell to be 0·025 ohm, determine the value of a suitable series resistance to give a charging current of 6 amps.

Total number of cells $= 6 \times 6$
$= 36$
Total internal resistance of cells $= 36 \times 0·025$
$= 0·9$ ohm
Total battery voltage $= 36 \times 1·8$
$= 64·8$ volts

Now, charging voltage = Supply volts − Total battery volts
$= 200 - 64·8$ volts

Therefore, $$R + r = \frac{E - e}{I}$$

$$R + 0{\cdot}9 = \frac{200 - 64{\cdot}8}{6}$$

$$R + 0{\cdot}9 = \frac{135{\cdot}2}{6}$$

$$R + 0{\cdot}9 = 22{\cdot}5$$

$$\therefore R = 22{\cdot}5 - 0{\cdot}9$$

$$= \underline{21{\cdot}4 \text{ ohms}}$$

The Alkaline Battery

The two main types of alkaline battery are the nickel–iron and the nickel–cadmium battery. In both types a steel container holds the positive plates of nickel peroxide, but the negative plates differ. In the nickel–iron battery the active material used for the negative plates is iron, for the nickel–cadmium battery cadmium is used. The plates are immersed in the electrolyte, which is a solution of caustic potash in water, the specific gravity of the electrolyte is 1·17 to 1·19 and the gravity remains constant during both charge and discharge.

Both batteries have a voltage of about 1·4 volts per cell charged and about 1·1 volts per cell discharged; they are assembled in banks of 5, 9 or 10 cells connected in series.

Chemical Action

When a nickel–iron battery is on charge the nickel oxide on the positive plates is converted into nickel peroxide, while the iron oxide on the negative plates becomes iron peroxide.

Although there is uncertainty about the exact chemical action of the nickel–cadmium battery, the following can be taken as a general guide.

On charge, the positive plates will become nickel peroxide and the negative plates will become pure cadmium.

On discharge, the positive plates change to nickel oxide and the cadmium plates become oxidized.

Fig. 16.11 shows the charge and discharge curves for lead–acid and alkaline batteries.

Magnetism

Magnetism is a form of energy and, as many students will know, we are able to show the application of this energy by means of the bar magnet (see Fig. 16.12). The bar magnet has a North Pole at one end and a South Pole at the other end, and either pole is able to attract unmagnetized iron or steel.

First Law of Magnetism

If a bar magnet is freely suspended in air and the north pole of another magnet is brought slowly towards the north pole of the suspended magnet, then the suspended magnet will swing away or be 'repelled' from the approaching magnet. In the same way, the south poles of two magnets will repel each other. The south pole of one magnet, however, will 'attract' the north pole of another magnet, and the north pole of one magnet will attract the south pole of another magnet.

Thus, we are able to state the important magnetic law:

Like poles repel: Unlike poles attract.

Magnetic Lines of Force and Fields

The magnetic force, causing magnetic effects, is assumed to emerge from the north pole of a magnet as invisible lines which appear to travel in a curved path through the surrounding space to the south pole, see Fig. 16.13. This can be shown by placing a sheet of paper over a bar magnet and sprinkling iron filings on the surface of the paper. When the paper is gently tapped, the iron filings will arrange themselves into definite lines known as **lines of force**.

These lines of force can be compared with stretched elastic bands which are therefore always trying to straighten themselves, and the force created by this attempt to straighten is used as a basis for starter motor operation. (See Part 2 of this book.) The strength of a magnet depends on the number of these lines of force in a given area, e.g. a powerful magnet has many more lines of force than a weak magnet.

The term magnetic field indicates an area covered by lines of force or any space subjected to a magnetic force. When a bar of soft iron is placed in a magnetic field the bar will also become a magnet. This kind of magnetism is called **induced magnetism**, i.e. magnetism which is 'brought about'. This induced magnetism, however, is only temporary, because the soft iron rapidly loses its magnetism when the bar is removed from the influence of the magnetic field. A bar of hardened alloy steel, however, will retain a considerable amount of its magnetic force after it has been removed from the magnetic field, and this is known as a **permanent magnet**.

The horseshoe magnet fitted to the rotating armature-type magneto is an excellent example of a permanent magnet. The magnetic strength or 'pull' of a permanent magnet can be reduced or practically destroyed by rough treatment, e.g. when hit with a hammer, dropped on the floor or heated to a bright red.

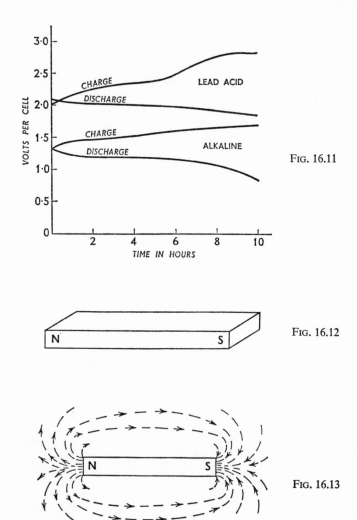

Fig. 16.11

Fig. 16.12

Fig. 16.13

Electromagnetism

Electromagnetism is the production of a magnetic field from an electric current or the production of an electric current from a magnetic field.

If a current is passed through a single wire, then a magnetic field is set up around the wire and the lines of force will form a number of circles all having their centre on the axis (centre) of the wire, see Fig. 16.14. The relationship between the direction of current flow in the wire

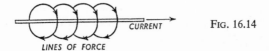

CURRENT

LINES OF FORCE

FIG. 16.14

and the direction of the lines of force set up around the wire can be represented by turning a right-hand screw with a screwdriver. If the direction of current flow is known, then the direction of the lines of force can be found.

The lengthwise movement of the screw represents the direction of current flow and the rotation given to the screw by the screwdriver represents the direction of the lines of force produced by the current. This is known as the **screwdriver rule**, i.e. when the screwdriver is turned clockwise the current goes 'away' from the screwdriver (usually indicated by the feather of an arrow), see Fig. 16.15 (a), and the lines

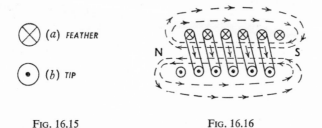

(a) FEATHER

(b) TIP

FIG. 16.15

FIG. 16.16

of force flow in a clockwise direction. If the screwdriver is turned anti-clockwise, however, the current comes 'toward' the screwdriver (usually indicated by the tip of an arrow), see Fig. 16.15(b), and the lines of force will flow in an anti-clockwise direction.

If instead of using a single wire we pass current through a coil of insulated wire, a much larger number of magnetic lines of force will be produced. These lines of force, however, will not take the form of circles as they did when a single wire only was used, but they will combine to give long lines of force which pass inside and outside the coil, see Fig. 16.16. In this way a complete magnetic field is formed with a north and a south pole to give, in effect, a bar magnet.

Electromagnets

If we go a stage further and wind a coil of insulated wire on a soft-iron bar or core and pass a current through the wire, the bar will become a powerful magnet, called an **electromagnet**, with the same properties as a bar magnet, i.e. the ability to attract unmagnetized iron or steel. Where the coil is wound with the wire in a clockwise direction and current is passed through the wire in a clockwise direction also, then the bar will become a magnet with a south pole at the positive end of the wire and a north pole at the negative end of the wire, see Fig. 16.17. If the current flow is reversed the north pole will be at the positive end and the south pole will be at the negative end of the wire, see Fig. 16.18.

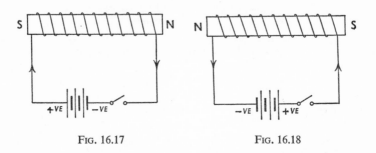

FIG. 16.17   FIG. 16.18

The magnetic strength of an electromagnet depends on the number of turns in the coil of insulated wire, usually called the winding, and the amount of current flowing. This strength is measured by the number of **ampere-turns**, i.e. the amount of current flowing in amperes (amps) multiplied by the number of turns in the winding; these are usually called 'amp-turns'.

When a current is passed through the winding of an electromagnet we say it is **energized**, i.e. the electromagnet is capable of doing work, and, as we shall see in the following pages, this ability to do work is used for the operation of regulators, cut-outs, horn relays, and so on.

Two types of electromagnet used in motor vehicle electrical equipment are:

(1) The open or **armature** type, see Fig. 16.19.

(2) The **solenoid** type, see Fig. 16.20.

The open type is generally used for the opening and closing of contacts, e.g. in cut-outs, voltage control regulators, and so on. When a current passes through the winding the iron core becomes energized; this iron core attracts a flat strip of iron, called an **armature**, and moves it against the tension of a return spring, see Fig. 16.19.

The solenoid type is generally used for mechanical movement in the starter switch, the electrically operated diaphragm petrol pump, and so on. When current energizes the winding a movable plunger is attracted; this plunger slides inside the barrel against the force of a return spring and thus performs its purpose, see Fig. 16.20.

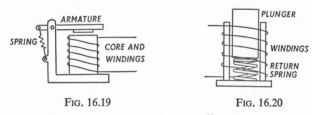

FIG. 16.19   FIG. 16.20

The foregoing are only two examples of the use of electromagnetism and most of the electrical equipment used in motor vehicles employ the principles of electromagnetism in one form or another. The application of these principles to the dynamo, the starter motor, and so on, is described in the second part of this book.

We have seen that an electric current can produce a magnetic field, and earlier in this chapter it was stated that a magnetic field is able to produce an electric current.

If a coil of insulated wire has its ends attached to a **galvanometer** (a sensitive current-measuring device), see Fig. 16.21, and a bar magnet

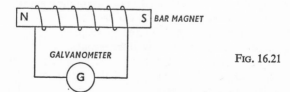

FIG. 16.21

is moved to and fro inside the coil, then the galvanometer needle will move to and fro also, thus showing that an electric current is flowing in the coil of wire. The current, however, will only flow while the magnet is actually moving and the reason for this is that to produce current, the turns of the coil of wire must 'cut' through the lines of force of the bar magnet. In order to do this 'cutting' the bar magnet must be moved or the coil must move.

Electromagnetic Induction

The term **induction** refers to the ability of one coil of wire with a current passing through it to induce another current in a second coil of wire when both coils are wound on the same soft-iron core: the coils are not connected electrically and they are insulated.

The process of induction was discovered by Faraday in 1831 by means of an experiment whose arrangement is shown in Fig. 16.22. A coil of insulated copper wire, called the **primary**, is wound on part of

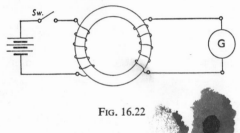

Fig. 16.22

a soft-iron ring and the ends of the coil are connected through a switch to a battery. When the switch is 'closed', current will flow through the coil and its value will rapidly 'build-up' from zero to maximum; at the same time the lines of force will also 'build-up' from zero to their maximum magnetic strength. Note that *all* the iron ring will be magnetized.

Another coil of insulated copper wire, called the **secondary**, is wound on the opposite side of the iron ring and the ends of the coil are connected to a galvanometer. During the build-up of the magnetic strength of the iron ring an increasing number of the lines of force will be 'cut' by the turns of the secondary coil and we can consider this action as equivalent to a bar magnet moving in the secondary coil. The result is, that an electric current is induced in the secondary coil; this induced current however does not register on the galvanometer after the magnetic build-up is completed.

If the primary circuit is broken by opening the switch, then the magnetism in the ring will gradually 'fall away' to give the same effect as withdrawing a magnet from the secondary coil. A current, therefore, will again be induced in the secondary coil and it will register on the galvanometer. Thus, by alternately making and breaking the primary circuit, by means of the switch, a current is induced in the secondary coil.

The operation of the ignition coil is based on these principles.

Exercise 16

1. In testing part of a starter motor circuit a current of 3·6 amps passed when a voltage of 6·9 was applied. Calculate (*a*) the resistance of the circuit in ohms, (*b*) the power used in watts.

((*a*) 1·916 ohms; (*b*) 24·84 watts; (N.C.T.E.C.)

2. State Ohm's Law.

Three conductors are placed in a circuit in series, their resistance being 2, 3 and 4 ohms respectively. What current flows in each when an e.m.f. of 12 volts is applied to the circuit?

If the conductors are now arranged in parallel in a circuit with the same voltage, what current will flow in each?

(1·33 amps in each; 6 amps; 4 amps and 3 amps) (E.M.E.U.)

3. (*a*) An electric car-heater is to operate off a 12-volt system and provide 100 watts heat output. What will be its resistance and what current will it take?

(*b*) If the same heater, with resistance as in (*a*), is connected to a six-volt system, what will be the current in amps and the output in watts?

((*a*) 1·44 ohms; 8·33 amps; (*b*) 4·16 amps; 24·96 watts) (I.M.I.)

4. Draw a wiring diagram showing how you would connect a 12-volt battery to four 12-volt lamps via three simple switches, two controlling one lamp each and a third controlling two lamps. (C. and G.)

5. Find the filament resistance of a 12-V 36-W bulb when in circuit with a battery whose e.m.f. is 12 volts, 12·5 volts and 11·5 volts.

(4 ohms; 4·16 ohms; 3·83 ohms)

6. Calculate the terminal p.d. and the current taken from a battery whose no-load e.m.f. is 12 volts, when carrying the following load:

2, 24-watt headlamps
2, 12-watt sidelamps
1, 6-watt tail-lamps

with 3-amp ignition coil. Assume the internal resistance to be 0·15 ohm.   (10·575 volts;   9·5 amps)   (I.M.I.)

7. (*a*) Name three substances which are good conductors of electricity and three which are good insulators.

(*b*) Write down the equation which you would use to enable you to calculate the current passing in a conductor if the resistance and voltage are known. A current of 11 amperes will just cause a fuse in a 12-volt circuit to fail. What is the resistance of the fuse?

(1·09 ohms)   (E.M.E.U.)

8. Explain the principle on which a solenoid works and name two pieces of apparatus in the equipment of a car in which solenoids are used.   (E.M.E.U.)

9. What are: (1) amperes, (2) volts?

Give reasons for the differences between the sizes of the leads from battery to starter and from induction coil to distributor and sparking plugs.   (E.M.E.U.)

10. The internal resistance of a generator, whose e.m.f. is 12 volts, is 0·01 ohm. What is the terminal voltage of the generator when supplying a current of 10 amps?   (11·9 volts)

11. (*a*) Explain the meaning of the terms 'ampere-hour' and 'internal resistance' when used in respect to secondary cells.

(*b*) A lead–acid accumulator having 14 discharged cells connected in series has to be charged from a 200-volt D.C. supply. The e.m.f. of each cell is 1·8 volts when discharged and the internal resistance of each cell can be assumed to be constant and equal to 0·02 ohms. If the charging current has to be maintained constant at 10 amps, calculate the initial value of the series resistance required.

(17·2 ohms)   (C. and G.)

12. Four accumulator cells are to be charged from a 110-volt D.C. supply using an electric lamp as a resistance. Assuming each cell to have an e.m.f. of 2·5 volts when on charge and that the charging current is to be 0·5 amps, find the voltage and wattage of the most suitable size lamp.

Draw a diagram of the circuit.

(100 volt, 50 watt)   (E.M.E.U.)

13. (*a*) What is meant by saying that the capacity of a battery is 80 ampere-hours?

(*b*) If a 6-volt battery is to provide current for 5 hours for two 36-watt and three 6-watt lamps, all in use at the same time, what must be its minimum capacity? What is the resistance of each of these lamps?

(100 Ah;   1 ohm;   6 ohm)   (E.M.E.U.)

14. (*a*) Give the current taken by each of the following lamps at rated voltage: 12-V 36-W, 12-V 18-W, 12-V 6-W, 6-V 6-W, 6-V 6-W.

(*b*) What is the resistance of each of the five lamps referred to in (*a*)?

(*c*) What total current would these five lamps take from a 12-volt secondary battery if the 12-volt lamps are connected in parallel, and if the two 6-volt lamps are connected in series, across the battery terminals.

(*d*) Using the result of (*c*), calculate the equivalent resistance of all the lamps connected as described. Check that this result agrees with that obtained by the more usual but much longer method of calculating the equivalent resistance of a combination of resistors from their separate resistances.

((*a*) 3 amps; 1·5 amps; 0·5 amps; 1 amp; 1 amp;

(*b*) 4 ohms; 8 ohms; 24 ohms; 6 ohms; 6 ohms;

(*c*) 6 amps; (*d*) 2 ohms) (C. and G.)

15. (*a*) State the composition of the plates and electrolyte when a battery is (1) charged, (2) discharged.

(*b*) What care does a battery require in order to give satisfactory service in a car? (U.L.C.I.)

16. Describe the construction of one type of alkaline battery. State the composition of the plates and electrolyte when this type of battery is (*a*) charged, (*b*) discharged.

17. A six-cell, 12-V battery gave an open-circuit voltage of 12·75 V. When supplying a current of 16 A the terminal voltage drops to 12·11 V. Calculate the internal resistance of the battery.

(0·04 ohms) (U.L.C.I.)

18. (*a*) State Ohm's Law.

(*b*) Determine the resistance of a 12-V starter if the current flow is 180 A, and there is a drop of 3 V at the motor terminals.

(*c*) How can this voltage drop be minimized?

((*b*) 0·016 ohm) (N.C.T.E.C.)

19. (*a*) A starter cable carrying current of 185 amps has a resistance of 0·0015 ohm. Calculate the voltage drop in the cable.

(*b*) How is the electrical resistance of a cable affected by:

    (i) shortening its length;

    (ii) increasing its temperature;

    (iii) reducing its diameter;

    (iv) using iron instead of copper?

((*a*) 0·2775 volt) (U.E.I.)

NATURAL SINES

°	0'	6'	12'	18'	24'	30'	36'	42'	48'	54'	1'	2'	3'	4'	5'
0	·0000	0017	0035	0052	0070	0087	0105	0122	0140	0157	3	6	9	12	15
1	·0175	0192	0209	0227	0244	0262	0279	0297	0314	0332	3	6	9	12	15
2	·0349	0366	0384	0401	0419	0436	0454	0471	0488	0506	3	6	9	12	15
3	·0523	0541	0558	0576	0593	0610	0628	0645	0663	0680	3	6	9	12	15
4	·0698	0715	0732	0750	0767	0785	0802	0819	0837	0854	3	6	9	12	14
5	·0872	0889	0906	0924	0941	0958	0976	0993	1011	1028	3	6	9	12	14
6	·1045	1063	1080	1097	1115	1132	1149	1167	1184	1201	3	6	9	12	14
7	·1219	1236	1253	1271	1288	1305	1323	1340	1357	1374	3	6	9	12	14
8	·1392	1409	1426	1444	1461	1478	1495	1513	1530	1547	3	6	9	12	14
9	·1564	1582	1599	1616	1633	1650	1668	1685	1702	1719	3	6	9	11	14
10	·1736	1754	1771	1788	1805	1822	1840	1857	1874	1891	3	6	9	11	14
11	·1908	1925	1942	1959	1977	1994	2011	2028	2045	2062	3	6	9	11	14
12	·2079	2096	2113	2130	2147	2164	2181	2198	2215	2233	3	6	9	11	14
13	·2250	2267	2284	2300	2317	2334	2351	2368	2385	2402	3	6	8	11	14
14	·2419	2436	2453	2470	2487	2504	2521	2538	2554	2571	3	6	8	11	14
15	·2588	2605	2622	2639	2656	2672	2689	2706	2723	2740	3	6	8	11	14
16	·2756	2773	2790	2807	2823	2840	2857	2874	2890	2907	3	6	8	11	14
17	·2924	2940	2957	2974	2990	3007	3024	3040	3057	3074	3	6	8	11	14
18	·3090	3107	3123	3140	3156	3173	3190	3206	3223	3239	3	6	8	11	14
19	·3256	3272	3289	3305	3322	3338	3355	3371	3387	3404	3	5	8	11	14
20	·3420	3437	3453	3469	3486	3502	3518	3535	3551	3567	3	5	8	11	14
21	·3584	3600	3616	3633	3649	3665	3681	3697	3714	3730	3	5	8	11	14
22	·3746	3762	3778	3795	3811	3827	3843	3859	3875	3891	3	5	8	11	13
23	·3907	3923	3939	3955	3971	3987	4003	4019	4035	4051	3	5	8	11	13
24	·4067	4083	4099	4115	4131	4147	4163	4179	4195	4210	3	5	8	11	13
25	·4226	4242	4258	4274	4289	4305	4321	4337	4352	4368	3	5	8	11	13
26	·4384	4399	4415	4431	4446	4462	4478	4493	4509	4524	3	5	8	10	13
27	·4540	4555	4571	4586	4602	4617	4633	4648	4664	4679	3	5	8	10	13
28	·4695	4710	4726	4741	4756	4772	4787	4802	4818	4833	3	5	8	10	13
29	·4848	4863	4879	4894	4909	4924	4939	4955	4970	4985	3	5	8	10	13
30	·5000	5015	5030	5045	5060	5075	5090	5105	5120	5135	3	5	8	10	13
31	·5150	5165	5180	5195	5210	5225	5240	5255	5270	5284	2	5	7	10	12
32	·5299	5314	5329	5344	5358	5373	5388	5402	5417	5432	2	5	7	10	12
33	·5446	5461	5476	5490	5505	5519	5534	5548	5563	5577	2	5	7	10	12
34	·5592	5606	5621	5635	5650	5664	5678	5693	5707	5721	2	5	7	10	12
35	·5736	5750	5764	5779	5793	5807	5821	5835	5850	5864	2	5	7	10	12
36	·5878	5892	5906	5920	5934	5948	5962	5976	5990	6004	2	5	7	9	12
37	·6018	6032	6046	6060	6074	6088	6101	6115	6129	6143	2	5	7	9	12
38	·6157	6170	6184	6198	6211	6225	6239	6252	6266	6280	2	5	7	9	11
39	·6293	6307	6320	6334	6347	6361	6374	6388	6401	6414	2	4	7	9	11
40	·6428	6441	6455	6468	6481	6494	6508	6521	6534	6547	2	4	7	9	11
41	·6561	6574	6587	6600	6613	6626	6639	6652	6665	6678	2	4	7	9	11
42	·6691	6704	6717	6730	6743	6756	6769	6782	6794	6807	2	4	6	9	11
43	·6820	6833	6845	6858	6871	6884	6896	6909	6921	6934	2	4	6	8	11
44	·6947	6959	6972	6984	6997	7009	7022	7034	7046	7059	2	4	6	8	10

°	0′	6′	12′	18′	24′	30′	36′	42′	48′	54′	1′	2′	3′	4′	5′
45	·7071	7083	7096	7108	7120	7133	7145	7157	7169	7181	2	4	6	8	10
46	·7193	7206	7218	7230	7242	7254	7266	7278	7290	7302	2	4	6	8	10
47	·7314	7325	7337	7349	7361	7373	7385	7396	7408	7420	2	4	6	8	10
48	·7431	7443	7455	7466	7478	7490	7501	7513	7524	7536	2	4	6	8	10
49	·7547	7559	7570	7581	7593	7604	7615	7627	7638	7649	2	4	6	8	9
50	·7660	7672	7683	7694	7705	7716	7727	7738	7749	7760	2	4	6	7	9
51	·7771	7782	7793	7804	7815	7826	7837	7848	7859	7869	2	4	5	7	9
52	·7880	7891	7902	7912	7923	7934	7944	7955	7965	7976	2	4	5	7	9
53	·7986	7997	8007	8018	8028	8039	8049	8059	8070	8080	2	3	5	7	9
54	·8090	8100	8111	8121	8131	8141	8151	8161	8171	8181	2	3	5	7	8
55	·8192	8202	8211	8221	8231	8241	8251	8261	8271	8281	2	3	5	7	8
56	·8290	8300	8310	8320	8329	8339	8348	8358	8368	8377	2	3	5	6	8
57	·8387	8396	8406	8415	8425	8434	8443	8453	8462	8471	2	3	5	6	8
58	·8480	8490	8499	8508	8517	8526	8536	8545	8554	8563	2	3	5	6	8
59	·8572	8581	8590	8599	8607	8616	8625	8634	8643	8652	1	3	4	6	7
60	·8660	8669	8678	8686	8695	8704	8712	8721	8729	8738	1	3	4	6	7
61	·8746	8755	8763	8771	8780	8788	8796	8805	8813	8821	1	3	4	6	7
62	·8829	8838	8846	8854	8862	8870	8878	8886	8894	8902	1	3	4	5	7
63	·8910	8918	8926	8934	8942	8949	8957	8965	8973	8980	1	3	4	5	6
64	·8988	8996	9003	9011	9018	9026	9033	9041	9048	9056	1	3	4	5	6
65	·9063	9070	9078	9085	9092	9100	9107	9114	9121	9128	1	2	4	5	6
66	·9135	9143	9150	9157	9164	9171	9178	9184	9191	9198	1	2	3	5	6
67	·9205	9212	9219	9225	9232	9239	9245	9252	9259	9265	1	2	3	4	6
68	·9272	9278	9285	9291	9298	9304	9311	9317	9323	9330	1	2	3	4	5
69	·9336	9342	9348	9354	9361	9367	9373	9379	9385	9391	1	2	3	4	5
70	·9397	9403	9409	9415	9421	9426	9432	9438	9444	9449	1	2	3	4	5
71	·9455	9461	9466	9472	9478	9483	9489	9494	9500	9505	1	2	3	4	5
72	·9511	9516	9521	9527	9532	9537	9542	9548	9553	9558	1	2	3	4	4
73	·9563	9568	9573	9578	9583	9588	9593	9598	9603	9608	1	2	2	3	4
74	·9613	9617	9622	9627	9632	9636	9641	9646	9650	9655	1	2	2	3	4
75	·9659	9664	9668	9673	9677	9681	9686	9690	9694	9699	1	1	2	3	4
76	·9703	9707	9711	9715	9720	9724	9728	9732	9736	9740	1	1	2	3	3
77	·9744	9748	9751	9755	9759	9763	9767	9770	9774	9778	1	1	2	3	3
78	·9781	9785	9789	9792	9796	9799	9803	9806	9810	9813	1	1	2	2	3
79	·9816	9820	9823	9826	9829	9833	9836	9839	9842	9845	1	1	2	2	3
80	·9848	9851	9854	9857	9860	9863	9866	9869	9871	9874	0	1	1	2	2
81	·9877	9880	9882	9885	9888	9890	9893	9895	9898	9900	0	1	1	2	2
82	·9903	9905	9907	9910	9912	9914	9917	9919	9921	9923	0	1	1	2	2
83	·9925	9928	9930	9932	9934	9936	9938	9940	9942	9943	0	1	1	1	2
84	·9945	9947	9949	9951	9952	9954	9956	9957	9959	9960	0	1	1	1	1
85	·9962	9963	9965	9966	9968	9969	9971	9972	9973	9974	0	0	1	1	1
86	·9976	9977	9978	9979	9980	9981	9982	9983	9984	9985	0	0	1	1	1
87	·9986	9987	9988	9989	9990	9990	9991	9992	9993	9993	0	0	0	0	0
88	·9994	9995	9995	9996	9996	9997	9997	9997	9998	9998	0	0	0	0	0
89	·9998	9999	9999	9999	9999	1·000	1·000	1·000	1·000	1·000	0	0	0	0	0

NATURAL COSINES

°	0′	6′	12′	18′	24′	30′	36′	42′	48′	54′	1′	2′	3′	4′	5′
0	1·000	1·000	1·000	1·000	1·000	1·000	**9999**	**9999**	**9999**	**9999**	0	0	0	0	0
1	·9998	9998	9998	9997	9997	9997	9996	9996	9995	9995	0	0	0	0	0
2	·9994	9993	9993	9992	9991	9990	9990	9989	9988	9987	0	0	0	0	0
3	·9986	9985	9984	9983	9982	9981	9980	9979	9978	9977	0	0	1	1	1
4	·9976	9974	9973	9972	9971	9969	9968	9966	9965	9963	0	0	1	1	1
5	·9962	9960	9959	9957	9956	9954	9952	9951	9949	9947	0	1	1	1	1
6	·9945	9943	9942	9940	9938	9936	9934	9932	9930	9928	0	1	1	1	2
7	·9925	9923	9921	9919	9917	9914	9912	9910	9907	9905	0	1	1	2	2
8	·9903	9900	9898	9895	9893	9890	9888	9885	9882	9880	0	1	1	2	2
9	·9877	9874	9871	9869	9866	9863	9860	9857	9854	9851	0	1	1	2	2
10	·9848	9845	9842	9839	9836	9833	9829	9826	9823	9820	1	1	2	2	3
11	·9816	9813	9810	9806	9803	9799	9796	9792	9789	9785	1	1	2	2	3
12	·9781	9778	9774	9770	9767	9763	9759	9755	9751	9748	1	1	2	3	3
13	·9744	9740	9736	9732	9728	9724	9720	9715	9711	9707	1	1	2	3	3
14	·9703	9699	9694	9690	9686	9681	9677	9673	9668	9664	1	1	2	3	4
15	·9659	9655	9650	9646	9641	9636	9632	9627	9622	9617	1	2	2	3	4
16	·9613	9608	9603	9598	9593	9588	9583	9578	9573	9568	1	2	2	3	4
17	·9563	9558	9553	9548	9542	9537	9532	9527	9521	9516	1	2	3	4	4
18	·9511	9505	9500	9494	9489	9483	9478	9472	9466	9461	1	2	3	4	5
19	·9455	9449	9444	9438	9432	9426	9421	9415	9409	9403	1	2	3	4	5
20	·9397	9391	9385	9379	9373	9367	9361	9354	9348	9342	1	2	3	4	5
21	·9336	9330	9323	9317	9311	9304	9298	9291	9285	9278	1	2	3	4	5
22	·9272	9265	9259	9252	9245	9239	9232	9225	9219	9212	1	2	3	4	6
23	·9205	9198	9191	9184	9178	9171	9164	9157	9150	9143	1	2	3	5	6
24	·9135	9128	9121	9114	9107	9100	9092	9085	9078	9070	1	2	4	5	6
25	·9063	9056	9048	9041	9033	9026	9018	9011	9003	8996	1	3	4	5	6
26	·8988	8980	8973	8965	8957	8949	8942	8934	8926	8918	1	3	4	5	6
27	·8910	8902	8894	8886	8878	8870	8862	8854	8846	8838	1	3	4	5	7
28	·8829	8821	8813	8805	8796	8788	8780	8771	8763	8755	1	3	4	6	7
29	·8746	8738	8729	8721	8712	8704	8695	8686	8678	8669	1	3	4	6	7
30	·8660	8652	8643	8634	8625	8616	8607	8599	8590	8581	1	3	4	6	7
31	·8572	8563	8554	8545	8536	8526	8517	8508	8499	8490	2	3	5	6	8
32	·8480	8471	8462	8453	8443	8434	8425	8415	8406	8396	2	3	5	6	8
33	·8387	8377	8368	8358	8348	8339	8329	8320	8310	8300	2	3	5	6	8
34	·8290	8281	8271	8261	8251	8241	8231	8221	8211	8202	2	3	5	7	8
35	·8192	8181	8171	8161	8151	8141	8131	8121	8111	8100	2	3	5	7	8
36	·8090	8080	8070	8059	8049	8039	8028	8018	8007	7997	2	3	5	7	9
37	·7986	7976	7965	7955	7944	7934	7923	7912	7902	7891	2	4	5	7	9
38	·7880	7869	7859	7848	7837	7826	7815	7804	7793	7782	2	4	5	7	9
39	·7771	7760	7749	7738	7727	7716	7705	7694	7683	7672	2	4	6	7	9
40	·7660	7649	7638	7627	7615	7604	7593	7581	7570	7559	2	4	6	8	9
41	·7547	7536	7524	7513	7501	7490	7478	7466	7455	7443	2	4	6	8	10
42	·7431	7420	7408	7396	7385	7373	7361	7349	7337	7325	2	4	6	8	10
43	·7314	7302	7290	7278	7266	7254	7242	7230	7218	7206	2	4	6	8	10
44	·7193	7181	7169	7157	7145	7133	7120	7108	7096	7083	2	4	6	8	10

Figures in **bold** type show change of integer

NATURAL COSINES

°	0'	6'	12'	18'	24'	30'	36'	42'	48'	54'	1'	2'	3'	4'	5'
45	·7071	7059	7046	7034	7022	7009	6997	6984	6972	6959	2	4	6	8	10
46	·6947	6934	6921	6909	6896	6884	6871	6858	6845	6833	2	4	6	8	11
47	·6820	6807	6794	6782	6769	6756	6743	6730	6717	6704	2	4	6	9	11
48	·6691	6678	6665	6652	6639	6626	6613	6600	6587	6574	2	4	7	9	11
49	·6561	6547	6534	6521	6508	6494	6481	6468	6455	6441	2	4	7	9	11
50	·6428	6414	6401	6388	6374	6361	6347	6334	6320	6307	2	4	7	9	11
51	·6293	6280	6266	6252	6239	6225	6211	6198	6184	6170	2	5	7	9	11
52	·6157	6143	6129	6115	6101	6088	6074	6060	6046	6032	2	5	7	9	12
53	·6018	6004	5990	5976	5962	5948	5934	5920	5906	5892	2	5	7	9	12
54	·5878	5864	5850	5835	5821	5807	5793	5779	5764	5750	2	5	7	9	12
55	·5736	5721	5707	5693	5678	5664	5650	5635	5621	5606	2	5	7	10	12
56	·5592	5577	5563	5548	5534	5519	5505	5490	5476	5461	2	5	7	10	12
57	·5446	5432	5417	5402	5388	5373	5358	5344	5329	5314	2	5	7	10	12
58	·5299	5284	5270	5255	5240	5225	5210	5195	5180	5165	2	5	7	10	12
59	·5150	5135	5120	5105	5090	5075	5060	5045	5030	5015	3	5	8	10	13
60	·5000	4985	4970	4955	4939	4924	4909	4894	4879	4863	3	5	8	10	13
61	·4848	4833	4818	4802	4787	4772	4756	4741	4726	4710	3	5	8	10	13
62	·4695	4679	4664	4648	4633	4617	4602	4586	4571	4555	3	5	8	10	13
63	·4540	4524	4509	4493	4478	4462	4446	4431	4415	4399	3	5	8	10	13
64	·4384	4368	4352	4337	4321	4305	4289	4274	4258	4242	3	5	8	11	13
65	·4226	4210	4195	4179	4163	4147	4131	4115	4099	4083	3	5	8	11	13
66	·4067	4051	4035	4019	4003	3987	3971	3955	3939	3923	3	5	8	11	13
67	·3907	3891	3875	3859	3843	3827	3811	3795	3778	3762	3	5	8	11	13
68	·3746	3730	3714	3697	3681	3665	3649	3633	3616	3600	3	5	8	11	14
69	·3584	3567	3551	3535	3518	3502	3486	3469	3453	3437	3	5	8	11	14
70	·3420	3404	3387	3371	3355	3338	3322	3305	3289	3272	3	5	8	11	14
71	·3256	3239	3223	3206	3190	3173	3156	3140	3123	3107	3	6	8	11	14
72	·3090	3074	3057	3040	3024	3007	2990	2974	2957	2940	3	6	8	11	14
73	·2924	2907	2890	2874	2857	2840	2823	2807	2790	2773	3	6	8	11	14
74	·2756	2740	2723	2706	2689	2672	2656	2639	2622	2605	3	6	8	11	14
75	·2588	2571	2554	2538	2521	2504	2487	2470	2453	2436	3	6	8	11	14
76	·2419	2402	2385	2368	2351	2334	2317	2300	2284	2267	3	6	8	11	14
77	·2250	2233	2215	2198	2181	2164	2147	2130	2113	2096	3	6	9	11	14
78	·2079	2062	2045	2028	2011	1994	1977	1959	1942	1925	3	6	9	11	14
79	·1908	1891	1874	1857	1840	1822	1805	1788	1771	1754	3	6	9	11	14
80	·1736	1719	1702	1685	1668	1650	1633	1616	1599	1582	3	6	9	11	14
81	·1564	1547	1530	1513	1495	1478	1461	1444	1426	1409	3	6	9	12	14
82	·1392	1374	1357	1340	1323	1305	1288	1271	1253	1236	3	6	9	12	14
83	·1219	1201	1184	1167	1149	1132	1115	1097	1080	1063	3	6	9	12	14
84	·1045	1028	1011	0993	0976	0958	0941	0924	0906	0889	3	6	9	12	14
85	·0872	0854	0837	0819	0802	0785	0767	0750	0732	0715	3	6	9	12	14
86	·0698	0680	0663	0645	0628	0610	0593	0576	0558	0541	3	6	9	12	15
87	·0523	0506	0488	0471	0454	0436	0419	0401	0384	0366	3	6	9	12	15
88	·0349	0332	0314	0297	0279	0262	0244	0227	0209	0192	3	6	9	12	15
89	·0175	0157	0140	0122	0105	0087	0070	0052	0035	0017	3	6	9	12	15

NATURAL TANGENTS

°	0′	6′	12′	18′	24′	30′	36′	42′	48′	54′	1′	2′	3′	4′	5′
0	·0000	0017	0035	0052	0070	0087	0105	0122	0140	0157	3	6	9	12	15
1	·0175	0192	0209	0227	0244	0262	0279	0297	0314	0332	3	6	9	12	15
2	·0349	0367	0384	0402	0419	0437	0454	0472	0489	0507	3	6	9	12	15
3	·0524	0542	0559	0577	0594	0612	0629	0647	0664	0682	3	6	9	12	15
4	·0699	0717	0734	0752	0769	0787	0805	0822	0840	0857	3	6	9	12	15
5	·0875	0892	0910	0928	0945	0963	0981	0998	1016	1033	3	6	9	12	15
6	·1051	1069	1086	1104	1122	1139	1157	1175	1192	1210	3	6	9	12	15
7	·1228	1246	1263	1281	1299	1317	1334	1352	1370	1388	3	6	9	12	15
8	·1405	1423	1441	1459	1477	1495	1512	1530	1548	1566	3	6	9	12	15
9	·1584	1602	1620	1638	1655	1673	1691	1709	1727	1745	3	6	9	12	15
10	·1763	1781	1799	1817	1835	1853	1871	1890	1908	1926	3	6	9	12	15
11	·1944	1962	1980	1998	2016	2035	2053	2071	2089	2107	3	6	9	12	15
12	·2126	2144	2162	2180	2199	2217	2235	2254	2272	2290	3	6	9	12	15
13	·2309	2327	2345	2364	2382	2401	2419	2438	2456	2475	3	6	9	12	15
14	·2493	2512	2530	2549	2568	2586	2605	2623	2642	2661	3	6	9	12	16
15	·2679	2698	2717	2736	2754	2773	2792	2811	2830	2849	3	6	9	13	16
16	·2867	2886	2905	2924	2943	2962	2981	3000	3019	3038	3	6	9	13	16
17	·3057	3076	3096	3115	3134	3153	3172	3191	3211	3230	3	6	10	13	16
18	·3249	3269	3288	3307	3327	3346	3365	3385	3404	3424	3	6	10	13	16
19	·3443	3463	3482	3502	3522	3541	3561	3581	3600	3620	3	7	10	13	16
20	·3640	3659	3679	3699	3719	3739	3759	3779	3799	3819	3	7	10	13	17
21	·3839	3859	3879	3899	3919	3939	3959	3979	4000	4020	3	7	10	13	17
22	·4040	4061	4081	4101	4122	4142	4163	4183	4204	4224	3	7	10	14	17
23	·4245	4265	4286	4307	4327	4348	4369	4390	4411	4431	3	7	10	14	17
24	·4452	4473	4494	4515	4536	4557	4578	4599	4621	4642	4	7	11	14	18
25	·4663	4684	4706	4727	4748	4770	4791	4813	4834	4856	4	7	11	14	18
26	·4877	4899	4921	4942	4964	4986	5008	5029	5051	5073	4	7	11	15	18
27	·5095	5117	5139	5161	5184	5206	5228	5250	5272	5295	4	7	11	15	18
28	·5317	5340	5362	5384	5407	5430	5452	5475	5498	5520	4	8	11	15	19
29	·5543	5566	5589	5612	5635	5658	5681	5704	5727	5750	4	8	12	15	19
30	·5774	5797	5820	5844	5867	5890	5914	5938	5961	5985	4	8	12	16	20
31	·6009	6032	6056	6080	6104	6128	6152	6176	6200	6224	4	8	12	16	20
32	·6249	6273	6297	6322	6346	6371	6395	6420	6445	6469	4	8	12	16	20
33	·6494	6519	6544	6569	6594	6619	6644	6669	6694	6720	4	8	13	17	21
34	·6745	6771	6796	6822	6847	6873	6899	6924	6950	6976	4	9	13	17	21
35	·7002	7028	7054	7080	7107	7133	7159	7186	7212	7239	4	9	13	18	22
36	·7265	7292	7319	7346	7373	7400	7427	7454	7481	7508	5	9	14	18	23
37	·7536	7563	7590	7618	7646	7673	7701	7729	7757	7785	5	9	14	18	23
38	·7813	7841	7869	7898	7926	7954	7983	8012	8040	8069	5	9	14	19	24
39	·8098	8127	8156	8185	8214	8243	8273	8302	8332	8361	5	10	15	20	24
40	·8391	8421	8451	8481	8511	8541	8571	8601	8632	8662	5	10	15	20	25
41	·8693	8724	8754	8785	8816	8847	8878	8910	8941	8972	5	10	16	21	26
42	·9004	9036	9067	9099	9131	9163	9195	9228	9260	9293	5	11	16	21	27
43	·9325	9358	9391	9424	9457	9490	9523	9556	9590	9623	6	11	17	22	28
44	·9657	9691	9725	9759	9793	9827	9861	9896	9930	9965	6	11	17	23	29

NATURAL TANGENTS

°	0'	6'	12'	18'	24'	30'	36'	42'	48'	54'	1'	2'	3'	4'	5'
45	1·0000	0035	0070	0105	0141	0176	0212	0247	0283	0319	6	12	18	24	30
46	1·0355	0392	0428	0464	0501	0538	0575	0612	0649	0686	6	12	18	25	31
47	1·0724	0761	0799	0837	0875	0913	0951	0990	1028	1067	6	13	19	25	32
48	1·1106	1145	1184	1224	1263	1303	1343	1383	1423	1463	7	13	20	26	33
49	1·1504	1544	1585	1626	1667	1708	1750	1792	1833	1875	7	14	21	28	34
50	1·1918	1960	2002	2045	2088	2131	2174	2218	2261	2305	7	14	22	29	36
51	1·2349	2393	2437	2482	2527	2572	2617	2662	2708	2753	8	15	23	30	38
52	1·2799	2846	2892	2938	2985	3032	3079	3127	3175	3222	8	16	24	31	39
53	1·3270	3319	3367	3416	3465	3514	3564	3613	3663	3713	8	16	25	33	41
54	1·3764	3814	3865	3916	3968	4019	4071	4124	4176	4229	9	17	26	34	43
55	1·4281	4335	4388	4442	4496	4550	4605	4659	4715	4770	9	18	27	36	45
56	1·4826	4882	4938	4994	5051	5108	5166	5224	5282	5340	10	19	29	38	48
57	1·5399	5458	5517	5577	5637	5697	5757	5818	5880	5941	10	20	30	40	50
58	1·6003	6066	6128	6191	6255	6319	6383	6447	6512	6577	11	21	32	43	53
59	1·6643	6709	6775	6842	6909	6977	7045	7113	7182	7251	11	23	34	45	56
60	1·7321	7391	7461	7532	7603	7675	7747	7820	7893	7966	12	24	36	48	60
61	1·8040	8115	8190	8265	8341	8418	8495	8572	8650	8728	13	26	38	51	64
62	1·8807	8887	8967	9047	9128	9210	9292	9375	9458	9542	14	27	41	55	68
63	1 9626	9711	9797	9883	9970	**0057**	**0145**	**0233**	**0323**	**0413**	15	29	44	58	73
64	2·0503	0594	0686	0778	0872	0965	1060	1155	1251	1348	16	31	47	63	78
65	2·1445	1543	1642	1742	1842	1943	2045	2148	2251	2355	17	34	51	68	85
66	2·2460	2566	2673	2781	2889	2998	3109	3220	3332	3445	18	37	55	73	92
67	2·3559	3673	3789	3906	4023	4142	4262	4383	4504	4627	20	40	60	79	99
68	2·4751	4876	5002	5129	5257	5386	5517	5649	5782	5916	22	43	65	87	108
69	2·6051	6187	6325	6464	6605	6746	6889	7034	7179	7326	24	47	71	95	118
70	2·7475	7625	7776	7929	8083	8239	8397	8556	8716	8878	26	52	78	104	130
71	2·9042	9208	9375	9544	9714	9887	**0061**	**0237**	**0415**	**0595**	29	58	87	116	145
72	3·0777	0961	1146	1334	1524	1716	1910	2106	2305	2506	32	64	96	129	161
73	3·2709	2914	3122	3332	3544	3759	3977	4197	4420	4646	36	72	108	144	180
74	3·4874	5105	5339	5576	5816	6059	6305	6554	6806	7062	41	81	122	163	203
75	3·7321	7583	7848	8118	8391	8667	8947	9232	9520	9812	Use interpolation				
76	4·0108	0408	0713	1022	1335	1653	1976	2303	2635	2972					
77	4·3315	3662	4015	4373	4737	5107	5483	5864	6252	6646					
78	4·7046	7453	7867	8288	8716	9152	9594	**0045**	**0504**	**0970**					
79	5·1446	1929	2422	2924	3435	3955	4486	5026	5578	6140					
80	5·6713	7297	7894	8502	9124	9758	**0405**	**1066**	**1742**	**2432**					
81	6·3138	3859	4596	5350	6122	6912	7720	8548	9395	**0204**					
82	7·1154	2066	3002	3962	4947	5958	6996	8062	9158	**0285**					
83	8·1443	2636	3863	5126	6427	7769	9152	**0579**	**2052**	**3572**					
84	9·5144	6768	8448	10·02	10·20	10·39	10·58	10·78	10·99	11·20					
85	11·43	11·66	11·91	12·16	12·43	12·71	13·00	13·30	13·62	13·95					
86	14·30	14·67	15·06	15·46	15·89	16·35	16·83	17·34	17·89	18·46					
87	19·08	19·74	20·45	21·20	22·02	22·90	23·86	24·90	26·03	27·27					
88	28·64	30·14	31·82	33·69	35·80	38·19	40·92	44·07	47·74	52·08					
89	57·29	63·66	71·62	81·85	95·49	114·6	143·2	191·0	286·5	573·c					

Figures in **bold type** show changes of integer

SQUARES

	0	1	2	3	4	5	6	7	8	9	1	2	3	4	5	6	7	8	9
10	1000	1020	1040	1061	1082	1103	1124	1145	1166	1188	2	4	6	8	10	13	15	17	19
11	1210	1232	1254	1277	1300	1323	1346	1369	1392	1416	2	5	7	9	11	14	16	18	21
12	1440	1464	1488	1513	1538	1563	1588	1613	1638	1664	2	5	7	10	12	15	17	20	22
13	1690	1716	1742	1769	1796	1823	1850	1877	1904	1932	3	5	8	11	13	16	19	22	24
14	1960	1988	2016	2045	2074	2103	2132	2161	2190	2220	3	6	9	12	14	17	20	23	26
15	2250	2280	2310	2341	2372	2403	2434	2465	2496	2528	3	6	9	12	15	19	22	25	28
16	2560	2592	2624	2657	2690	2723	2756	2789	2822	2856	3	7	10	13	16	20	23	26	30
17	2890	2924	2958	2993	3028	3063	3098	3133	3168	3204	3	7	10	14	17	21	24	28	31
18	3240	3276	3312	3349	3386	3423	3460	3497	3534	3572	4	7	11	15	18	22	26	30	33
19	3610	3648	3686	3725	3764	3803	3842	3881	3920	3960	4	8	12	16	19	23	27	31	35
20	4000	4040	4080	4121	4162	4203	4244	4285	4326	4368	4	8	12	16	20	25	29	33	37
21	4410	4452	4494	4537	4580	4623	4666	4709	4752	4796	4	9	13	17	21	26	30	34	39
22	4840	4884	4928	4973	5018	5063	5108	5153	5198	5244	4	9	13	18	22	27	31	36	40
23	5290	5336	5382	5429	5476	5523	5570	5617	5664	5712	5	9	14	19	23	28	33	38	42
24	5760	5808	5856	5905	5954	6003	6052	6101	6150	6200	5	10	15	20	24	29	34	39	44
25	6250	6300	6350	6401	6452	6503	6554	6605	6656	6708	5	10	15	20	25	31	36	41	46
26	6760	6812	6864	6917	6970	7023	7076	7129	7182	7236	5	11	16	21	26	32	37	42	48
27	7290	7344	7398	7453	7508	7563	7618	7673	7728	7784	5	11	16	22	27	33	38	44	49
28	7840	7896	7952	8009	8066	8123	8180	8237	8294	8352	6	11	17	23	28	34	40	46	51
29	8410	8468	8526	8585	8644	8703	8762	8821	8880	8940	6	12	18	24	30	35	41	47	53
30	9000	9060	9120	9181	9242	9303	9364	9425	9486	9548	6	12	18	24	31	37	43	49	55
31	9610	9672	9734	9797	9860	9923	9986				6	13	19	25	31	38	44	50	56
31								1005	1011	1018	1	1	2	3	3	4	5	5	6
32	1024	1030	1037	1043	1050	1056	1063	1069	1076	1082	1	1	2	3	3	4	5	5	6
33	1089	1096	1102	1109	1116	1122	1129	1136	1142	1149	1	1	2	3	3	4	5	5	6
34	1156	1163	1170	1176	1183	1190	1197	1204	1211	1218	1	1	2	3	3	4	5	6	6
35	1225	1232	1239	1246	1253	1260	1267	1274	1282	1289	1	1	2	3	4	4	5	6	6
36	1296	1303	1310	1318	1325	1332	1340	1347	1354	1362	1	1	2	3	4	4	5	6	7
37	1369	1376	1384	1391	1399	1406	1414	1421	1429	1436	1	2	2	3	4	5	5	6	7
38	1444	1452	1459	1467	1475	1482	1490	1498	1505	1513	1	2	2	3	4	5	5	6	7
39	1521	1529	1537	1544	1552	1560	1568	1576	1584	1592	1	2	2	3	4	5	6	6	7
40	1600	1608	1616	1624	1632	1640	1648	1656	1665	1673	1	2	2	3	4	5	6	6	7
41	1681	1689	1697	1706	1714	1722	1731	1739	1747	1756	1	2	2	3	4	5	6	7	7
42	1764	1772	1781	1789	1798	1806	1815	1823	1832	1840	1	2	3	3	4	5	6	7	8
43	1849	1858	1866	1875	1884	1892	1901	1910	1918	1927	1	2	3	3	4	5	6	7	8
44	1936	1945	1954	1962	1971	1980	1989	1998	2007	2016	1	2	3	4	4	5	6	7	8
45	2025	2034	2043	2052	2061	2070	2079	2088	2098	2107	1	2	3	4	5	5	6	7	8
46	2116	2125	2134	2144	2153	2162	2172	2181	2190	2200	1	2	3	4	5	6	7	7	8
47	2209	2218	2228	2237	2247	2256	2266	2275	2285	2294	1	2	3	4	5	6	7	8	9
48	2304	2314	2323	2333	2343	2352	2362	2372	2381	2391	1	2	3	4	5	6	7	8	9
49	2401	2411	2421	2430	2440	2450	2460	2470	2480	2490	1	2	3	4	5	6	7	8	9
50	2500	2510	2520	2530	2540	2550	2560	2570	2581	2591	1	2	3	4	5	6	7	8	9
51	2601	2611	2621	2632	2642	2652	2663	2673	2683	2694	1	2	3	4	5	6	7	8	9
52	2704	2714	2725	2735	2746	2756	2767	2777	2788	2798	1	2	3	4	5	6	7	8	9
53	2809	2820	2830	2841	2852	2862	2873	2884	2894	2905	1	2	3	4	5	6	7	9	10
54	2916	2927	2938	2948	2959	2970	2981	2992	3003	3014	1	2	3	4	5	7	8	9	10

The position of the decimal point should be found by inspection

SQUARES

	0	1	2	3	4	5	6	7	8	9	1 2 3 4	5	6 7 8 9
55	3025	3036	3047	3058	3069	3080	3091	3102	3114	3125	1 2 3 4	6	7 8 9 10
56	3136	3147	3158	3170	3181	3192	3204	3215	3226	3238	1 2 3 5	6	7 8 9 10
57	3249	3260	3272	3283	3295	3306	3318	3329	3341	3352	1 2 3 5	6	7 8 9 10
58	3364	3376	3387	3399	3411	3422	3434	3446	3457	3469	1 2 4 5	6	7 8 9 11
59	3481	3493	3505	3516	3528	3540	3552	3564	3576	3588	1 2 4 5	6	7 8 10 11
60	3600	3612	3624	3636	3648	3660	3672	3684	3697	3709	1 2 4 5	6	7 8 10 11
61	3721	3733	3745	3758	3770	3782	3795	3807	3819	3832	1 2 4 5	6	7 9 10 11
62	3844	3856	3869	3881	3894	3906	3919	3931	3944	3956	1 3 4 5	6	8 9 10 11
63	3969	3982	3994	4007	4020	4032	4045	4058	4070	4083	1 3 4 5	6	8 9 10 11
64	4096	4109	4122	4134	4147	4160	4173	4186	4199	4212	1 3 4 5	6	8 9 10 12
65	4225	4238	4251	4264	4277	4290	4303	4316	4330	4343	1 3 4 5	7	8 9 10 12
66	4356	4369	4382	4396	4409	4422	4436	4449	4462	4476	1 3 4 5	7	8 9 11 12
67	4489	4502	4516	4529	4543	4556	4570	4583	4597	4610	1 3 4 5	7	8 9 11 12
68	4624	4638	4651	4665	4679	4692	4706	4720	4733	4747	1 3 4 5	7	8 10 11 12
69	4761	4775	4789	4802	4816	4830	4844	4858	4872	4886	1 3 4 6	7	8 10 11 13
70	4900	4914	4928	4942	4956	4970	4984	4998	5013	5027	1 3 4 6	7	8 10 11 13
71	5041	5055	5069	5084	5098	5112	5127	5141	5155	5170	1 3 4 6	7	9 10 11 13
72	5184	5198	5213	5227	5242	5256	5271	5285	5300	5314	1 3 4 6	7	9 10 12 13
73	5329	5344	5358	5373	5388	5402	5417	5432	5446	5461	1 3 4 6	7	9 10 12 13
74	5476	5491	5506	5520	5535	5550	5565	5580	5595	5610	1 3 4 6	7	9 10 12 13
75	5625	5640	5655	5670	5685	5700	5715	5730	5746	5761	2 3 5 6	8	9 11 12 14
76	5776	5791	5806	5822	5837	5852	5868	5883	5898	5914	2 3 5 6	8	9 11 12 14
77	5929	5944	5960	5975	5991	6006	6022	6037	6053	6068	2 3 5 6	8	9 11 12 14
78	6084	6100	6115	6131	6147	6162	6178	6194	6209	6225	2 3 5 6	8	9 11 13 14
79	6241	6257	6273	6288	6304	6320	6336	6352	6368	6384	2 3 5 6	8	10 11 13 14
80	6400	6416	6432	6448	6464	6480	6496	6512	6529	6545	2 3 5 6	8	10 11 13 14
81	6561	6577	6593	6610	6626	6642	6659	6675	6691	6708	2 3 5 7	8	10 11 13 15
82	6724	6740	6757	6773	6790	6806	6823	6839	6856	6872	2 3 5 7	8	10 12 13 15
83	6889	6906	6922	6939	6956	6972	6989	7006	7022	7039	2 3 5 7	8	10 12 13 15
84	7056	7073	7090	7106	7123	7140	7157	7174	7191	7208	2 3 5 7	8	10 12 14 15
85	7225	7242	7259	7276	7293	7310	7327	7344	7362	7379	2 3 5 7	9	10 12 14 15
86	7396	7413	7430	7448	7465	7482	7500	7517	7534	7552	2 3 5 7	9	10 12 14 16
87	7569	7586	7604	7621	7639	7656	7674	7691	7709	7726	2 4 5 7	9	11 12 14 16
88	7744	7762	7779	7797	7815	7832	7850	7868	7885	7903	2 4 5 7	9	11 12 14 16
89	7921	7939	7957	7974	7992	8010	8028	8046	8064	8082	2 4 5 7	9	11 13 14 16
90	8100	8118	8136	8154	8172	8190	8208	8226	8245	8263	2 4 5 7	9	11 13 14 16
91	8281	8299	8317	8336	8354	8372	8391	8409	8427	8446	2 4 5 7	9	11 13 15 16
92	8464	8482	8501	8519	8538	8556	8575	8593	8612	8630	2 4 6 7	9	11 13 15 17
93	8649	8668	8686	8705	8724	8742	8761	8780	8798	8817	2 4 6 7	9	11 13 15 17
94	8836	8855	8874	8892	8911	8930	8949	8968	8987	9006	2 4 6 8	9	11 13 15 17
95	9025	9044	9063	9082	9101	9120	9139	9158	9178	9197	2 4 6 8	10	11 13 15 17
96	9216	9235	9254	9274	9293	9312	9332	9351	9370	9390	2 4 6 8	10	12 14 15 17
97	9409	9428	9448	9467	9487	9506	9526	9545	9565	9584	2 4 6 8	10	12 14 16 18
98	9604	9624	9643	9663	9683	9702	9722	9742	9761	9781	2 4 6 8	10	12 14 16 18
99	9801	9821	9841	9860	9880	9900	9920	9940	9960	9980	2 4 6 8	10	12 14 16 18

The position of the decimal point should be found by inspection

SQUARE ROOTS

	0	1	2	3	4	5	6	7	8	9	1 2 3 4	5	6 7 8 9
10	1000	1005	1010	1015	1020	1025	1030	1034	1039	1044	0 1 1 2	2	3 3 4 4
	3162	3178	3194	3209	3225	3240	3256	3271	3286	3302	2 3 5 6	8	9 11 12 14
11	1049	1054	1058	1063	1068	1072	1077	1082	1086	1091	0 1 1 2	2	3 3 4 4
	3317	3332	3347	3362	3376	3391	3406	3421	3435	3450	1 3 4 6	7	9 10 12 13
12	1095	1100	1105	1109	1114	1118	1122	1127	1131	1136	0 1 1 2	2	3 3 4 4
	3464	3479	3493	3507	3521	3536	3550	3564	3578	3592	1 3 4 6	7	9 10 11 13
13	1140	1145	1149	1153	1158	1162	1166	1170	1175	1179	0 1 1 2	2	3 3 3 4
	3606	3619	3633	3647	3661	3674	3688	3701	3715	3728	1 3 4 5	7	8 10 11 12
14	1183	1187	1192	1196	1200	1204	1208	1212	1217	1221	0 1 1 2	2	3 3 3 4
	3742	3755	3768	3782	3795	3808	3821	3834	3847	3860	1 3 4 5	7	8 9 10 12
15	1225	1229	1233	1237	1241	1245	1249	1253	1257	1261	0 1 1 2	2	3 3 3 4
	3873	3886	3899	3912	3924	3937	3950	3962	3975	3987	1 3 4 5	6	8 9 10 11
16	1265	1269	1273	1277	1281	1285	1288	1292	1296	1300	0 1 1 2	2	2 3 3 4
	4000	4012	4025	4037	4050	4062	4074	4087	4099	4111	1 2 4 5	6	7 9 10 11
17	1304	1308	1311	1315	1319	1323	1327	1330	1334	1338	0 1 1 2	2	2 3 3 3
	4123	4135	4147	4159	4171	4183	4195	4207	4219	4231	1 2 4 5	6	7 8 10 11
18	1342	1345	1349	1353	1356	1360	1364	1367	1371	1375	0 1 1 1	2	2 3 3 3
	4243	4254	4266	4278	4290	4301	4313	4324	4336	4347	1 2 3 5	6	7 8 9 10
19	1378	1382	1386	1389	1393	1396	1400	1404	1407	1411	0 1 1 1	2	2 3 3 3
	4359	4370	4382	4393	4405	4416	4427	4438	4450	4461	1 2 3 5	6	7 8 9 10
20	1414	1418	1421	1425	1428	1432	1435	1439	1442	1446	0 1 1 1	2	2 2 3 3
	4472	4483	4494	4506	4517	4528	4539	4550	4561	4572	1 2 3 4	6	7 8 9 10
21	1449	1453	1456	1459	1463	1466	1470	1473	1476	1480	0 1 1 1	2	2 2 3 3
	4583	4593	4604	4615	4626	4637	4648	4658	4669	4680	1 2 3 4	5	6 7 9 10
22	1483	1487	1490	1493	1497	1500	1503	1507	1510	1513	0 1 1 1	2	2 2 3 3
	4690	4701	4712	4722	4733	4743	4754	4764	4775	4785	1 2 3 4	5	6 7 8 10
23	1517	1520	1523	1526	1530	1533	1536	1539	1543	1546	0 1 1 1	2	2 2 3 3
	4796	4806	4817	4827	4837	4848	4858	4868	4879	4889	1 2 3 4	5	6 7 8 9
24	1549	1552	1556	1559	1562	1565	1568	1572	1575	1578	0 1 1 1	2	2 2 3 3
	4899	4909	4919	4930	4940	4950	4960	4970	4980	4990	1 2 3 4	5	6 7 8 9
25	1581	1584	1587	1591	1594	1597	1600	1603	1606	1609	0 1 1 1	2	2 2 3 3
	5000	5010	5020	5030	5040	5050	5060	5070	5079	5089	1 2 3 4	5	6 7 8 9
26	1612	1616	1619	1622	1625	1628	1631	1634	1637	1640	0 1 1 1	2	2 2 2 3
	5099	5109	5119	5128	5138	5148	5158	5167	5177	5187	1 2 3 4	5	6 7 8 9
27	1643	1646	1649	1652	1655	1658	1661	1664	1667	1670	0 1 1 1	1	2 2 2 3
	5196	5206	5215	5225	5235	5244	5254	5263	5273	5282	1 2 3 4	5	6 7 8 9
28	1673	1676	1679	1682	1685	1688	1691	1694	1697	1700	0 1 1 1	1	2 2 2 3
	5292	5301	5310	5320	5329	5339	5348	5357	5367	5376	1 2 3 4	5	6 7 7 8
29	1703	1706	1709	1712	1715	1718	1720	1723	1726	1729	0 1 1 1	1	2 2 2 3
	5385	5394	5404	5413	5422	5431	5441	5450	5459	5468	1 2 3 4	5	6 6 7 8
30	1732	1735	1738	1741	1744	1746	1749	1752	1755	1758	0 1 1 1	1	2 2 2 3
	5477	5486	5495	5505	5514	5523	5532	5541	5550	5559	1 2 3 4	5	5 6 7 8
31	1761	1764	1766	1769	1772	1775	1778	1780	1783	1786	0 1 1 1	1	2 2 2 2
	5568	5577	5586	5595	5604	5612	5621	5630	5639	5648	1 2 3 4	4	5 6 7 8
32	1789	1792	1794	1797	1800	1803	1806	1808	1811	1814	0 1 1 1	1	2 2 2 2
	5657	5666	5675	5683	5692	5701	5710	5718	5727	5736	1 2 3 4	4	5 6 7 8

The position of the decimal point and the first significant figure should be found by inspection.

SQUARE ROOTS

	0	1	2	3	4	5	6	7	8	9	1	2	3	4	5	6	7	8	9
32	1789	1792	1794	1797	1800	1803	1806	1808	1811	1814	0	1	1	1	1	2	2	2	3
	5657	5666	5675	5683	5692	5701	5710	5718	5727	5736	1	2	3	4	4	5	6	7	8
33	1817	1819	1822	1825	1828	1830	1833	1836	1838	1841	0	1	1	1	1	2	2	2	2
	5745	5753	5762	5771	5779	5788	5797	5805	5814	5822	1	2	3	3	4	5	6	7	8
34	1844	1847	1849	1852	1855	1857	1860	1863	1865	1868	0	1	1	1	1	2	2	2	2
	5831	5840	5848	5857	5865	5874	5882	5891	5899	5908	1	2	3	3	4	5	6	7	8
35	1871	1873	1876	1879	1881	1884	1887	1889	1892	1895	0	1	1	1	1	2	2	2	2
	5916	5925	5933	5941	5950	5958	5967	5975	5983	5992	1	2	3	3	4	5	6	7	8
36	1897	1900	1903	1905	1908	1910	1913	1916	1918	1921	0	1	1	1	1	2	2	2	2
	6000	6008	6017	6025	6033	6042	6050	6058	6066	6075	1	2	2	3	4	5	6	7	7
37	1924	1926	1929	1931	1934	1936	1939	1942	1944	1947	0	1	1	1	1	2	2	2	2
	6083	6091	6099	6107	6116	6124	6132	6140	6148	6156	1	2	2	3	4	5	6	6	7
38	1949	1952	1954	1957	1960	1962	1965	1967	1970	1972	0	1	1	1	1	2	2	2	2
	6164	6173	6181	6189	6197	6205	6213	6221	6229	6237	1	2	2	3	4	5	6	6	7
39	1975	1977	1980	1982	1985	1987	1990	1992	1995	1997	0	1	1	1	1	1	2	2	2
	6245	6253	6261	6269	6277	6285	6293	6301	6309	6317	1	2	2	3	4	5	6	6	7
40	2000	2002	2005	2007	2010	2012	2015	2017	2020	2022	0	0	1	1	1	1	2	2	2
	6325	6332	6340	6348	6356	6364	6372	6380	6387	6395	1	2	2	3	4	5	5	6	7
41	2025	2027	2030	2032	2035	2037	2040	2042	2045	2047	0	0	1	1	1	1	2	2	2
	6403	6411	6419	6427	6434	6442	6450	6458	6465	6473	1	2	2	3	4	5	5	6	7
42	2049	2052	2054	2057	2059	2062	2064	2066	2069	2071	0	0	1	1	1	1	2	2	2
	6481	6488	6496	6504	6512	6519	6527	6535	6542	6550	1	2	2	3	4	5	5	6	7
43	2074	2076	2078	2081	2083	2086	2088	2090	2093	2095	0	0	1	1	1	1	2	2	2
	6557	6565	6573	6580	6588	6595	6603	6611	6618	6626	1	2	2	3	4	5	5	6	7
44	2098	2100	2102	2105	2107	2110	2112	2114	2117	2119	0	0	1	1	1	1	2	2	2
	6633	6641	6648	6656	6663	6671	6678	6686	6693	6701	1	1	2	3	4	5	6	7	7
45	2121	2124	2126	2128	2131	2133	2135	2138	2140	2142	0	0	1	1	1	1	2	2	2
	6708	6716	6723	6731	6738	6745	6753	6760	6768	6775	1	1	2	3	4	4	5	6	7
46	2145	2147	2149	2152	2154	2156	2159	2161	2163	2166	0	0	1	1	1	1	2	2	2
	6782	6790	6797	6804	6812	6819	6826	6834	6841	6848	1	1	2	3	4	4	5	6	7
47	2168	2170	2173	2175	2177	2179	2182	2184	2186	2189	0	0	1	1	1	1	2	2	2
	6856	6863	6870	6877	6885	6892	6899	6907	6914	6921	1	1	2	3	4	4	5	6	6
48	2191	2193	2195	2198	2200	2202	2205	2207	2209	2211	0	0	1	1	1	1	2	2	2
	6928	6935	6943	6950	6957	6964	6971	6979	6986	6993	1	1	2	3	4	4	5	6	6
49	2214	2216	2218	2220	2223	2225	2227	2229	2232	2234	0	0	1	1	1	1	2	2	2
	7000	7007	7014	7021	7029	7036	7043	7050	7057	7064	1	1	2	3	4	4	5	6	6
50	2236	2238	2241	2243	2245	2247	2249	2252	2254	2256	0	0	1	1	1	1	2	2	2
	7071	7078	7085	7092	7099	7106	7113	7120	7127	7134	1	1	2	3	3	4	5	6	6
51	2258	2261	2263	2265	2267	2269	2272	2274	2276	2278	0	0	1	1	1	1	2	2	2
	7141	7148	7155	7162	7169	7176	7183	7190	7197	7204	1	1	2	3	3	4	5	6	6
52	2280	2283	2285	2287	2289	2291	2293	2296	2298	2300	0	0	1	1	1	1	2	2	2
	7211	7218	7225	7232	7239	7246	7253	7259	7266	7273	1	1	2	3	3	4	5	6	6
53	2302	2304	2307	2309	2311	2313	2315	2317	2319	2322	0	0	1	1	1	1	2	2	2
	7280	7287	7294	7301	7308	7314	7321	7328	7335	7342	1	1	2	3	3	4	5	5	6
54	2324	2326	2328	2330	2332	2335	2337	2339	2341	2343	0	0	1	1	1	1	1	2	2
	7348	7355	7362	7369	7376	7382	7389	7396	7403	7409	1	1	2	3	3	4	5	5	6

The position of the decimal point and the first significant figure should be found by inspection.

	0	1	2	3	4	5	6	7	8	9	1 2 3 4	5	6 7 8 9
55	2345	2347	2349	2352	2354	2356	2358	2360	2362	2364	0 0 1 1	1	1 1 2 2
	7416	7423	7430	7436	7443	7450	7457	7463	7470	7477	1 1 2 3	3	4 5 5 6
56	2366	2369	2371	2373	2375	2377	2379	2381	2383	2385	0 0 1 1	1	1 1 2 2
	7483	7490	7497	7503	7510	7517	7523	7530	7537	7543	1 1 2 3	3	4 5 5 6
57	2387	2390	2392	2394	2396	2398	2400	2402	2404	2406	0 0 1 1	1	1 1 2 2
	7550	7556	7563	7570	7576	7583	7589	7596	7603	7609	1 1 2 3	3	4 5 5 6
58	2408	2410	2412	2415	2417	2419	2421	2423	2425	2427	0 0 1 1	1	1 1 2 2
	7616	7622	7629	7635	7642	7649	7655	7662	7668	7675	1 1 2 3	3	4 5 5 6
59	2429	2431	2433	2435	2437	2439	2441	2443	2445	2447	0 0 1 1	1	1 1 2 2
	7681	7688	7694	7701	7707	7714	7720	7727	7733	7740	1 1 2 3	3	4 5 5 6
60	2449	2452	2454	2456	2458	2460	2462	2464	2466	2468	0 0 1 1	1	1 1 2 2
	7746	7752	7759	7765	7772	7778	7785	7791	7797	7804	1 1 2 3	3	4 4 5 6
61	2470	2472	2474	2476	2478	2480	2482	2484	2486	2488	0 0 1 1	1	1 1 2 2
	7810	7817	7823	7829	7836	7842	7849	7855	7861	7868	1 1 2 3	3	4 4 5 6
62	2490	2492	2494	2496	2498	2500	2502	2504	2506	2508	0 0 1 1	1	1 1 2 2
	7874	7880	7887	7893	7899	7906	7912	7918	7925	7931	1 1 2 3	3	4 4 5 6
63	2510	2512	2514	2516	2518	2520	2522	2524	2526	2528	0 0 1 1	1	1 1 2 2
	7937	7944	7950	7956	7962	7969	7975	7981	7987	7994	1 1 2 3	3	4 4 5 6
64	2530	2532	2534	2536	2538	2540	2542	2544	2546	2548	0 0 1 1	1	1 1 2 2
	8000	8006	8012	8019	8025	8031	8037	8044	8050	8056	1 1 2 2	3	4 4 5 6
65	2550	2551	2553	2555	2557	2559	2561	2563	2565	2567	0 0 1 1	1	1 1 2 2
	8062	8068	8075	8081	8087	8093	8099	8106	8112	8118	1 1 2 2	3	4 4 5 6
66	2569	2571	2573	2575	2577	2579	2581	2583	2585	2587	0 0 1 1	1	1 1 2 2
	8124	8130	8136	8142	8149	8155	8161	8167	8173	8179	1 1 2 2	3	4 4 5 5
67	2588	2590	2592	2594	2596	2598	2600	2602	2604	2606	0 0 1 1	1	1 1 2 2
	8185	8191	8198	8204	8210	8216	8222	8228	8234	8240	1 1 2 2	3	4 4 5 5
68	2608	2610	2612	2613	2615	2617	2619	2621	2623	2625	0 0 1 1	1	1 1 2 2
	8246	8252	8258	8264	8270	8276	8283	8289	8295	8301	1 1 2 2	3	4 4 5 5
69	2627	2629	2631	2632	2634	2636	2638	2640	2642	2644	0 0 1 1	1	1 1 2 2
	8307	8313	8319	8325	8331	8337	8343	8349	8355	8361	1 1 2 2	3	4 4 5 5
70	2646	2648	2650	2651	2653	2655	2657	2659	2661	2663	0 0 1 1	1	1 1 2 2
	8367	8373	8379	8385	8390	8396	8402	8408	8414	8420	1 1 2 2	3	4 4 5 5
71	2665	2666	2668	2670	2672	2674	2676	2678	2680	2681	0 0 1 1	1	1 1 1 2
	8426	8432	8438	8444	8450	8456	8462	8468	8473	8479	1 1 2 2	3	4 4 5 5
72	2683	2685	2687	2689	2691	2693	2694	2696	2698	2700	0 0 1 1	1	1 1 1 2
	8485	8491	8497	8503	8509	8515	8521	8526	8532	8538	1 1 2 2	3	3 4 5 5
73	2702	2704	2706	2707	2709	2711	2713	2715	2717	2718	0 0 1 1	1	1 1 1 2
	8544	8550	8556	8562	8567	8573	8579	8585	8591	8597	1 1 2 2	3	3 4 5 5
74	2720	2722	2724	2726	2728	2729	2731	2733	2735	2737	0 0 1 1	1	1 1 1 2
	8602	8608	8614	8620	8626	8631	8637	8643	8649	8654	1 1 2 2	3	3 4 5 5
75	2739	2740	2742	2744	2746	2748	2750	2751	2753	2755	0 0 1 1	1	1 1 1 2
	8660	8666	8672	8678	8683	8689	8695	8701	8706	8712	1 1 2 2	3	3 4 5 5
76	2757	2759	2760	2762	2764	2766	2768	2769	2771	2773	0 0 1 1	1	1 1 1 2
	8718	8724	8729	8735	8741	8746	8752	8758	8764	8769	1 1 2 2	3	3 4 5 5
77	2775	2777	2778	2780	2782	2784	2786	2787	2789	2791	0 0 1 1	1	1 1 1 2
	8775	8781	8786	8792	8798	8803	8809	8815	8820	8826	1 1 2 2	3	3 4 5 5

The position of the decimal point and the first significant figure should be found by inspection.

SQUARE ROOTS

	0	1	2	3	4	5	6	7	8	9	1 2 3 4	5	6 7 8 9
77	2775	2777	2778	2780	2782	2784	2786	2787	2789	2791	0 0 1 1	1	1 1 1 2
	8775	8781	8786	8792	8798	8803	8809	8815	8820	8826	1 1 2 2	3	3 4 5 5
78	2793	2795	2796	2798	2800	2802	2804	2805	2807	2809	0 0 1 1	1	1 1 1 2
	8832	8837	8843	8849	8854	8860	8866	8871	8877	8883	1 1 2 2	3	3 4 4 5
79	2811	2812	2814	2816	2818	2820	2821	2823	2825	2827	0 0 1 1	1	1 1 1 2
	8888	8894	8899	8905	8911	8916	8922	8927	8933	8939	1 1 2 2	3	3 4 4 5
80	2828	2830	2832	2834	2835	2837	2839	2841	2843	2844	0 0 1 1	1	1 1 1 2
	8944	8950	8955	8961	8967	8972	8978	8983	8989	8994	1 1 2 2	3	3 4 4 5
81	2846	2848	2850	2851	2853	2855	2857	2858	2860	2862	0 0 1 1	1	1 1 1 2
	9000	9006	9011	9017	9022	9028	9033	9039	9044	9050	1 1 2 2	3	3 4 4 5
82	2864	2865	2867	2869	2871	2872	2874	2876	2877	2879	0 0 1 1	1	1 1 1 2
	9055	9061	9066	9072	9077	9083	9088	9094	9099	9105	1 1 2 2	3	3 4 4 5
83	2881	2883	2884	2886	2888	2890	2891	2893	2895	2897	0 0 1 1	1	1 1 1 2
	9110	9116	9121	9127	9132	9138	9143	9149	9154	9160	1 1 2 2	3	3 4 4 5
84	2898	2900	2902	2903	2905	2907	2909	2910	2912	2914	0 0 1 1	1	1 1 1 2
	9165	9171	9176	9182	9187	9192	9198	9203	9209	9214	1 1 2 2	3	3 4 4 5
85	2915	2917	2919	2921	2922	2924	2926	2927	2929	2931	0 0 1 1	1	1 1 1 2
	9220	9225	9230	9236	9241	9247	9252	9257	9263	9268	1 1 2 2	3	3 4 4 5
86	2933	2934	2936	2938	2939	2941	2943	2944	2946	2948	0 0 1 1	1	1 1 1 2
	9274	9279	9284	9290	9295	9301	9306	9311	9317	9322	1 1 2 2	3	3 4 4 5
87	2950	2951	2953	2955	2956	2958	2960	2961	2963	2965	0 0 1 1	1	1 1 1 2
	9327	9333	9338	9343	9349	9354	9359	9365	9370	9375	1 1 2 2	3	3 4 4 5
88	2966	2968	2970	2972	2973	2975	2977	2978	2980	2982	0 0 0 1	1	1 1 1 2
	9381	9386	9391	9397	9402	9407	9413	9418	9423	9429	1 1 2 2	3	3 4 4 5
89	2983	2985	2987	2988	2990	2992	2993	2995	2997	2998	0 0 0 1	1	1 1 1 1
	9434	9439	9445	9450	9455	9460	9466	9471	9476	9482	1 1·2 2	3	3 4 4 5
90	3000	3002	3003	3005	3007	3008	3010	3012	3013	3015	0 0 0·1	1	1 1 1 1
	9487	9492	9497	9503	9508	9513	9518	9524	9529	9534	1 1 2 2	3	3 4 4 5
91	3017	3018	3020	3022	3023	3025	3027	3028	3030	3032	0 0 0 1	1	1 1 1 1
	9539	9545	9550	9555	9560	9566	9571	9576	9581	9586	1 1 2 2	3	3 4 4 5
92	3033	3035	3036	3038	3040	3041	3043	3045	3046	3048	0 0 0 1	1	1 1 1·1
	9592	9597	9602	9607	9612	9618	9623	9628	9633	9638	1 1 2 2	3	3 4 4 5
93	3050	3051	3053	3055	3056	3058	3059	3061	3063	3064	0 0 0 1	1	1 1 1 1
	9644	9649	9654	9659	9664	9670	9675	9680	9685	9690	1 1 2 2	3	3 4 4 5
94	3066	3068	3069	3071	3072	3074	3076	3077	3079	3081	0 0 0 1	1	1 1 1 1
	9695	9701	9706	9711	9716	9721	9726	9731	9737	9742	1 1 2 2	3	3 4 4 5
95	3082	3084	3085	3087	3089	3090	3092	3094	3095	3097	0 0 0 1	1	1 1 1 1
	9747	9752	9757	9762	9767	9772	9778	9783	9788	9793	1 1 2 2	3	3 4 4 5
96	3098	3100	3102	3103	3105	3106	3108	3110	3111	3113	0 0 0 1	1	1 1 1 1
	9798	9803	9808	9813	9818	9823	9829	9834	9839	9844	1 1 2 2	3	3 4 4 5
97	3114	3116	3118	3119	3121	3122	3124	3126	3127	3129	0 0 0 1	1	1 1·1 1
	9849	9854	9859	9864	9869	9874	9879	9884	9889	9894	0 1 1 2	2	3 3 4 4
98	3130	3132	3134	3135	3137	3138	3140	3142	3143	3145	0 0 0 1	1	1 1 1 1
	9899	9905	9910	9915	9920	9925	9930	9935	9940	9945	0 1 1 2	2	3 3 4 4
99	3146	3148	3150	3151	3153	3154	3156	3158	3159	3161	0 0 0 1	1	1· 1 1 1
	9950	9955	9960	9965	9970	9975	9980	9985	9990	9995	0 1 1 2	2	3 3 4 4

The position of the decimal point and the first significant figure should be found by inspection.

Index

Index